DIMITRIOS NTOUNIAS

The CryptoEaz Curriculum

A Beginner's Guide to Understanding Digital Finance

First published by CryptoEaz 2025

This book contains the complete educational curriculum of the CryptoEaz platform. It is designed to take anyone from an absolute beginner to an expert-level participant in the world of cryptocurrency and decentralized finance. The lessons are structured to build upon each other, creating a clear and comprehensive learning path.

First edition

This book was professionally typeset on Reedsy.
Find out more at reedsy.com

Contents

1

Foreword: Your Guide to Digital Finance

Welcome to the CryptoEaz Curriculum. You're holding a guide designed to take you from zero knowledge to a point of confidence and safety in the world of digital finance. In an industry filled with hype and complexity, my mission is to provide simple, transparent, and foundational education. This book is structured to build your understanding step-by-step.

I will not just tell you what something is; I will try to explain why it matters and how it works. Whether you're here to understand the future of money, learn how to invest safely, or explore the cutting edge of Web3, your journey starts now.

2

Level 1: Beginner

Goal: Take someone with zero knowledge to a point of confidence, safety, and basic understanding.

Module 1: Foundations of Finance & Investing

Module Introduction:

Before you can understand digital money, you need to understand money itself. This module demystifies the core ideas of finance, from inflation and market cycles to the psychology of investing. These ten lessons are the bedrock of your entire education.

Lesson 01 - What is Money?

An Introduction to the Tool We Never Question

Before we can explore the groundbreaking world of digital currencies, we must ask a more fundamental question: what *is* money, really? It's a tool we use every single day to buy coffee, pay rent, and save for the future, yet we rarely question what it is or why it works. Understanding the story of money—this incredible social technology—is the first and most crucial step in grasping the revolution that Bitcoin and cryptocurrency represent. This lesson will change how you see the dollar in your pocket forever.

The Core Explanation: An Agreement of Value

At its core, money is not an object; it's an agreement. It is a tool we invented to solve the problems of barter and to exchange value with one another efficiently. For this tool to work, it must reliably perform three key functions:

1. **A Medium of Exchange:** This is its most basic job. Money allows you to trade something you have (your time and skills at work) for something you want (groceries) without the hassle of bartering. Imagine a web developer trying to trade coding services for a loaf of bread—it's inefficient. Money acts as the universal intermediary.
2. **A Unit of Account:** Money provides a common yardstick to measure the value of everything. We can say a coffee costs $4 and a car costs $40,000. This allows us to compare the value of different goods and services easily and conduct business on a large scale.
3. **A Store of Value:** This means that money should retain its purchasing power over time. If you earn $100 today, you should be able to spend it a month from now and buy a roughly equivalent amount of goods. As we'll see in the next lesson, this function is where modern money often struggles.

Historically, we've seen two major types of money:

- **Commodity Money:** This is money that has its own intrinsic value. The object itself is useful. Ancient societies used items like salt, cattle, shells, and grains because they had a practical purpose. The most successful commodity money in history is gold, valued for its rarity, durability, and beauty.
- **Fiat Money:** This is the money we use today, like the Australian Dollar. Its value comes not from the material it's made of, but from a government decree, or "fiat" (Latin for "let it be done"). We accept a $20 note not because the polymer is valuable, but because we have collective trust that the government will keep it stable and that others will accept it as payment.

Historical Example: The Fall of the Gold Standard

For much of modern history, many fiat currencies were linked to a commodity—gold. This was known as the "Gold Standard." A country's government could only print as much money as it had in gold reserves. This provided a hard anchor for the value of the currency.

The pivotal case study is the United States in 1971. President Nixon officially severed the U.S. Dollar's link to gold. From that moment on, the U.S. Dollar became a pure fiat currency, backed by nothing but the "full faith and credit" of the U.S. government. Most of the world's currencies followed suit. This gave governments immense flexibility to manage their economies, but it also opened the door for the value of money to be more easily diluted over time—a concept we will explore with inflation.

Practical Application: The Wallet in Your Pocket

Look in your wallet or check your bank account. The physical notes you hold are fiat money, valuable only because of a shared belief system. The number you see in your banking app is even more abstract—it's just a digital entry in a bank's private ledger.

This demonstrates that we are already deeply comfortable with abstract, even digital, forms of value. The idea of money has already evolved from a physical object (a gold coin) to a societal promise (a fiat banknote) to a digital entry (your bank balance). This long history of abstraction sets the stage for the next logical step: decentralized digital currencies that are not controlled by any single government or bank.

Key Takeaways

- **Money is a Technology:** Think of money as a social technology designed to serve three functions: a medium of exchange, a unit of account, and a store of value.
- **Value is an Agreement:** Commodity money (like gold) has intrinsic value, while fiat money (like the AUD) derives its value purely from our collective trust in the issuing government.
- **The Story is Still Unfolding:** The evolution from commodity to fiat to digital bank entries is a clear historical progression. Decentralized cryptocurrencies represent a new and potentially disruptive chapter in this story.

Bridge to the Next Lesson

We've established that modern money is based on trust.

But what happens when that trust is tested? What happens when the value of the money in your bank account silently decreases every single year? This powerful, often invisible, force is called inflation. In our next lesson, we will explore what inflation is and why it is the single most important concept for understanding the need to invest.

Lesson 02 - Inflation and Purchasing Power

An Introduction to the Silent Tax on Your Savings

Imagine a thief who sneaks into your bank account every night and steals a tiny fraction of a cent. You'd never notice it day-to-day, but over years, the accumulated loss would be enormous. That, in essence, is inflation. It is the silent and invisible tax on your savings that guarantees the cash you hold today will be worth less tomorrow. Understanding this concept isn't just academic; it's the fundamental reason why learning to invest is no longer a luxury, but a necessity for financial survival.

The Core Explanation: Why Your Money Buys Less

Inflation is the rate at which the general level of prices for goods and services in an economy is rising, and as a result, the purchasing power of your money is falling. Put simply, inflation means your dollar doesn't go as far as it used to.

The most common way this is measured is through the Consumer Price Index (CPI), which tracks the average price of a basket of common household goods and services. When you hear that inflation is at 5%, it means that, on average, that basket of goods is 5% more expensive than it was a year ago.

- **Real-World Example:** If a typical basket of your weekly groceries cost $100 last year, and inflation is 5%, that exact same basket of groceries will now cost you $105. You haven't received more goods, but you must spend more money to get them. This is a direct loss of your money's purchasing power.

This is why holding cash over the long term is a losing strategy. While it feels safe, cash is a melting ice cube; its value is constantly being eroded by inflation. Central banks around the world, including the Reserve Bank of Australia, often target a small and steady rate of inflation (usually 2-3%) to encourage spending and economic activity. While this may be healthy for the economy, it is detrimental to your savings unless you do something about it.

Historical Example: The Hyperinflation of the Weimar Republic

To see the destructive power of inflation in its most extreme form, we can look at the Weimar Republic (Germany) in the early 1920s. After World War I, the German government, burdened by war reparations, began printing massive amounts of money to pay its debts.

This led to hyperinflation on a scale that is hard to comprehend. Prices began doubling every few days. A loaf of bread that cost 250 marks in January 1923 cost 200 *billion* marks by November 1923. People's life savings were wiped out in a matter of months. Workers would demand to be paid twice a day so they could rush to the stores and spend their money before it became worthless by dinnertime. This historical trauma illustrates the ultimate consequence of a complete loss of faith in a fiat currency and the devastating impact of out-of-control inflation.

Practical Application: The Goal of Investing

The primary goal of investing is to grow your wealth at a rate that is higher than the rate of inflation. This is how you increase your *real* wealth and purchasing power over time.

- **Try This How-To:**

Find an online inflation calculator for Australia (the RBA has one on its website). Enter $100 and set the start year to 20 years ago from today. See what that amount is equivalent to in today's dollars. The result is often shocking and makes the concept of lost purchasing power tangible. This simple exercise makes it clear: to build wealth, your money must be put to work in assets that have the potential to grow faster than inflation.

Key Takeaways

- **Inflation Erodes Value:** Inflation is the steady increase in the price of goods, which directly reduces the purchasing power of your money.
- **Cash is a Risky Long-Term Hold:** While it feels safe, holding cash over long periods is a guaranteed way to lose real value due to the persistent effects of inflation.
- **Investing is the Antidote:** The core purpose of investing is to generate returns that outpace the rate of inflation, allowing you to grow your real wealth and purchasing power over time.

Bridge to the Next Lesson

If holding cash is a losing game, where do people traditionally put their money to work to fight inflation? For generations, investors have relied on a few core asset classes. In our next lesson, we'll introduce the "big three" of traditional investing: stocks, bonds, and real estate. Understanding them is essential to see where crypto fits into the bigger picture.

Lesson 03 - Stocks, Bonds, and Real Estate

An Introduction to the Classic Wealth-Building Toolkit

For over a century, the path to building wealth was paved with three key asset classes: owning businesses, loaning money, and buying property. These are the traditional pillars of the financial world. Before you can truly appreciate the unique nature of cryptocurrency, you need to understand this classic toolkit. This lesson will demystify Stocks, Bonds, and Real Estate, showing you how they work and giving you the context to see where crypto fits in as the new kid on the block.

The Core Explanation: The Three Pillars

Before crypto, investors primarily used these traditional asset classes to grow their wealth and preserve their purchasing power against inflation. Each serves a different purpose and has a different risk profile.

- **Stocks (also called Equities):** When you buy a stock, you are buying a small piece of ownership in a company. If you buy a share of Apple, you are a part-owner of the company. As an owner, you have a claim on the company's profits. If the company succeeds and grows, the value of your share can increase, and the company might also pay you a portion of its profits directly, known as a dividend. Stocks offer the potential for high growth but also come with higher risk, as a company can perform poorly or even go bankrupt.

- **Bonds:** A bond is essentially a loan you give to a government or a large corporation. In exchange for your capital, the entity promises to pay you back the full amount (the "principal") on a specific future date (the "maturity date"). Along the way, they will pay you regular, fixed interest payments. Bonds are generally considered much safer than stocks because you are a lender, not an owner. Your return is more predictable, but the potential for high growth is also much lower.
- **Real Estate:** This is the most tangible asset class: physical property like land, a house, or a commercial building. Real estate can build wealth in two ways: through appreciation (the value of the property going up over time) and through rental income. It's often seen as a stable, long-term investment, but it is also highly illiquid, meaning you can't sell it quickly or easily like a stock.

Market Example: The 60/40 Portfolio

A classic investment strategy for decades was the "60/40 portfolio." This involved allocating 60% of your portfolio to stocks (for growth) and 40% to bonds (for stability and income). The idea was that in times of economic uncertainty, the stable bonds would cushion the portfolio from the volatility of the stock market.

For example, during the 2008 Global Financial Crisis, stock markets around the world plummeted. However, many types of government bonds held their value or even increased as investors fled to safety. Someone with a 60/40 portfolio would have had a difficult year, but they would have been protected from the catastrophic losses experienced by those who were 100% invested in stocks. This historical model demonstrates the traditional approach to balancing risk and reward.

Practical Application: Where Does Crypto Fit?

Now, think about cryptocurrency as a completely new, digital asset class with its own unique properties. It doesn't behave quite like a stock, a bond, or real estate.

- It has the high-growth potential of a technology stock.
- Some assets, like Bitcoin, have the scarcity properties of a commodity like gold.
- Other assets allow you to earn a yield, like a bond.
- **Try This How-To:**

Go to a financial website like Yahoo Finance or Google Finance. Look up the "ticker symbol" for a company you admire (e.g., AAPL for Apple, TSLA for Tesla). Look at its stock chart over the last five years. Now, look up the price of Gold (GC=F) over the same period. This will give you a visual sense of the different performance and volatility between a growth stock and a traditional store-of-value asset.

Key Takeaways

- **Stocks are Ownership:** Buying a stock makes you a part-owner of a business, giving you a claim on its future profits and growth potential.

- **Bonds are Loans:** Buying a bond means you are lending money to an entity in exchange for regular interest payments and the return of your principal.
- **Crypto is a New Asset Class:** Cryptocurrency is an emerging digital asset class with a unique blend of properties that differentiate it from traditional investments.

Bridge to the Next Lesson

We've talked about "risk" and "reward" as general concepts. But what does that relationship mean, and how does it apply across these different asset classes? In our next lesson, we will dive deep into the unbreakable law of investing: the Risk vs. Reward spectrum. Understanding this will be the key to building a portfolio that aligns with your personal financial goals.

Lesson 04 - What is an investment? Risk vs. Reward

An Introduction to the Unbreakable Law of Finance

At its core, an investment is a simple act: using your money today with the hope of having more money in the future. But this simple act is governed by a powerful and unbreakable law—the relationship between risk and reward. Many people chase high returns without understanding this principle, and it's the fastest way to lose money. This lesson will instil in you the single most important concept in all of finance, a mental model that will guide every investment decision you ever make.

The Core Explanation: The Risk-Reward Spectrum

An investment is the act of allocating money with the expectation of generating a future income or profit. You are putting your capital to work, accepting some level of risk in exchange for the potential of a positive return.

The fundamental law is this: the higher the potential reward an investment offers, the higher the risk it carries. There is no such thing as a high-return, low-risk investment. Anyone who promises you one is either mistaken or trying to scam you.

It's best to visualize this as a spectrum:

- **Low-Risk / Low-Reward:** At this end, you have assets like government bonds or high-interest savings accounts. The risk of losing your initial capital is extremely low. As a result, the returns they offer are also very low, sometimes not even keeping pace with inflation.
- **Medium-Risk / Medium-Reward:** This is where you might find assets like a diversified stock market index fund or residential real estate. Over the long term, they have a good chance of providing solid returns, but they also come with the risk of significant downturns.
- **High-Risk / High-Reward:** At the far end of the spectrum are assets like individual startup stocks, speculative commodities, and, of course, most cryptocurrencies. These assets have the potential for explosive, life-changing returns. However, they also carry a very high risk of volatility and the potential to lose your entire investment.

Case Study: The Dot-Com Bubble of the Late 1990s

The late 1990s saw the rise of the internet and a massive speculative bubble in "dot-com" stocks. Companies with

".com" in their name, many with no profits and sometimes no revenue, saw their stock prices soar to astronomical levels. The promise of high rewards was intoxicating, and investors poured money in, ignoring the immense risks.

When the bubble burst in 2000-2001, the results were catastrophic. Companies like Pets.com and Webvan, which had been market darlings, went bankrupt, and their stocks became worthless. The NASDAQ stock index, which was full of these tech companies, lost nearly 80% of its value. This event serves as a powerful historical lesson on what happens when the pursuit of high rewards leads to a collective blindness to risk.

Practical Application: Know Thyself

Before you can build an investment portfolio, you must first understand your own **personal risk tolerance**. This is a combination of your financial ability to withstand losses and your emotional ability to handle market volatility without panicking.

- **Try This How-To:**

Ask yourself these questions and write down the answers:

1. If I invested $1,000 and the market dropped, at what point would I start to feel genuinely anxious? Down 10% ($100)? Down 30% ($300)? Down 50% ($500).
2. What is my investment timeline? Do I need this money in one year, or in thirty years? (A longer timeline generally allows for a higher risk tolerance).
3. What is my financial goal for this investment? (Saving for a house deposit requires a lower-risk approach than

speculative growth).

Answering these questions honestly will give you a clear picture of where you sit on the risk-reward spectrum and will be your most valuable guide in choosing the right investments.

Key Takeaways

- **No Free Lunch:** The relationship between risk and reward is a fundamental law of finance. Higher potential returns always come with higher risk.
- **Investing is a Spectrum:** Assets exist on a spectrum from low-risk/low-reward to high-risk/high-reward.
- **Understand Your Tolerance:** Knowing your personal risk tolerance is the essential first step before allocating a single dollar to any investment.

Bridge to the Next Lesson

There is one force in finance that is so powerful it can turn small, consistent investments into life-changing wealth over time. Albert Einstein allegedly called it the "8th wonder of the world." In our next lesson, we will explore the magic of compound interest and why time is the most valuable asset an investor has.

Lesson 05 - The 8th Wonder of the World

An Introduction to the Power of Compounding

What if you could earn money not just on your initial investment, but also on the earnings that your investment generates? This powerful, snowball-like effect is called compound interest, and it is the single most important engine for long-term wealth creation. It's a concept that seems simple on the surface, but its effects are so profound that it can make the difference between a modest nest egg and true financial freedom. This lesson will show you why time, not timing, is your greatest ally in investing.

The Core Explanation: Earning Interest on Your Interest

To understand the magic of compounding, we first need to distinguish it from its less powerful sibling, simple interest.

- **Simple Interest:** This is interest that is calculated only on your initial investment amount (the "principal").

Example: If you invest $1,000 at 10% simple interest, you will earn $100 every single year. After 20 years, you'll have your original $1,000 plus $2,000 in interest ($100 x 20 years), for a total of $3,000.

- **Compound Interest:** This is interest that is calculated on your principal amount plus all the accumulated interest from previous periods. It's "interest on your interest."

Example: If you invest $1,000 at 10% compound interest:

- **Year 1:** You earn $100. Your new balance is $1,100.

- **Year 2:** You earn 10% on $1,100, which is $110. Your new balance is $1,210.
- **Year 3:** You earn 10% on $1,210, which is $121. Your new balance is $1,331.

This difference seems small at first, but over time, the growth becomes exponential. After 20 years, your initial $1,000 would have grown to **$6,727**. That's more than double the return from simple interest, with the extra wealth generated purely from the effect of compounding.

Case Study: The Warren Buffett Anecdote

Warren Buffett is one of the most successful investors in history, with a net worth of over $100 billion. The fascinating part of his story is how he built that wealth. It is often reported that over 99% of his net worth was earned after his 50th birthday.

This isn't because he suddenly became a much better investor in his later years. It's because he started investing early (he bought his first stock at age 11) and let his capital compound for many, many decades. His wealth wasn't built on a few lucky bets; it was built on consistent, good returns amplified by the unstoppable force of compound interest over an incredibly long-time horizon. His career is a real-world testament to the power of starting early and staying invested.

Practical Application: The Rule of 72

The "Rule of 72" is a simple mental shortcut to estimate how long it will take for an investment to double in value, given a fixed annual rate of return. The formula is:

72 ÷ (Your Annual Interest Rate) = Years to Double

- **Try This How-To:**

1. If your investment earns a 6% annual return, it will take approximately 12 years to double (72 ÷ 6 = 12).
2. If your investment earns a 10% annual return, it will take approximately 7.2 years to double (72 ÷ 10 = 7.2).

This rule is not just for stocks; it applies directly to crypto. Many crypto activities, such as staking or lending, allow you to earn a yield on your assets. By understanding the Rule of 72, you can quickly estimate the power of compounding on your crypto holdings and see how different yield rates can dramatically affect how quickly your assets grow.

Key Takeaways

- **Compounding Creates Exponential Growth:** Compound interest, or "interest on interest," allows your wealth to grow at an accelerating rate over time.
- **Time is Your Most Valuable Asset:** The longer your investment has to compound, the more dramatic the results will be. Starting early is one of the biggest advantages an investor can have.
- **The Rule of 72 is a Powerful Shortcut:** Use this simple formula to quickly estimate how long it will take for your investments to double at a given rate of return.

Bridge to the Next Lesson

Understanding the mathematical forces that drive wealth is crucial. But financial markets are also driven by human emotion and language. To navigate the world of investing, you need to speak the language. In our next lesson, we'll define some of the most common terms you'll hear every day: "bulls," "bears," and the all-important metric used to measure an asset's size, the "market cap."

Lesson 06 - Bulls vs. Bears, and Market Caps

An Introduction to the Language of the Market

To navigate any new territory, you must first learn the language. In the world of finance, conversations are dominated by talk of "bulls" and "bears," and assets are constantly ranked by a metric called "market cap." These aren't just jargon; they are fundamental concepts that describe the market's mood and an asset's scale. This lesson will teach you to speak the language of the market, allowing you to understand the financial news and analyse assets like a professional.

The Core Explanation: Market Mood and Asset Size

Financial markets are driven by the collective sentiment of their participants, which tends to move in broad cycles. These cycles are described using two powerful animal analogies:

1. **A Bull Market:** This is a period when prices are generally rising, and investor sentiment is overwhelmingly optimistic. Confidence is high, and participants expect prices to continue going up. The name comes from the way a bull thrusts its horns upwards in an attack.
2. **A Bear Market:** This is the opposite—a period when prices are generally falling, and sentiment is pessimistic. Fear is the dominant emotion, and participants expect prices to continue dropping. The name comes from the

way a bear swipes its paws downwards in an attack.

Beyond the market's mood, we need a way to measure the size and significance of an asset. The universal metric for this is Market Capitalization **(Market Cap)**. It represents the total value of all the coins or shares of an asset in existence. The formula is simple: **Market Cap = Current Price × Circulating Supply**

An asset with a large market cap (like Bitcoin) is often called a "large-cap" and is generally considered more established and less volatile than an asset with a small market cap (a "small-cap"), which might have more room for growth but also carries significantly more risk.

Case Study: The 2021 Bull Run vs. The 2022 Bear Market

The crypto market provided a textbook example of these cycles recently.

- **The Bull Market (2020-2021):** Following a period of uncertainty, crypto prices began to soar. Bitcoin broke its previous all-time highs, and a wave of retail and institutional interest flooded the market. News headlines were positive, social media was euphoric with stories of massive gains, and the dominant feeling was that prices would go up forever. This was a classic bull market.
- **The Bear Market (2022):** The sentiment shifted dramatically. Macroeconomic pressures and internal crypto failures led to a sharp decline in prices. Confidence evaporated, fear became the prevailing emotion, and headlines turned negative. Many of the high-flying assets from the bull run lost 80-90% of their value. This painful downturn was a classic bear market.

This recent history shows how quickly the market's mood can swing from one extreme to the other.

Practical Application: Sizing Up the Market

Understanding market cap gives you an instant snapshot of the crypto landscape. It helps you differentiate the giants from the speculative startups.

- **Try This How-To:**

1. Go to a crypto data website like CoinGecko or CoinMarketCap.
2. On the homepage, you'll see a list of cryptocurrencies ranked by market cap.
3. Compare the market cap of Bitcoin (BTC) to the asset ranked #10, and then to the asset ranked #100.

Notice the staggering difference in value. This exercise immediately gives you a sense of the market's hierarchy and the relative scale and risk of different projects. A $500 million market cap project is not the same as a $500 billion one.

Key Takeaways

- **Bulls Rise, Bears Fall:** A bull market is a period of rising prices and optimism, while a bear market is a period of falling prices and pessimism.
- **Market Cap is a Measure of Size:** It's the total value of an asset, calculated by multiplying the price by the circulating supply.
- **Size Often Correlates with Risk:** Large-cap assets are

typically more established and less volatile, while small-cap assets are generally higher-risk, higher-reward investments.

Bridge to the Next Lesson

Now that we know how to measure the size of different assets, how should we combine them in a portfolio to manage risk? The next lesson introduces one of the most crucial concepts for long-term survival in investing: diversification.

Lesson 07 - Introduction to Diversification

An Introduction to Not Losing Everything

"Don't put all your eggs in one basket." It's a piece of wisdom so old it has become a cliché. Yet, in the world of investing, it is the single most important rule for risk management and long-term survival. Diversification is the practical application of this wisdom. It's not about finding the next big winner; it's about building a resilient portfolio that can withstand shocks and prevent a single bad outcome from wiping you out. This lesson is your guide to building that resilience.

The Core Explanation: Spreading Your Bets to Reduce Risk

Diversification is the strategy of spreading your investments across a variety of different assets to reduce your overall risk. The core principle is that the poor performance of a single investment will be less likely to devastate your entire portfolio if it's just one small part of a larger whole.

A well-constructed portfolio uses two main types of diversification:

1. **Diversification Across Asset Classes:** This is the most important type. It means owning a mix of different kinds of assets that don't always move in the same direction. For example, a portfolio might contain stocks, bonds, real estate, and cryptocurrencies. Historically, when stocks have performed poorly, bonds have often performed well, cushioning the portfolio. By owning different asset classes, you smooth out your returns and reduce your dependence on the success of any single market.
2. **Diversification Within an Asset Class:** This means not putting all your eggs in one basket *within* a specific category. For crypto, it means not investing 100% of your capital into a single cryptocurrency. A diversified crypto portfolio might hold Bitcoin, Ethereum, and a few other promising altcoins, rather than betting everything on one project.

The goal of diversification is not to maximize returns—in fact, it will likely prevent you from capturing the explosive gains of a single lucky bet. Its true goal is to provide a more consistent journey and, most importantly, to protect you from catastrophic, unrecoverable losses.

Case Study: The Terra (LUNA) Collapse

In May 2022, the crypto world witnessed the catastrophic collapse of the Terra ecosystem and its native token, LUNA. At its peak, it was one of the largest cryptocurrencies in the world. Many investors, convinced by its high returns and charismatic founder, had allocated huge portions—sometimes 100%—of their crypto portfolios to it.

When the system failed, the price of LUNA fell by over 99.9% in a matter of days. Investors who had put all their eggs in that one basket were completely wiped out, losing their life savings. However, a diversified investor who had perhaps only a 5% allocation to LUNA, with the rest of their portfolio in assets like Bitcoin and Ethereum, would have taken a painful hit but would have survived. Their other assets would have cushioned the blow. This event became the most brutal and effective lesson in the importance of diversification in crypto history.

Practical Application: Sketching Your Own Diversified Portfolio

Thinking about how to allocate capital is the first step towards building a sound strategy.

- **Try This How-To:**

1. Imagine you have $1,000 to invest for the long term.
2. On a piece of paper, decide what percentage you would put into different asset classes. For example: 60% in a stock market index fund, 10% in bonds, and 30% in crypto.
3. Now, take your crypto allocation ($300 in this example) and decide how you would diversify *within* it. For example: 50% in Bitcoin ($150), 35% in Ethereum ($105), and 15% in another altcoin ($45).

This simple exercise forces you to think deliberately about risk and allocation, which is the core practice of a disciplined investor.

Key Takeaways

- **Don't Put All Your Eggs in One Basket:** Diversification is the cornerstone of risk management, designed to protect your portfolio from the failure of a single investment.
- **Diversify Across and Within:** The most effective strategies involve diversifying across different asset classes (stocks, crypto) and within each asset class (multiple cryptocurrencies).
- **The Goal is Resilience, Not Maximum Gain:** Diversification protects you from catastrophic losses and provides a smoother investment journey, even if it means missing out on the highest possible return from a single lucky bet.

Bridge to the Next Lesson

Managing risk through diversification is a logical strategy. But what about the illogical, emotional forces that can wreck even the best-laid plans? In our next lesson, we'll confront the two biggest enemies of every investor: FOMO and FUD.

Lesson 08 - Your Biggest Enemy: FOMO & FUD

An Introduction to the Battle Within

In the investing arena, your greatest opponent is not the market, not a shadowy hedge fund, and not a bad financial advisor. Your greatest opponent is the person staring back at you in the mirror. The human mind is wired with powerful emotional biases that can turn a perfectly logical investor into their own worst enemy. This lesson is about identifying and defending against the two most destructive emotions in finance: the greed-driven "Fear Of Missing Out" (FOMO) and the fear-driven "Fear, Uncertainty, and Doubt" (FUD).

The Core Explanation: The Two-Headed Dragon of Emotion

Successful investing requires a calm and rational mind, but the market is a chaotic environment designed to provoke emotional reactions. The two most powerful are:

1. **FOMO (Fear Of Missing Out):** This is the intense, anxious feeling that arises when you see an asset's price skyrocketing without you. Everyone seems to be getting rich, and the urge to jump on the bandwagon becomes overwhelming. FOMO is a powerful form of social proof and greed that short-circuits your logical thinking. It is the single biggest reason why investors buy high. They abandon their strategy and pile in at the peak of a bubble, just as the smart money is selling.
2. **FUD (Fear, Uncertainty, and Doubt):** This is the wave of panic that washes over you when the market is crashing. Prices are in freefall, the news is filled with apocalyptic headlines, and your portfolio is bleeding. FUD is a potent cocktail of fear and doubt that makes you question all your previous decisions. It is the single biggest reason why investors sell low. They capitulate at the point of maximum pain, locking in their losses and abandoning their long-term strategy right at the bottom.

These two emotions are opposite sides of the same coin, and

they work together to create the classic investor trap: "buy high, sell low."

Case Study: The Psychology of a Market Cycle

The "Wall Street Cheat Sheet: Psychology of a Market Cycle" is a famous chart that perfectly illustrates how these emotions drive investor behaviour.

- As a market begins to rise, there is **Optimism**, which turns into **Excitement**, then **Thrill**. As the price goes vertical, the market enters a state of **Euphoria**. This is the point of maximum financial risk, and it is precisely where FOMO is at its peak, sucking in the last buyers.
- After the top, the price begins to fall. Investors feel **Anxiety** and go into **Denial**. As the losses mount, this turns into **Fear**, then **Desperation**, and finally **Panic**. At the very bottom of the market, as investors sell everything to "make the pain stop," this is called **Capitulation** and **Despair**. This is the point of maximum financial opportunity, and it is where FUD is at its most powerful.

This cycle repeats in all financial markets because human psychology does not change.

Practical Application: Creating an Emotional Circuit Breaker

The best defence against emotional decision-making is to have a pre-defined plan and to create systems that force you to pause before acting.

- **Try This How-To:**

Create a simple "Investment Checklist" that you must consult *before* making any buy or sell decision. It could include questions like:

1. Why am I making this decision? (Is it based on my strategy or an emotion?)
2. Does this align with my long-term financial goals?
3. Have I done my own research on this asset?
4. If I'm buying, am I comfortable if the price immediately drops 20%?
5. If I'm selling, am I doing it as part of my plan (e.g., taking profits) or because I am afraid?

Forcing yourself to answer these questions acts as a "circuit breaker." It re-engages the logical part of your brain and can be the crucial pause that saves you from a disastrous, emotion-driven mistake.

Key Takeaways

- **You Are Your Own Biggest Risk:** The emotional biases of FOMO (greed) and FUD (fear) are the primary drivers of poor investment decisions.
- **FOMO Leads to Buying High:** The fear of missing out tempts investors to buy into assets at the peak of a bubble.
- **FUD Leads to Selling Low:** Fear, uncertainty, and doubt cause investors to panic and sell their assets at the bottom of a market crash.
- **A Plan is Your Best Defence:** A disciplined investment strategy, created during a time of calm, is your most powerful weapon against making emotional decisions in the heat of the moment.

Bridge to the Next Lesson

Controlling your emotions is half the battle. The other half is being able to interpret the market's data objectively. The most fundamental piece of data is an asset's price history, which is displayed on a price chart. In our next lesson, we'll learn the basics of how to read one of these charts, turning a confusing wall of data into a clear story.

Lesson 09 - How to Read a Basic Price Chart

An Introduction to the Market's Footprint

A price chart can look intimidating at first—a chaotic jumble of lines, bars, and colours. But in reality, a chart is simply a story. It is the historical footprint of an asset's journey, showing every battle fought between buyers and sellers. Learning to read a basic chart is like learning to read a map in a foreign land. It gives you context, helps you identify landmarks, and allows you to make more informed decisions about where you are and where you might be going. This lesson will demystify the most common type of chart and give you the foundational skills to start reading the market's story.

The Core Explanation: Anatomy of a Candlestick Chart

While there are many types of charts, the most popular and useful by far is the candlestick chart. Each "candle" on the chart represents the price action over a specific period (e.g., one hour, one day, or one week).

The two most important elements of any chart are the axes:

- The **horizontal axis (x-axis)** represents **Time**.

- The **vertical axis (y-axis)** represents **Price**.

Each individual candle tells you four key pieces of information for its time period:

1. **The Opening Price:** The price at the start of the period.
2. **The Closing Price:** The price at the end of the period.
3. **The High:** The highest price the asset reached during the period.
4. **The Low:** The lowest price the asset reached during the period.

The "body" of the candle represents the range between the open and close, while the thin lines (the "wicks" or "shadows") show the full range from the high to the low. The most important feature for a beginner is the colour:

- **Green Candle (Bullish):** This means the price closed higher than it opened. Buyers were in control during this period.
- **Red Candle (Bearish):** This means the price closed lower than it opened. Sellers were in control during this period.

By looking at a series of these candles, you can start to see patterns, such as an uptrend (a series of higher highs and higher lows) or a downtrend.

Case Study: Bitcoin's 2021 Price Action

If you look at a daily candlestick chart of Bitcoin during 2021, you can clearly see the market's story told in candles.

- **Early 2021:** You would see a long series of large green candles, indicating strong and consistent buying pressure. This was the heart of the bull run. The uptrend is clear and powerful.

- **Mid-2021:** You would see a period of large red candles, indicating a sharp sell-off, followed by a period of smaller green and red candles moving sideways. This shows the market losing its upward momentum and entering a period of uncertainty.
- **Late 2021:** You would see another series of strong green candles as the price surged to a new all-time high, followed by a series of decisive red candles as the final peak was reached and the trend began to reverse.

This simple visual story is far more immediate and intuitive than reading a spreadsheet of historical prices.

Practical Application: Spotting a Trend

The most basic skill in chart reading is identifying the primary trend. You don't need to be an expert analyst to do this.

- **Try This How-To:**

1. Go to a charting website like TradingView (it has a free version).
2. In the search bar, type BTCUSD to bring up the Bitcoin/US Dollar chart.
3. Set the time frame to "1D" (one day). This means each candle represents one day of trading.
4. Zoom out to look at the last 2-3 years of price history.
5. Simply with your eyes, can you identify the major uptrends (long periods where the price was generally

moving from the bottom-left to the top-right) and the major downtrends (periods where it was moving from the top-left to the bottom-right)?

This exercise trains your eye to see the big picture and identify the market's main direction, which is the foundational skill of chart analysis.

Key Takeaways

- **Charts Tell a Story:** A price chart is a visual history of an asset's price movements over time.
- **Candlesticks Show the Battle:** Each candle shows the open, close, high, and low price for a period, with the colour indicating whether buyers (green) or sellers (red) won.
- **Trends are the Big Picture:** The most important initial skill is to zoom out and identify the primary direction of the market's trend.

Bridge to the Next Lesson

We've learned how to manage our emotions and how to read the market's past. But before we invest a single dollar based on any of this, we need to answer the most important question of all: *Why* are we investing in the first place? In our final lesson of this module, we'll cover the critical importance of setting clear financial goals.

Lesson 10 - Setting Clear Financial Goals

An Introduction to Your Financial North Star

We have reached the final and most important lesson of our foundational module. We've discussed money, risk, emotion, and analysis. But none of it matters without a destination. Investing without a goal is like setting sail without a map or a compass—you'll be tossed about by the waves and are unlikely to end up anywhere you want to be. This lesson is about crafting your "Financial North Star." It's about defining *why* you are investing, because your "why" will determine your entire strategy and give you the strength to navigate the inevitable storms ahead.

The Core Explanation: Your "Why" Defines Your "How"

Before you ever choose an investment, you must first define your financial goals. A goal is not a vague desire like "I want to be rich." A proper financial goal is specific, measurable, and has a clear timeline.

Your financial goals are the single most important factor because they determine three critical components of your investment strategy:

1. **Your Timeline:** How soon do you need the money? A goal with a long timeline (e.g., retirement in 30 years) can withstand much more market volatility than a goal with a short timeline (e.g., a house deposit in 3 years).
2. **Your Risk Tolerance:** Your timeline directly influences how much risk you should take. Money needed in the short term should be kept in low-risk assets, as you don't have time to recover from a market crash. Capital for long-term goals can be allocated to higher-risk,

higher-growth assets.

3. **Your Investment Strategy:** Your goals will dictate your strategy. Are you aiming for capital preservation, steady income, or aggressive growth? The answer will change which assets you choose to buy and how you manage them.

Without this clarity, you are simply speculating. With it, you are investing with purpose.

Case Study: Two Different Investors

Let's consider two hypothetical investors, both with $10,000 to invest:

- **Investor A: Sarah.** Sarah is 30 years old and her primary goal is to save for retirement at age 65. Her timeline is 35 years. Because her timeline is so long, she can afford to take on more risk for higher potential growth. She might build a portfolio that is heavily weighted towards growth assets like stocks and cryptocurrencies. She is not concerned with short-term price swings because she knows she has decades to let her investments compound.
- **Investor B: David.** David is 40 years old and is saving for his daughter's university tuition, which he will need in 4 years. His timeline is very short. It would be extremely irresponsible for David to put this money into high-risk assets. A major bear market could wipe out a significant portion of his savings with no time to recover. David should build a low-risk portfolio focused on capital preservation, likely consisting of bonds and other stable assets.

Both are "investing," but their clearly defined goals lead them to completely different and appropriate strategies.

Practical Application: The S.M.A.R.T. Goal Framework

A powerful way to set effective goals is to use the S.M.A.R.T. framework. Your goals should be: **S**pecific, **M**easurable, **A**chievable, **R**elevant, and **T**ime-bound.

- **Try This How-To:**

1. Take out a piece of paper or open a new document.
2. Write down one of your major financial goals.
3. Now, rewrite it using the S.M.A.R.T. framework.

- Bad Goal: "I want to save for a house."
- S.M.A.R.T. Goal: "I will save a $50,000 (Measurable) down payment for my first home (Specific). I will do this by investing $600 per month into a low-risk portfolio (Achievable). This is my top financial priority (Relevant). I will achieve this goal in 5 years (Time-bound)."

This exercise transforms a vague wish into an actionable plan. This plan becomes your anchor, providing discipline and focus, especially when markets become volatile and emotions run high.

Key Takeaways

- **Know Your Destination:** You must define your financial goals before you start investing. Investing without a clear goal is just gambling.
- **Goals Define Strategy:** Your goals, and specifically your

timeline, are the primary factors that should determine your risk tolerance and your overall investment strategy.
- **Clarity Creates Discipline:** Having specific, written goals is the ultimate defence against making emotional, short-sighted decisions. It is your North Star in the chaos of the market.

3

Module 1 Recap

Congratulations, you've completed the first and most important module of your journey. You now have a solid foundation in the timeless principles of finance.

- You've learned that money is a technology that has evolved over time, and that the fiat money we use today is based on trust.
- You understand that inflation is a silent force that erodes the value of your savings, making investing a necessity to build real wealth.
- You can identify the classic asset classes and, most importantly, you grasp the unbreakable law of risk vs. reward.
- You know that your own emotions, **FOMO and FUD**, are your greatest enemies, and that a disciplined plan based on clear goals is your greatest defence.

You are now ready to step into the world of digital finance,

not as a speculator, but as an informed and prepared investor.

Module 2 - Introduction to Blockchain & Crypto

Module Introduction: Now that you have a firm grasp on the principles of investing, it's time to open the door to the digital frontier. This module demystifies the revolutionary technology that underpins the entire crypto ecosystem. We will move from abstract concepts to concrete understanding, exploring what a blockchain is, what gives cryptocurrencies their value, and the practical steps for buying and securing your first digital assets safely. By the end of this module, you will have both the knowledge and the confidence to take your first steps as a sovereign individual in this new financial world.

Lesson 01 - What is Web3?

An Introduction to the Next Internet

Have you ever felt that the internet, once a place of open exploration, now feels like a handful of walled gardens? We create, share, and live our digital lives on platforms owned by a few giant corporations. They own our data, they set the rules, and they reap the rewards. Web3 is a vision to fix this. It's not just an update; it's a fundamental reimagining of how the internet works, built on the revolutionary idea that users—not corporations—should be in control. This lesson will explain that powerful vision and why it represents one of the most significant technological shifts of our generation.

The Core Explanation: The Evolution of the Web

To understand Web3, you must first understand its predecessors. The internet has evolved in distinct phases:

1. **Web1 (The "Read-Only" Internet | ~1990-2004):** This was the era of static, brochure-like websites. Information flowed in one direction—from the website to the user. You could read, but you couldn't easily contribute. It was a decentralized and open protocol, but with limited functionality, like a global, digital library.
2. **Web2 (The "Read-Write" Internet | ~2004-Present):** This is the interactive and social web we use today. The rise of platforms like Facebook, Google, YouTube, and X (Twitter) allowed anyone to become a creator. We could now write, publish, and share content with the world. However, this came at a cost. In exchange for these "free" services, we handed over control of our data to the centralized companies that own the platforms.
3. **Web3 (The "Read-Write-Own" Internet):** Web3 aims to combine the decentralized ethos of Web1 with the rich, interactive experience of Web2, adding a powerful new ingredient: ownership. Built on blockchain technology, Web3 introduces a shared, open, and trust less backend. This allows for the creation of applications where users have true, provable ownership over their digital assets, data, and identity. It shifts the power from the platform back to the user.

Case Study: Your Social Media Profile

Consider your profile on a platform like Instagram or X (Twitter). You've spent years building your audience, curating your content, and creating a digital identity. But you don't *own* it.

- The platform can delete your account for any reason, and you lose everything.
- You cannot take your followers with you to another platform.
- The platform monetizes your data and your content, and you see very little of that value.

In a Web3 world, your social identity could be an NFT that you own in your crypto wallet. Your content and your "social graph" (your list of followers) would be tied to *you*, not the platform. You could then grant different applications permission to access this data, moving freely between them without losing the network you've built. This is the promise of digital ownership in action.

Practical Application: Experiencing Web3 Today

While the full vision of Web3 is still being built, you can touch and feel its early versions today.

- **Try This How-To:**

Instead of using a standard browser like Chrome, try downloading **Brave**. Brave is a Web3-native browser with a built-in crypto wallet and features that block trackers by default. It even allows you to earn a cryptocurrency (BAT) for opting into privacy-respecting ads. Using Brave for a day will give you a tangible sense of how Web3 tools aim to shift the user experience towards privacy and user rewards.

Key Takeaways

- **Web3 is About Ownership:** The defining feature of Web3 is its shift from corporate-controlled platforms to user-owned networks, enabled by blockchain technology.
- **An Evolution from Read-Only to Read-Write-Own:** The internet has progressed from a static information source (Web1) to an interactive social layer (Web2), and is now moving towards a user-owned economy (Web3).
- **It's a Work in Progress:** Web3 is not a single product but a growing ecosystem of protocols and applications that are building a more decentralized, open, and user-centric internet.

Bridge to the Next Lesson

We've talked a lot about how Web3 is "built on the blockchain." But what exactly *is* a blockchain? It's the foundational technology that makes all this possible, yet it remains a mysterious concept for many. In our next lesson, we will demystify the blockchain once and for all, using a simple analogy that will make you understand its genius.

Lesson 02 - What is a Blockchain?

An Introduction to the Trust Machine

What if we could create a system for recording information that was impossible to cheat? A system so secure and transparent that we wouldn't need banks, lawyers, or other middlemen to verify things for us? That is the profound promise of a blockchain. It is often called a "trust machine" because it allows a global network of strangers to agree on a single source of truth without needing to trust each other. This lesson will break down how this revolutionary technology works using a simple, powerful analogy.

The Core Explanation: The Shared Digital Notebook

At its core, a blockchain is a decentralized, digital ledger. Let's break that down with an analogy:

Imagine a special notebook that is shared among thousands of people around the world. Every person has an identical copy.

1. **Adding a New Page (a "Block"):** When someone wants to make a new entry (a transaction), they announce it to everyone. The participants in the network gather a list of these new transactions and put them onto a fresh page, which is called a block.
2. **Sealing the Page (Cryptography):** Before this new page can be added to the notebook, it must be "sealed" with a unique, complex cryptographic code called a hash. This hash acts like a digital fingerprint for all the data on the page. If even a single letter on the page were changed, the fingerprint would change completely.
3. **Linking the Pages (the "Chain"):** Here is the crucial step. The cryptographic seal (hash) for this new page also includes the seal from the *previous* page. This creates a powerful, unbreakable link between them. Each page is chained to the one before it, all the way back to the very first page.

This structure is what makes a blockchain so secure. Because every copy of the notebook is the same and every page is cryptographically linked, for someone to alter a past transaction, they would have to rewrite that page, reseal it, and then rewrite and reseal *every single page that came after it*, across thousands of computers, all at the same time. This is practically impossible, making the history of the ledger effectively immutable, or unchangeable.

Historical Example: The Problem of Double-Spending

Before Bitcoin, creating a purely digital cash system faced a major hurdle known as the "double-spending problem." With a digital file (like an MP3 or a photo), you can make infinite perfect copies. If digital money was just a file, how could you stop someone from spending the same "digital dollar" over and over again?

For decades, the only solution was to have a trusted central party, like a bank, keep a central ledger of who owns what. They were the ones who would verify that you couldn't spend the same money twice.

Satoshi Nakamoto's breakthrough with the Bitcoin blockchain was solving the double-spending problem *without* a central authority. The public, decentralized, and immutable ledger of the blockchain makes it so that the entire network can see and agree on every transaction. Once a transaction is confirmed in a block, it cannot be undone or re-spent. This was the key innovation that made a truly peer-to-peer electronic cash system possible for the first time in history.

Practical Application: Verifying for Yourself

The transparency of a blockchain is one of its most powerful features. You don't need to take anyone's word for it; you can check the ledger yourself.

- **Try This How-To:**

Go to a block explorer website like blockchain.com for Bitcoin. You can see a live feed of new blocks being created and new transactions being added to the ledger in real-time. You can click on any transaction to see its details—the sender, the receiver, and the amount. This is the "shared digital notebook" in action, open for the entire world to see and verify.

Key Takeaways

- **A Blockchain is a Distributed Ledger:** It's like a shared digital notebook that is copied across thousands of computers, making it decentralized and resilient.
- **Blocks are Linked with Cryptography:** Data is stored in "blocks" that are sealed and linked together in a "chain," making the historical record virtually impossible to tamper with.
- **It Solves the Double-Spend Problem:** Blockchains allow for the transfer of digital value without a central intermediary by creating a transparent, public, and immutable record of transactions.

Bridge to the Next Lesson

Now that we understand the underlying technology of the blockchain, we can properly explore the first and most famous application built on top of it: cryptocurrency. What is it, what gives it value, and how is it different from the digital money we already have in our bank accounts? Our next lesson will provide the answer.

Lesson 03 - What is Cryptocurrency?

An Introduction to Decentralized Digital Money

We talk about "digital money" all the time—the numbers in our bank accounts, credit card taps, online transfers. But that's just a digital representation of government-issued currency. Cryptocurrency is something fundamentally different. It is a new form of money that is native to the internet itself, designed from the ground up to be secure, global, and free from the control of any single company or government. This lesson will explore the core properties that make cryptocurrencies a potential paradigm shift in the history of finance.

The Core Explanation: Money Secured by Math

A cryptocurrency is a digital or virtual currency that is secured by cryptography, making it nearly impossible to counterfeit or double-spend. Unlike the digital dollars in your bank account, which are entries in a private bank ledger, cryptocurrencies are bearer assets that exist on a public blockchain.

There are two defining characteristics of most cryptocurrencies:

1. **They are Secured by Cryptography:** The "crypto" in cryptocurrency refers to the advanced cryptographic techniques used to secure the network and verify transactions. This is what protects the system from fraud and ensures the integrity of the ledger. Instead of relying on

a bank's security systems, it relies on the verifiable and universal laws of mathematics.

2. **They are Decentralized:** This is the most crucial difference. Cryptocurrencies are not issued or controlled by any central authority like a government or a central bank. They operate on distributed networks of computers, meaning no single entity can shut them down, freeze your account, or arbitrarily create more of the currency to devalue it. This decentralization makes them theoretically immune to government interference or manipulation, a property that is impossible with traditional fiat currencies.

Bitcoin and Ethereum are the two most prominent examples, but thousands of others now exist, each with its own specific design and purpose.

Case Study: The 2013 Cyprus "Bail-In"

In 2013, the small European nation of Cyprus faced a severe banking crisis. To secure an international bailout, the Cypriot government took a drastic and shocking step: they imposed a "bail-in." This meant they forcibly seized a significant percentage of the savings from all bank accounts holding more than €100,000.

Overnight, people's life savings were taken from their "safe" bank accounts to prop up the failing banking system. This event sent shockwaves through the financial world and became a powerful real-world case study for the value proposition of Bitcoin. The price of Bitcoin surged at the time, as people sought a financial asset that was outside the control of any government—an asset that could not be unilaterally seized or frozen. It was a stark demonstration of the risks of centralized financial systems and the appeal of a decentralized alternative.

Practical Application: The Global Nature of Crypto

The decentralized and permissionless nature of cryptocurrency makes it a powerful tool for global transactions.

- **Real-World Connection:** Imagine you need to send $500 to a friend or family member in another country. Using the traditional banking system, this would involve multiple intermediary banks, take 3-5 business days to clear, and incur significant fees for currency conversion and processing.
- With a cryptocurrency like Bitcoin or a stablecoin, you can send that same $500 directly to their crypto wallet. The transaction would be confirmed in minutes (or seconds, depending on the blockchain), 24/7, for a fraction of the cost, without needing permission from any bank. This borderless, peer-to-peer nature is one of the most tangible benefits of cryptocurrency today.

Key Takeaways

- **Digital Money Secured by Cryptography:** Cryptocurrencies are protected by complex math, not the policies of a central institution, making them highly secure and difficult to counterfeit.
- **Decentralization is the Key Feature:** The lack of a central controlling entity makes cryptocurrencies censorship-resistant and immune to the monetary policies of any single government.

- **Global and Permissionless:** Cryptocurrencies operate on a global, 24/7 network, allowing for fast, low-cost, peer-to-peer value transfer across borders without the need for intermediaries.

Bridge to the Next Lesson

The world of cryptocurrency is vast, but it all started with one. The original creation that solved the double-spending problem and kickstarted this entire industry remains the most important and valuable of them all. In our next lesson, we will explore the story and purpose of the original cryptocurrency: Bitcoin.

Lesson 04 - Bitcoin: The First Digital Gold

An Introduction to the Original

In the wake of the 2008 financial crisis, as trust in the traditional banking system evaporated, an anonymous creator named Satoshi Nakamoto released a whitepaper for a "peer-to-peer electronic cash system." This system was called Bitcoin. It wasn't just an idea; it was a complete, working solution to the problem of digital money without a central authority. More than a decade later, Bitcoin is not just a technology; it's a global phenomenon. This lesson explores what makes it unique and why it has earned the nickname "digital gold."

The Core Explanation: A New Form of Hard Money

Bitcoin was the very first cryptocurrency, a direct response to the failures of the centralized financial system. While it can be used for payments, its primary value proposition has evolved into being a **decentralized store of value**, an asset designed to preserve wealth over the long term.

Three core properties give Bitcoin its "digital gold" characteristics:

1. **Provable Scarcity:** This is its most important feature. There will only ever be **21 million Bitcoin** created. This hard cap is enforced by the network's code and cannot be changed. Unlike fiat currencies, which can be printed endlessly by central banks, Bitcoin's supply is absolutely finite, making it a truly scarce asset.
2. **Decentralization:** Bitcoin is the most decentralized and secure blockchain network in the world. It is not controlled by any single person, company, or government. Its network is run by thousands of independent node operators and miners across the globe, making it incredibly resilient to attack or censorship.
3. **Durability & Portability:** Like gold, Bitcoin is durable (it doesn't degrade). But unlike gold, it is incredibly portable. You can move a billion dollars' worth of Bitcoin across the world in minutes with just an internet connection, a feat impossible with a physical commodity.

Case Study: The "Immaculate Conception"

Bitcoin's launch is often referred to as the "immaculate conception" because it was arguably the fairest launch of any financial asset in history. When Satoshi Nakamoto mined the first block (the "genesis block") in January 2009, there was no pre-sale, no venture capital funding, and no insider allocation.

For the first year, Bitcoin was essentially worthless, mined only by a small group of cypherpunks and hobbyists who were intrigued by the technology. Anyone with a computer could participate on equal footing. This organic, grassroots distribution is a key part of its story and a major reason why many consider it to be a truly neutral monetary asset, free from the influence of early, centralized stakeholders.

Practical Application: Internalizing Scarcity

The 21 million supply cap can feel abstract. Let's make it tangible.

- **Try This How-To:**

1. There are roughly 8 billion people in the world.
2. There will only ever be 21 million Bitcoin.
3. This means there isn't even enough Bitcoin for every millionaire in the world to own one whole coin.
4. Divide 21 million by 8 billion. The result shows that if Bitcoin were distributed evenly, no one could have more than 0.002625 BTC.

This simple exercise demonstrates just how scarce Bitcoin is on a global scale, which is the entire foundation of its value as a long-term store of wealth.

Key Takeaways

- **Bitcoin is Digital Scarcity:** Its unbreakable 21 million supply cap makes it a hedge against inflation and currency debasement.
- **The Most Decentralized Network:** Bitcoin's security and

censorship resistance come from its massive, globally distributed network of miners and nodes.

- **A Fair and Neutral Launch:** Its "immaculate conception" without pre-mined coins for insiders gives it a unique claim as a neutral monetary asset.

Bridge to the Next Lesson

Bitcoin was designed to be a simple and robust store of value, like digital gold. But what if you could take the underlying blockchain technology and make it programmable? What if money itself could be coded? In our next lesson, we'll explore the revolutionary invention that did just that: Ethereum.

Lesson 05 - Ethereum: The World Computer & Smart Contracts

An Introduction to Programmable Money

If Bitcoin is digital gold—simple, secure, and a store of value—then Ethereum is digital oil. It's a powerful, flexible resource that fuels a whole new digital economy. Launched in 2015, Ethereum asked a revolutionary question: what if we could use blockchain technology for more than just money? The answer to that question was the "smart contract," an invention that transformed the blockchain from a simple ledger into a global, decentralized computer, and it powers almost everything in Web3 today.

The Core Explanation: The Vending Machine of the Inter-

net

While Ethereum has its own cryptocurrency, **Ether (ETH)**, its true innovation is the **'smart contract'**. A smart contract is a self-executing contract with the terms of the agreement written directly into lines of code.

- **The Vending Machine Analogy:** A vending machine is the perfect real-world example of a smart contract. It operates based on a simple, programmed rule: **IF** you insert the correct amount of money, **THEN** it will dispense your chosen snack. There's no need for a cashier. The code of the machine enforces the agreement automatically.

Smart contracts do the same for digital value. They allow developers to create decentralized applications (dApps) that run on the blockchain without any intermediaries. This programmable money is the engine behind:

- **Decentralized Finance (DeFi):** Building lending, borrowing, and trading services without banks.
- **Non-Fungible Tokens (NFTs):** Creating unique, ownable digital items.
- **Decentralized Autonomous Organizations (DAOs):** Forming internet-native organizations governed by code.

Ethereum, therefore, isn't just a payment network; it's a global, open-source platform for developers to build and deploy these unstoppable applications.

Case Study: The DAO Hack and the Ethereum Fork

In 2016, one of the first major projects on Ethereum was "The DAO," a decentralized venture capital fund. It raised over $150 million worth of ETH, but there was a bug in its smart contract code. An attacker exploited this bug and began to drain the funds.

This created a massive crisis. The code was law, and the smart contract was executing exactly as it was written, even though it was being exploited. To reverse the theft, the Ethereum community made a controversial decision: they performed a "hard fork"—a network upgrade that essentially turned back the clock on the blockchain to a point before the hack, creating a new version of the chain where the theft never occurred.

A small part of the community disagreed, arguing that code should be law no matter what. They continued to run the original, unaltered chain, which is now known as "Ethereum Classic" (ETC). The main chain became the Ethereum (ETH) we know today. This event is a powerful case study of the immense power of smart contracts, the risks of bugs in immutable code, and the human element of governance in decentralized systems.

Practical Application: Exploring the dApp Ecosystem

The world of dApps built on Ethereum and other smart contract platforms is vast and growing daily.

- **Try This How-To:**

1. Go to a website like **DappRadar**. This site acts as a directory for thousands of dApps across many blockchains.
2. Explore the different categories: "DeFi," "Games," "Marketplaces."

3. Click on a few of the top-ranked dApps. You don't need to connect a wallet or use them.
4. Simply browse their websites to get a sense of the incredible variety of applications being built—from decentralized exchanges and lending platforms to blockchain-based games and art markets. This will give you a real sense of what a "world computer" enables.

Key Takeaways

- **Ethereum is a Platform:** More than just a cryptocurrency, Ethereum is a global, decentralized platform for running smart contracts and building dApps.
- **Smart Contracts are Automated Agreements:** They are "if-then" statements written in code that execute automatically on the blockchain without intermediaries.
- **The Engine of Web3:** Ethereum's smart contract capability is the foundational technology that powers the vast majority of the DeFi, NFT, and DAO ecosystems.

Bridge to the Next Lesson

You now understand the two giants of the crypto world, Bitcoin and Ethereum. But how do you actually acquire them? The next step in our journey is the most practical one yet: learning how to use a centralized exchange, the primary "on-ramp" from the traditional financial world into the digital one.

Lesson 06 - How to Buy Your First Crypto (Exchanges)

An Introduction to the On-Ramp

The world of cryptocurrency can feel like a separate, digital nation with its own currency. To enter that nation, you first need to go through a currency exchange. In the crypto world, these are the primary on-ramps where you can trade your government-issued money, like Australian Dollars, for digital assets like Bitcoin and Ethereum. Understanding how these platforms work is the essential first step to building your portfolio.

The Core Explanation: The Digital Currency Broker

The simplest and most common way for a beginner to buy cryptocurrency is through a **Centralized Exchange (CEX)**. Think of a CEX as a traditional brokerage or a digital marketplace. It's a company that provides a platform for users to easily buy, sell, and trade a wide variety of cryptocurrencies. Popular and reputable examples include **Coinbase, Binance, and Kraken**.

The process for getting started is generally standardized across all major exchanges:

1. **Sign Up:** You create an account on the exchange's website or mobile app, just like you would for any other online service.
2. **Verify Your Identity (KYC):** Due to global anti-money laundering regulations, you will be required to complete an identity verification process known as **KYC ("Know Your Customer")**. This typically involves providing your name, address, and a photo of your government-issued ID.

3. **Deposit Funds:** You connect your bank account or use a debit card to deposit your local fiat currency (e.g., AUD) into your exchange account.
4. **Buy Crypto:** Once your funds have cleared, you can navigate to the trading section of the platform and place an order to buy the cryptocurrency of your choice.

These platforms are designed to be user-friendly, providing a crucial and accessible bridge from the world of traditional finance into the crypto ecosystem.

Case Study: The Mt. Gox Collapse - A Cautionary Tale

In the early days of crypto, one exchange called Mt. Gox handled over 70% of all Bitcoin transactions worldwide. It was *the* place to buy Bitcoin. In 2014, the exchange abruptly shut down and filed for bankruptcy, announcing that it had been hacked and had lost hundreds of thousands of Bitcoin belonging to its customers.

The collapse of Mt. Gox was a catastrophic event that triggered a major bear market. More importantly, it taught the crypto world a brutal lesson: when you leave your crypto on a centralized exchange, you do not truly own it. You are trusting the exchange's security and solvency. This event became the foundational argument for self-custody, a concept we will explore in the coming lessons.

Practical Application: Getting Familiar with the Interface

Even before you're ready to invest, you can take the first step by getting comfortable with the environment.

- **Try This How-To:**

1. Choose a large, reputable exchange that operates in

your country (a quick search for "best crypto exchanges Australia" will provide a list).
2. Go through the process of creating an account and completing the identity verification.
3. **Do not deposit any money yet.**
4. Simply spend some time navigating the user dashboard. Find the "deposit" and "withdraw" sections. Look at the trading interface. Find the list of available assets.

This no-risk exercise will demystify the platform and make you feel much more confident and prepared when you eventually decide to make your first purchase.

Key Takeaways

- **Exchanges are the On-Ramp:** Centralized exchanges are the most common and beginner-friendly way to convert fiat currency (like AUD) into cryptocurrency.
- **KYC is Standard:** Be prepared to verify your identity on any major exchange as part of global regulatory compliance.
- **Exchange Risk is Real:** Leaving your crypto on an exchange means you are trusting that company with your assets. It is convenient but comes with risks, as shown by historical failures like Mt. Gox.

Bridge to the Next Lesson

Once you buy crypto on an exchange, you have a choice: leave it there, or move it into your own possession. To truly own your digital assets, you need a "wallet." In our next lesson, we will explore what a crypto wallet is and the critical difference between your public and private keys.

Lesson 07 - What is a Crypto Wallet? (Public vs. Private Keys)

An Introduction to Digital Property Rights

In the physical world, possession is nine-tenths of the law. If you hold a gold coin in your hand, it's yours. But how do you "hold" a digital asset? The answer is a crypto wallet. A wallet is the tool that gives you true ownership and control over your digital property. Understanding how it works is not just a technical detail—it's the most critical piece of knowledge for securing your assets and becoming a sovereign individual in the digital economy.

The Core Explanation: The Keeper of Your Keys

A common misconception is that a crypto wallet "stores" your coins. This isn't quite right. Your coins always exist on the blockchain itself. A crypto wallet is a tool that stores your cryptographic keys—the secret information that proves you are the owner of the coins at a specific address on the blockchain.

Every non-custodial wallet is built around two types of keys:

1. **The Public Key (Your Address):** Think of this as your bank account number. It is a long string of letters and numbers that you can safely share with anyone. When someone wants to send you cryptocurrency, they send it to this address. It is derived from your public key,

and it's what you see when you click "Receive" in your wallet.

2. **The Private Key (Your Password & Signature):** This is the single most important piece of information in all of crypto. Think of your private key as your secret password, your PIN, and your legally binding signature all rolled into one. It is the master key that grants the ability to spend or send the funds associated with your public address. **Whoever knows the private key** has absolute control over the funds.

This is why you must **NEVER, EVER share your private key with anyone**. It is the mathematical proof of your ownership. Losing it means you lose your crypto forever. There is no "forgot password" service on the blockchain.

Case Study: The Man Who Threw Away a Fortune

In 2013, a Welsh IT worker named James Howells accidentally threw away a computer hard drive. This wasn't just any old hard drive; it contained the private keys to a wallet holding approximately 8,000 Bitcoins. At the time, they were worth a few million dollars. Today, they would be worth hundreds of millions.

For years, he has been petitioning his local council for permission to excavate the landfill where the hard drive is buried, even offering a massive reward. So far, they have refused due to environmental concerns. His story is a tragic and world-famous case study on the absolute importance of the private key. He knows the coins are his, the world knows they are his, but without the private key stored on that hard drive, he has no way to access them. They are lost forever unless he can find that physical key.

Practical Application: Finding Your Public Address

Every crypto user needs to know how to safely find and share their public address to receive funds.

- **Try This How-To (Conceptually):**

1. Imagine you have just set up a new crypto wallet app on your phone.
2. Open the app and look for a button that says "Receive" or "Deposit."
3. The next screen will show you your wallet's public address for a specific cryptocurrency (e.g., Bitcoin). It will display a long string of characters (like bc1q...) and a corresponding QR code.
4. Notice the "Copy" button next to the address. This is the button you would use to copy your address to your clipboard to safely share it with a sender.

Familiarizing yourself with this simple process is a core skill for transacting in crypto.

Key Takeaways

- **Wallets Store Keys, Not Coins:** A crypto wallet's primary job is to securely manage your private keys, which in turn give you control over your coins on the blockchain.
- **Public is for Receiving, Private is for Spending:** Your public key (address) is like a bank account number and is safe to share. Your private key is like your secret password and must never be shared.
- **Absolute Ownership, Absolute Responsibility:** The pri-

vate key gives you total control, but it also means you are solely responsible for its security. If you lose it, your funds are irrecoverable.

Bridge to the Next Lesson

Now that you understand the crucial role of private keys, we can discuss the most important choice you will make as a crypto owner: who holds them? Your decision will place you into one of two categories: using a custodial or a non-custodial wallet. Our next lesson will break down this critical difference.

Lesson 08 - Custodial vs. Non-Custodial Wallets

An Introduction to "Not Your Keys, Not Your Coins"

You've bought your first crypto on an exchange. Now you face the single most important decision for the security of your assets: where do you store it? This choice boils down to one question: **Who holds the private keys?** The answer determines whether you are merely the beneficiary of your crypto or its true, sovereign owner. This lesson will explain the fundamental difference between custodial and non-custodial wallets and introduce you to the most famous mantra in all of crypto.

The Core Explanation: The Line Between Trust and Control

There are two primary categories of crypto wallets, and the difference between them is everything.

1. **Custodial Wallets (Someone Else Holds Your Keys):**

A custodial wallet is one where a third party (a "custodian") holds and manages your private keys on your behalf.

- **Where you find them:** When you leave your crypto on a centralized exchange like Coinbase, Binance, or Kraken, you are using a custodial wallet.
- **Pros:** They are extremely convenient and user-friendly. If you forget your password to the exchange, you can go through a recovery process, just like with a bank. The user experience is familiar.
- **Cons:** You are placing 100% trust in that third party. You are trusting their security, their solvency, and their willingness to let you access your funds. If the exchange is hacked, goes bankrupt, or freezes your account, you can lose everything. You do not have final control.

1. **Non-Custodial Wallets (You Hold Your Keys):**

A non-custodial wallet is one where you, and only you, have exclusive possession and control of your private keys.

- **Where you find them:** Examples include software wallets like MetaMask and hardware wallets like Ledger or Trezor.
- **Pros:** You have absolute control and true, censorship-resistant ownership of your assets. No one can seize your funds or prevent you from making a transaction. You are your own bank.
- **Cons:** This control comes with absolute personal respon-

sibility. If you lose your private keys or the seed phrase that backs them up, there is no customer support to call. Your funds are permanently and irretrievably lost.

This critical distinction leads to the famous crypto mantra: **"Not your keys, not your coins."** It's a constant reminder that if you are not in direct possession of the private keys, you are relying on a promise, not on the mathematical certainty of the blockchain.

Case Study: The FTX & Celsius Collapses (2022)

The year 2022 provided a brutal, real-world lesson on the risks of custodial platforms. Two massive centralized crypto companies, Celsius (a lending platform) and FTX (an exchange), collapsed and declared bankruptcy.

Hundreds of thousands of users who had left their crypto on these platforms—believing it was safe in their custodial wallets—suddenly found their accounts frozen. They could not withdraw their funds. In the subsequent bankruptcy proceedings, these users were legally classified as "unsecured creditors," meaning they are at the back of the line to maybe, someday, get a fraction of their money back.

Crucially, users who had been interacting with decentralized protocols using their own non-custodial wallets were completely unaffected by these company failures. Their assets remained secure in their own possession. This was the ultimate validation for the "not your keys, not your coins" ethos.

Practical Application: The Sovereignty Test

How can you quickly tell if you are using a custodial or non-custodial service?

- **Try This How-To:**

Ask yourself one simple question: "When I set this up, was I given a secret phrase of 12 or 24 words that I was told to write down and keep safe?"

1. If the answer is **YES**, you are likely using a non-custodial wallet. That phrase is your master key, and you have self-sovereignty.
2. If the answer is **NO**, and you just have a username and password to log into a website, you are using a custodial service. You are trusting that company with your keys.

This simple test is the clearest way to understand who is ultimately in control of your digital assets.

Key Takeaways

- **The Key Question is Control:** The difference between wallet types is who controls the private keys—a third-party company (custodial) or you (non-custodial).
- **Custodial is Convenient but Trust-Based:** Leaving funds on an exchange is easy but requires you to trust that the company is secure and solvent.
- **Non-Custodial is Sovereign but Requires Responsibility:** Holding your own keys gives you true ownership but means you are solely responsible for securing them.
- **"Not Your Keys, Not Your Coins":** This is the most important security principle in cryptocurrency.

Bridge to the Next Lesson

For those who choose the path of self-sovereignty, the first step is usually setting up a software-based non-custodial wallet. These are often called "hot wallets." In our next lesson, we will walk through what a hot wallet is and the single most important security procedure you must follow when setting one up.

Lesson 09 - Setting Up a Hot Wallet (e.g., MetaMask)

An Introduction to Your Digital "Checking Account"

If you've decided to take control of your assets with a non-custodial wallet, your journey will almost certainly begin with a "hot wallet." This type of wallet is like your everyday physical wallet or a bank checking account: it's designed for convenience and frequent use, holding the funds you need for daily transactions. Setting one up is your entry ticket to the interactive world of Web3, but it comes with a critical security step that you absolutely must get right.

The Core Explanation: Convenient, Connected, and Vulnerable

A 'hot wallet' is a type of non-custodial wallet that is constantly connected to the internet. They typically exist as software in the form of a mobile app or a web browser extension. The most popular and widely used hot wallet for the Ethereum ecosystem is MetaMask.

- **Pros:** Their internet connection makes them extremely convenient. They allow you to quickly and easily send transactions and connect to thousands of dApps, from

DeFi protocols to NFT marketplaces. They are your active portal to Web3.

- **Cons:** Their constant internet connection also makes them vulnerable to online threats. If your computer or phone is infected with malware or you fall for a phishing scam, a hot wallet is at risk of being compromised. This is why it's best practice not to store your entire life savings in a hot wallet.

The single most important moment in a hot wallet's lifecycle is its creation. When you first set one up, the wallet will generate and present to you a 12 or 24-word 'seed phrase' (also called a recovery phrase or mnemonic phrase). This phrase is the master key to your entire wallet.

Case Study: The Phishing Scams

Phishing scams are the most common way that hot wallets are compromised. A scammer will create a fake website that looks identical to a popular dApp, like the decentralized exchange Uniswap. They will promote this fake site via social media or a direct message.

An unsuspecting user will navigate to the fake site and try to connect their MetaMask wallet. A pop-up will appear, but instead of the normal transaction approval, it will be a fake error message that says something like, "Wallet sync error. Please re-enter your 12-word seed phrase to reconnect."

The moment the user types their seed phrase into this box, the scammer captures it. Within seconds, they use the phrase to restore the user's wallet on their own computer and drain it of all its funds. This happens every single day and serves as a brutal reminder: No legitimate service will ever ask you for your seed phrase.

Practical Application: The Seed Phrase Security Drill

Your seed phrase is the master key to your financial sovereignty. Securing it properly is the most important skill in self-custody.

- **Try This How-To:**

This is the most critical "how-to" in this entire module.

- **Write It Down on Paper:** When your wallet gives you the seed phrase, write it down carefully on a piece of paper. Number each word. Double-check the spelling and order.

- **NEVER Store It Digitally:** Do not take a photo of it. Do not save it in a text file, a notes app, an email draft, or a password manager. Any digital storage method is a target for hackers. It must be kept 100% offline.

- **Store It Securely:** Store the piece of paper in a secure, private location where it is safe from fire, water damage, and prying eyes (e.g., a home safe). For added security, consider making two copies and storing them in separate, secure locations.

Treating your seed phrase with this level of seriousness is non-negotiable for anyone who values their assets.

Key Takeaways

- **Hot Wallets are for Daily Use:** They are internet-connected software wallets that offer convenience for transactions but come with higher security risks.
- **The Seed Phrase is Everything:** Your 12 or 24-word seed phrase is the master backup key to your wallet. Anyone who has it has full control of your funds.
- **Offline Storage is the Golden Rule:** Your seed phrase must be written down and stored in a secure, physical, offline location. Never store it digitally.

Bridge to the Next Lesson

Hot wallets are perfect for everyday spending and small amounts. But where should you store your long-term holdings and significant savings? For that, you need to move your assets from a "checking account" to a high-security vault. In our next lesson, we'll introduce the gold standard of crypto security: cold storage.

Lesson 10 - Introduction to Cold Storage (e.g., Ledger, Trezor)

An Introduction to Your Digital Fortress

A hot wallet is perfect for everyday transactions, like a checking account. But you wouldn't keep your entire life savings in a checking account, would you? For long-term holdings and significant value, you need a vault—a place of maximum security, isolated from daily threats. In the crypto world, this vault is called "cold storage." This lesson will introduce you to the gold standard of cryptocurrency security, the single best way to protect your assets for the long run.

The Core Explanation: Taking Your Keys Offline

'Cold storage' refers to the practice of storing your cryptocurrency private keys in a completely offline environment. The goal is to create an "air gap" between your keys and the internet, making them immune to the online threats that can affect hot wallets, such as viruses, malware, and phishing attacks.

The most common and user-friendly form of cold storage is the hardware wallet. This is a small, physical device, often resembling a USB stick, that is specifically designed for one purpose: to keep your private keys secure. The most popular brands are **Ledger and Trezor**.

Here is how a hardware wallet achieves its superior security:

1. **Key Generation & Storage:** When you set up the device, your private keys (and the corresponding seed phrase) are generated and stored within a specialized, secure chip inside the device itself. These keys never leave the device.
2. **Transaction Signing:** When you want to send crypto, you connect the hardware wallet to your computer or phone. Your software wallet (like MetaMask) creates the transaction details and sends them to the hardware device.
3. **Offline Confirmation:** You then verify the transaction details (amount and recipient address) on the hardware wallet's small, trusted screen. To approve the transac-

tion, you must physically press a button on the device. This action "signs" the transaction internally using your private keys, without ever exposing them to your internet-connected computer. The signed transaction is then broadcast to the network.

This process ensures that even if your computer is completely compromised with a virus, your funds cannot be stolen, because the final, physical approval step cannot be faked by a remote hacker.

Case Study: The Sophisticated Malware Attack

Consider a real-world scenario that has affected many crypto users. A trader downloads what they think is a legitimate piece of software, but it contains sophisticated malware. The malware sits silently on their computer, waiting.

When the trader uses their hot wallet (like MetaMask) to send a transaction, the malware springs into action at the last second. It intercepts the transaction and swaps the intended recipient's address with the hacker's address. The user, looking at their computer screen, might not notice the last-second change and approves the transaction, sending their funds to the thief.

However, a user with a hardware wallet would be protected. The malware could still try to alter the transaction on the computer screen, but the user's process is to check the final address on the hardware device's trusted screen. When they see a mismatch between what their computer says and what the secure device says, they will reject the transaction, and the theft is foiled. This illustrates the power of an independent, offline verification step.

Practical Application: Researching Your Fortress

While you may not be ready to buy one today, understanding how these devices work is a key piece of security knowledge.

- **Try This How-To:**

1. Go to the official website for either Ledger or Trezor. Crucially, never buy a hardware wallet from a second-hand source like eBay, as it could be tampered with.
2. Navigate to their "Products" section and choose their flagship model (e.g., Ledger Nano S Plus or Trezor Model One).
3. Watch the official "Getting Started" or "How it Works" video on their site. This will give you a clear, visual demonstration of the setup process, how it connects to a computer, and how it's used to approve transactions safely.

Key Takeaways

- **Cold Storage Means Keys are Offline:** The core principle is to isolate your private keys from the internet and its associated risks.
- **Hardware Wallets are the Gold Standard:** These physical devices are the most secure and user-friendly way to implement a cold storage strategy.
- **Security Through Physical Verification:** Hardware wallets protect you by requiring you to physically verify and approve all transactions on the device itself, protecting you from online hacks.

Bridge to the Next Lesson

Now that you understand the different ways to store your crypto, from exchanges to hot and cold wallets, it's time to learn the practical rules of the road for moving it. In our next lesson, we'll cover the essential safety checks for sending and receiving crypto.

Lesson 11 - How to Send and Receive Crypto Safely

An Introduction to Irreversible Transactions

In traditional finance, mistakes can often be reversed. You can cancel a bank transfer or dispute a credit card charge. In the world of crypto, there is no such safety net. Blockchain transactions are **final and irreversible**. This gives the system its strength and censorship resistance, but it also means the responsibility for accuracy falls entirely on you. This lesson is your "measure twice, cut once" guide to transacting safely, ensuring your assets always end up exactly where you intend them to go.

The Core Explanation: A Process of Precision

Moving crypto is a straightforward process, but it demands careful attention to detail at every step.

- How to Receive Crypto Safely:

1. **Open Your Wallet:** Access the wallet where you want to receive the funds.
2. **Find Your Public Address:** Look for a "Receive" or "Deposit" button. The wallet will display your public address for the specific coin you wish to receive (e.g., your

Bitcoin address will be different from your Ethereum address).

3. **Copy and Share Carefully:** Use the "Copy" button to copy the full address to your clipboard. Share this exact address with the person sending you the funds. It's often best to double-check with them that the address they received matches the one you sent.

- How to Send Crypto Safely:

1. **Obtain the Recipient's Address:** Get the correct public address from the person or service you are paying.
2. **Copy and Paste:** Never type an address by hand. They are long, case-sensitive, and complex. Always use the copy and paste functions to transfer the address into the "Send" field of your wallet.
3. **VERIFY. VERIFY. VERIFY:** This is the most critical step. Before you hit "Send," you must visually verify that the address you pasted is correct. The best practice is the "First and Last Check." Compare the first 4-5 characters and the last 4-5 characters of the pasted address with the original source provided by the recipient.

Case Study: The Clipboard Hijacking Malware

One of the most insidious types of malwares targets this exact process. A "clipboard hijacker" is a malicious program that runs silently in the background of an infected computer.

It is programmed to detect when a user copies a string of characters that looks like a cryptocurrency address. When it detects this, it instantly and secretly replaces the contents of the clipboard with the hacker's own crypto address.

The user's workflow is this:

1. They copy the correct address from their friend.
2. They go to their wallet and paste the address.
3. They enter the amount and hit "Send," believing they have sent it to their friend.

But because the malware swapped the address in the clipboard, the funds are sent directly to the hacker, never to be seen again. This is why the manual "First and Last Check" is not just a suggestion; it is a critical defence against this very real threat.

Practical Application: The Test Transaction Method

For any transaction that is significant to you—whether it's $100 or $100,000—there is a golden rule that will eliminate the risk of a catastrophic mistake.

- **Try This How-To (The Test Transaction):**

1. Before you send the full amount, first send a very small, trivial amount (e.g., $1 worth) to the recipient's address, following all the verification steps.
2. Wait for the transaction to be confirmed on the blockchain.
3. Contact the recipient and have them personally confirm that they have received the small test amount in their wallet.
4. Only after you have received this confirmation should you proceed to send the full, intended amount to that same, now-verified address.

This patient, two-step process takes a few extra minutes but provides complete peace of mind and can save you from a devastating loss.

Key Takeaways

- **Crypto Transactions are Final:** There is no "undo" button on the blockchain. The responsibility for accuracy is entirely yours.
- **Copy, Paste, and Verify:** Always copy and paste addresses, and always perform the "First and Last Check" to confirm the address is correct before sending.
- **The Test Transaction is Your Best Friend:** For any significant amount, sending a small test transaction first is the ultimate safety net.

Bridge to the Next Lesson

Every transaction you send comes with a fee. But who are you paying, and why does the price seem to change every time you make a transaction? In our next lesson, we'll demystify the concept of transaction fees, often called 'gas' on the Ethereum network.

Lesson 12 - Understanding Transaction Fees (Gas)

An Introduction to Paying for the Network

When you use a bank, you often pay fees for services. When you use a blockchain, you also pay fees, but they work in a completely different way. These fees aren't profit for a corporation; they are the economic lifeblood that keeps the entire decentralized network secure and running. Understanding what these fees are, who they go to, and why they fluctuate is key to understanding the economics of a blockchain. This lesson will explain the crucial role of transaction fees, also known as "gas."

The Core Explanation: The Incentive Layer of the Blockchain

Why aren't crypto transactions free? Because a decentralized network is not run by a single company; it's run by a global, distributed group of participants called miners (in Proof-of-Work) or validators (in Proof-of-Stake). These participants use their own resources (computing power or staked capital) to process transactions, bundle them into blocks, and secure the network.

The transaction fee is a direct payment from you, the user, to the validator who includes your transaction in a new block. This fee serves two primary purposes:

1. **It creates an economic incentive:** It rewards validators for their work, encouraging them to continue contributing their resources to keep the network secure and operational.
2. **It prevents spam:** If transactions were free, anyone could endlessly send tiny, useless transactions to clog up the network. Fees make this kind of spam attack economically unfeasible.

On the Ethereum network, this fee is famously called "Gas." Just as a car needs gasoline to drive, a transaction needs a certain amount of gas to be executed by the network. The price of this gas is not fixed; it operates like a real-time auction.

Case Study: The NFT Boom and Soaring Gas Prices

The concept of fluctuating gas fees was put on dramatic display during the NFT boom of 2021. When a highly anticipated NFT project like the Bored Ape Yacht Club or a new collection by a famous artist was launched, thousands of people would rush to "mint" (create) the new NFTs at the exact same time.

This created a massive, sudden spike in demand for the limited space in each Ethereum block. It became a frantic bidding war. Users who wanted to ensure their transaction was included quickly had to offer validators a very high gas fee. At the peak of this hype, gas prices on Ethereum skyrocketed. A simple transaction that might have cost $10 on a normal day could suddenly cost $200, $500, or even more. This period was a powerful real-world demonstration of how network congestion directly impacts the price of gas based on simple supply and demand.

Practical Application: Checking the Gas Price

You don't have to guess what the current network fee is. There are tools that allow you to see the real-time cost of transacting.

- **Try This How-To:**

1. Go to a website called the Etherscan Gas Tracker.
2. This page shows the current recommended gas price for the Ethereum network, measured in a small unit of ETH called "Gwei."
3. It will typically show prices for three levels: Low (cheaper, but your transaction will be slow), Average

(the standard price for a reasonably fast transaction), and High (a premium price to get your transaction confirmed very quickly).

4. Bookmark this site. Checking it before you plan to make a transaction can help you choose a time when the network is less congested and fees are lower.

Key Takeaways

- **Fees Secure the Network:** Transaction fees are an essential economic incentive that rewards the validators who process transactions and keep the blockchain secure.
- **Gas is the Fee on Ethereum:** On the Ethereum network, transaction fees are known as "Gas."
- **Fees Fluctuate with Demand:** The price of gas is not fixed. It operates like an auction, where prices rise during times of high network congestion and fall when the network is quiet.

Bridge to the Next Lesson

The crypto world has its own unique economy, but unfortunately, it also attracts its own unique type of criminal. The permissionless nature of the technology means you must be your own line of defence. In our next lesson, we'll cover the most common scams and how to protect yourself.

Lesson 13 - Common Scams and How to Avoid Them

An Introduction to Staying Safe on the Frontier

The world of crypto is a new and exciting frontier, full of innovation and opportunity. But like any frontier, it is also home to scammers and thieves looking to take advantage of newcomers. In a decentralized world where you are your own bank, you must also be your own security guard. This lesson is your security briefing. It will arm you with the knowledge to spot the most common scams so you can navigate the ecosystem safely and confidently.

The Core Explanation: The Scammer's Playbook

While scams can come in many forms, most of them rely on a few simple psychological tricks and target your most valuable asset: your private key or seed phrase. Here are the most common types to watch out for:

1. **Phishing Scams:** This is the most common threat. Scammers create fake websites, emails, or social media accounts that look identical to a legitimate service (like MetaMask, OpenSea, or your favourite exchange). They will lure you to their fake site and then try to trick you into entering your secret seed phrase or private key, often with a fake pop-up that claims you need to "verify your wallet" or "fix a sync error." **The Golden Rule: No legitimate service will EVER ask for your seed phrase.**
2. **Giveaway Scams:** You will see these all-over social media. A scammer will impersonate a well-known figure like Elon Musk or a famous crypto project. They will post a message saying, "To celebrate, we are giving away 10 BTC! Send 0.1 BTC to this address to participate,

and we will send you 0.2 BTC back!" This is **always** a scam. They are simply trying to get you to send them your crypto. You will receive nothing in return.

3. **Pump and Dump Schemes:** This is a form of market manipulation. A group of insiders will buy a large amount of a new, unknown, and worthless coin. They will then use social media to create a massive amount of fake hype and "shill" the coin to unsuspecting newcomers. As people FOMO in and buy the coin, the price skyrockets. The original insiders then "dump" all their coins at the peak, crashing the price to zero and leaving everyone else holding a worthless asset.

Case Study: The 2020 Twitter Hack

In July 2020, the world witnessed one of the most audacious scams in crypto history. Hackers gained access to Twitter's internal systems and took control of dozens of the most high-profile accounts on the platform, including those of Barack Obama, Joe Biden, Elon Musk, Bill Gates, Apple, and Uber.

From these verified, trusted accounts, they all began tweeting the same simple message: a classic giveaway scam. They promised to double any Bitcoin sent to a specific address within the next 30 minutes. Because the messages were coming from some of the most famous and trusted names in the world, many people fell for it, believing it was a legitimate promotion. The hackers made off with over $100,000 in a matter of hours. This event was a stark lesson that you should be sceptical of a deal that sounds too good to be true, even if it appears to be coming from a trusted source.

Practical Application: Your Personal Security Checklist

Your best defence is a healthy dose of scepticism and a

consistent security routine.

- **Try This How-To:**

Create a personal security checklist that you mentally run through before any major action.

1. **Am I on the Official Site?** "I will always double-check the URL in my browser's address bar to ensure it is the correct, official website and not a phishing clone."
2. **Is Someone Asking for My Secrets?** "I will NEVER, under any circumstances, type my 12 or 24-word seed phrase into a website or give it to anyone who asks."
3. **Does This Seem Too Good to Be True?** "I will treat any promise of free money, guaranteed high returns, or 'double your crypto' giveaways as a scam 100% of the time."

Internalizing these three rules will protect you from the vast majority of scams in the crypto space.

Key Takeaways

- **Guard Your Seed Phrase:** Your seed phrase is the master key to your funds. Never share it or type it into any website.
- **If It's Too Good to Be True, It Is:** The promise of free, easy, or guaranteed high returns is always a red flag for a scam.
- **Trust but Verify... Everything:** Be sceptical of unsolicited messages, verify information through official channels,

and always double-check URLs.

Bridge to the Next Lesson

While we must be vigilant against scams and volatility, there is a class of cryptocurrencies designed specifically to avoid price swings. In our next lesson, we'll explore the essential tool that provides a safe haven in the market and powers the DeFi ecosystem: stablecoins.

Lesson 14 - Introduction to Stablecoins (USDT, USDC)

An Introduction to Crypto's Stability Anchor

One of the biggest challenges for cryptocurrencies like Bitcoin and Ethereum is their price volatility. How can you use an asset for daily payments if its value can swing by 10% in a single day? The solution to this problem is one of the most important and widely used innovations in the entire ecosystem: stablecoins. These are a special class of digital asset designed to be a stability anchor in the often-stormy seas of the crypto market.

The Core Explanation: Pegged to Stability

A stablecoin is a type of cryptocurrency whose value is pegged, or tied, to another, more stable asset. In most cases, they are pegged 1-to-1 to a major fiat currency, like the US Dollar. The goal is to create a digital asset that has the stability of traditional money but can move on the rails of a global, decentralized blockchain.

The most common type of stablecoin is **fiat-collateralized**. Here's how it works:

1. A central, regulated company (the issuer) creates the stablecoin token (e.g., **USDC** or **USDT**).
2. For every one token they issue, they hold one US Dollar (or a highly liquid, equivalent asset like a short-term government bond) in a real-world, audited bank account or reserve.
3. This 1-to-1 backing ensures that the token should always be redeemable for $1, which keeps its market price stable at around $1.

Stablecoins are the bedrock of the crypto economy. They serve three crucial roles:

- **A Safe Haven:** Traders use them to move out of volatile assets like Bitcoin during market downturns without having to convert their funds back to a traditional bank.
- **A Unit of Account:** Most trading pairs on crypto exchanges are priced in stablecoins, and they are the primary currency used for lending and borrowing in DeFi.
- **A Bridge to Traditional Finance:** They provide a simple and efficient way to move value between the traditional banking system and the crypto ecosystem.

Case Study: The Tale of Two Stablecoins (USDC vs. UST)

Not all stablecoins are created equal. The way they maintain their peg is critically important.

- **USDC (USD Coin)** is a leading example of a fiat-collateralized stablecoin. It is issued by a regulated US company called Circle. For every USDC, Circle holds an equivalent amount of cash and short-term

U.S. government bonds in reserves, and these reserves are regularly audited by third-party accounting firms. This model is designed for maximum transparency and stability.

- **UST (TerraUSD)**, in contrast, was an "algorithmic" stablecoin. It was not backed by real-world assets. Instead, it tried to maintain its peg using a complex algorithm and a sister token called LUNA. In May 2022, this system failed catastrophically. UST lost its peg and its value collapsed to near zero, wiping out tens of billions of dollars in value.

This event was a powerful lesson that the quality of the reserves and the mechanism behind a stablecoin are of the utmost importance. Asset-backed stablecoins are, by a huge margin, considered safer than their experimental algorithmic counterparts.

Practical Application: Seeing Stablecoins in Action

The scale of stablecoins shows just how essential they are to the crypto market's daily operations.

- **Try This How-To:**

1. Go to a crypto data site like CoinGecko.
2. In the list of top cryptocurrencies by market cap, look for **Tether (USDT)** and **USD Coin (USDC)**.
3. Notice their market caps, which are in the tens of billions of dollars. They are consistently ranked among the top cryptocurrencies in the world.
4. This massive scale demonstrates their role as the primary liquidity, settlement, and trading assets for the entire global crypto market.

Key Takeaways

- **Stablecoins are Pegged for Stability:** They are cryptocurrencies designed to maintain a stable value by being tied to an asset like the US Dollar.
- **The Bridge of the Crypto World:** They act as a safe haven from volatility and are the primary unit of account for trading and DeFi.
- **The Backing Matters Most:** Fiat-collateralized stablecoins (like USDC), which are backed by audited, real-world assets, are considered much safer and more reliable than other experimental models.

Bridge to the Next Lesson

We've covered technology, security, and the assets themselves. But there's one principle that underpins everything you do in this space, a mindset that separates successful participants from victims. In our final lesson of this module, we'll cover the most important rule in all of crypto: **Do Your Own Research**.

Lesson 15 - The Most Important Rule: DYOR

An Introduction to Self-Sovereignty

In the world of traditional finance, there are regulators, advisors, and consumer protection agencies designed to shield you from the worst outcomes. In the decentralized world of crypto, those safety nets are largely absent. This is a feature, not a bug—it's a world built on the principles of self-sovereignty and personal responsibility. To thrive here, you must adopt the mindset of a sovereign individual. This brings us to the most important, three-word principle in the entire industry: **Do Your Own Research (DYOR).**

The Core Explanation: The Investor's Prime Directive

DYOR is the ethos that you should never blindly trust what other people say about an investment; you must take responsibility for investigating and verifying information for yourself before putting your capital at risk.

Why is this so critical in crypto?

- **A World of Hype and Shills:** The crypto market is heavily influenced by social media. There are thousands of anonymous accounts and paid influencers who are financially incentivized to "shill" or promote certain projects, regardless of their quality. Trusting them is a recipe for disaster.
- **Complex Technology:** The underlying technology can be complex and difficult to understand, making it easy for bad actors to make false claims that sound plausible to a newcomer.
- **No Recourse:** If you invest in a project that turns out to be a scam or a failure based on someone else's recommendation, there is no one to blame and no way to get your money back. The responsibility is yours alone.

Doing your own research is the process of moving from a state of trust to a state of understanding.

Case Study: The Bitconnect Ponzi Scheme

Bitconnect, which rose to prominence during the 2017 bull run, is the textbook case study for the importance of DYOR.

The platform promised impossibly high and "guaranteed" daily returns on investment, generated by a secret "trading bot." It had a massive marketing push, a cult-like community, and a multi-level referral system that rewarded people for bringing in new users.

To anyone with a basic understanding of finance, the promises were obvious red flags for a classic Ponzi scheme. The "guaranteed" high returns were mathematically impossible. However, thousands of investors, caught up in the hype and the promises of easy wealth, poured their money in without doing any critical research.

When the scheme inevitably collapsed in early 2018, the token's value went to zero, and an estimated $4 billion of investor capital was wiped out. It was a brutal lesson that if you don't do your own basic research, you are at the mercy of the market's most manipulative actors.

Practical Application: Your DYOR Starter Checklist

You don't need to be a technology expert to do basic research. You just need to know what questions to ask.

- **Try This How-To:**

Before ever considering an investment in a new crypto project, create and use a simple checklist to get the basic facts.

1. **The Whitepaper & Website:** "Have I read the project's official website and at least the introduction of its whitepaper? Do I understand, in simple terms, what problem this project is trying to solve?"
2. **The Team:** "Who is the team behind this project? Are they public with their real identities and photos? Do

they have relevant experience on their LinkedIn profiles? (Anonymous teams are a major red flag)."
3. **The Tokenomics:** "What is the purpose of the project's token? Is it used for something essential within the ecosystem? What is its total supply, and how was it distributed? (A large percentage given to the team and insiders can be a red flag)."
4. **The Community:** "Have I looked at their Discord and Twitter? Is the community having intelligent discussions about the project, or is it 99% hype, memes, and people asking 'wen moon?'"

This simple, four-part check will help you filter out many low-quality projects and scams.

Key Takeaways

- **DYOR is the Golden Rule:** In a decentralized and unregulated market, you are solely responsible for your investment decisions.
- **Don't Trust, Verify:** Cultivate a healthy scepticism towards hype and claims made on social media. Always seek out primary sources of information.
- **A Basic Framework is Your Best Tool:** You don't need to be an expert to do good research. A simple checklist focusing on the project's purpose, team, tokenomics, and community will protect you from most major risks.

4

Module 2 Recap

You have now completed a crucial module that takes you from theory to practice.

- You've learned about the grand vision of **Web3** and the foundational technology of the **blockchain** that makes it all possible.
- You understand the difference between **Bitcoin (digital gold)** and **Ethereum (the world computer)**.
- You now know the practical steps for buying crypto on an exchange and the critical importance of security, from understanding your public and private keys to choosing between custodial and non-custodial wallets.
- You are armed with a security-first mindset, knowing how to transact safely, understand **gas fees**, spot common scams, and, most importantly, the foundational principle of **Doing Your Own Research**.

You are no longer just an observer; you have the foun-

dational knowledge and skills to safely enter the crypto ecosystem.

5

Module 3 - Entering the Ecosystem

Module Introduction: You've built your foundation in finance and you understand the core technology of the blockchain. Now, it's time to step inside the house you've been observing from the outside. This module is all about practical application. You will learn about the key pillars of the Web3 world—NFTs, DeFi, and DAOs—and, more importantly, how to interact with them. We'll guide you through making your first trade on a decentralized exchange, understanding crypto taxes, and exploring the culture of this vibrant new ecosystem.

Lesson 01 - What are NFTs (Non-Fungible Tokens)?

An Introduction to Digital Ownership

You've probably heard of NFTs, most likely in the context of multi-million-dollar digital art or cartoon animal avatars. But behind the hype is a simple and profoundly important technological breakthrough: the ability to prove ownership of a unique item in the digital world. For the first time, the concept of "yours" can be applied to an item that exists only as data. This lesson will explain what NFTs truly are and why they represent a fundamental building block for the future of the internet.

The Core Explanation: Unique vs. Interchangeable

An NFT, or Non-Fungible Token, is a unique digital certificate of ownership that is recorded and secured on a blockchain. The key to understanding them lies in the term "non-fungible."

- **Fungible:** An item is fungible if it is interchangeable with another identical item. A $10 note is fungible; if we swap one for another, we both still have $10. A Bitcoin is fungible; one Bitcoin is the same as any other Bitcoin.
- **Non-Fungible:** An item is non-fungible if it is unique and cannot be replaced one-for-one. Your house deed is non-fungible; it represents ownership of one specific property. A ticket to a specific seat at a concert is non-fungible. The original Mona Lisa painting is non-fungible.

An NFT is simply a token on the blockchain that acts as the digital equivalent of that unique deed or ticket. The blockchain's public ledger provides an unbreakable, universally verifiable record of who owns that specific token. While anyone can copy the image or song an NFT points to, only one person can own the official token that represents the authentic original. It can represent ownership of a specific digital or physical asset, like art, music, or a collectible.

Case Study: Beeple's "Everydays" at Christie's

For a long time, digital art was seen as having little value because it could be infinitely copied. How could you own a JPG if anyone could right-click and save it? NFTs changed this.

In March 2021, the traditional art world was turned upside down when auction house Christie's sold a digital artwork by an artist named Beeple. The piece, "Everydays: The First 5000 Days," was an NFT representing a collage of all the images he had created daily for 13 years. It sold for a staggering $69.3 million.

This event was a watershed moment. It wasn't just about the price; it was about one of the most prestigious and historic auction houses in the world validating an NFT as a legitimate medium for fine art. It proved that the market was willing to attribute immense value to the provable ownership of a digital file, completely separate from the file's reproducibility.

Practical Application: The Art Gallery Analogy

Understanding the difference between an NFT and the image it represents is key.

- **Try This How-To:**

1. Go to the website of a major art museum, like the Louvre or the Met.
2. Find the page for a famous painting, like the Mona Lisa. You can view a high-resolution image of it, download it, and set it as your desktop background.
3. However, you do not own the Mona Lisa. The Louvre owns the physical painting, the one-of-a-kind original.

An NFT functions in the same way. You can download the image of a CryptoPunk, but the NFT is the digital "deed of ownership" that is stored in the owner's wallet. It is the provable link to the authentic original in a world of infinite copies.

Key Takeaways

- **NFTs are Proof of Uniqueness:** A Non-Fungible Token is a unique digital asset that proves ownership of a one-of-a-kind item on the blockchain.
- **Fungible vs. Non-Fungible:** Money is fungible (interchangeable), while items like art, real estate, and collectibles are non-fungible (unique and not interchangeable).
- **Ownership, Not the Object:** The NFT is not the image or file itself; it is the unbreakable, verifiable record of ownership of that file.

Bridge to the Next Lesson

NFTs represent the "ownership" pillar of the Web3 ecosystem. The other major pillar is a new, open financial system built on code rather than corporations. In our next lesson, we'll explore the revolutionary world of Decentralized Finance, or DeFi.

Lesson 02 - What is DeFi (Decentralized Finance)?

An Introduction to Banking Without Banks

Imagine a financial system that is open to anyone, anywhere, 24/7. A system where you can lend, borrow, trade, and earn interest without needing to ask a bank for permission. A system that is transparent, where all the rules are written in open-source code for the world to see. This isn't a futuristic dream; it's **Decentralized Finance (DeFi)**, and it's one of the most powerful and fast-growing sectors in the crypto ecosystem. This lesson will explain how DeFi is rebuilding the world of finance from the ground up.

The Core Explanation: Finance Powered by Code

DeFi is an umbrella term for an ecosystem of financial services that are built on top of blockchain technology, primarily using smart contracts. The core mission of DeFi is to disintermediate traditional finance by replacing centralized middlemen (like banks, brokers, and exchanges) with automated code.

This new financial system is built on several key principles:

1. **Open and Permissionless:** Anyone with an internet connection and a crypto wallet can access DeFi services. There are no gatekeepers, no credit checks, and no one can deny you service based on your location or background.
2. **Transparent:** Every transaction and every piece of the protocol's logic is recorded on the public blockchain. This creates a level of transparency that is impossible in the opaque world of traditional finance. You can see exactly how the system works and tracks the flow of funds in real-time.
3. **User Custody:** In most DeFi applications, you are always in control of your own assets. You interact with smart contracts directly from your non-custodial wallet, so you never have to hand over your funds to a central

company. This aligns with the crypto ethos of "not your keys, not your coins."

These principles combine to create a more open, efficient, and accessible global financial system where you can lend, borrow, trade, and earn interest on your crypto.

Case Study: The Rise of Uniswap

Before DeFi, trading new and obscure crypto assets was difficult. You had to rely on centralized exchanges to list the token, a process that could take months and involved high fees.

Then came Uniswap, a protocol that pioneered a new model called the Automated Market Maker **(AMM)**, which we'll explore in Level 2. In essence, Uniswap allowed any user to create a trading market for any two Ethereum-based tokens, instantly and without permission. It also allowed any user to contribute their assets to these markets (provide liquidity) and earn trading fees in return.

This was a paradigm shift. It democratized market making, which was previously the exclusive domain of large financial institutions. The success of Uniswap kicked off an explosion of innovation in DeFi, a period known as "DeFi Summer" in 2020, and established the DEX as a cornerstone of the on-chain economy.

Practical Application: Measuring the DeFi Economy

The scale of the DeFi ecosystem is a tangible measure of its growth and adoption.

- **Try This How-To:**

1. Go to a DeFi analytics website like DeFiLlama.

2. The main number you'll see on the homepage is the Total Value Locked **(TVL)**. This metric represents the billions of dollars of assets that users have deposited into DeFi protocols.
3. Browse the list of protocols ranked by TVL. You will see different categories like DEXs, Lending, and Liquid Staking.

Exploring this data gives you a real-time snapshot of the DeFi economy, showing you which applications are attracting the most capital and user trust.

Key Takeaways

- **DeFi is an Open Financial System:** It uses smart contracts on the blockchain to offer traditional financial services like lending and trading without centralized intermediaries.
- **Built on Transparency and User Control:** DeFi is defined by its open-access, transparent nature, and the principle that users should always maintain custody of their own assets.
- **A Multi-Billion Dollar Ecosystem:** The Total Value Locked (TVL) in DeFi protocols represents a significant and growing parallel financial system.

Bridge to the Next Lesson

One of the most popular activities in DeFi is putting your assets to work to earn a return, much like earning interest in a bank. In our next lesson, we'll explore the foundational method for earning this "passive income" in the crypto world: staking.

Lesson 03 - What is Staking? (Earning Passive Income)

An Introduction to Productive Digital Assets

Your money in a bank earns a tiny amount of interest because the bank lends it out. But what if your digital assets could do more? What if they could earn a return simply by helping to secure their own network? This is the core idea behind staking. It's a way to transform your crypto from an idle asset into a productive one, allowing you to earn rewards for actively participating in the health and security of a blockchain. This lesson will explain how you can earn passive income with your crypto.

The Core Explanation: Earning Rewards for Securing the Network

Staking is the process of locking up a certain amount of cryptocurrency to actively participate in a blockchain's network operations and security. This process is specific to blockchains that use a consensus mechanism called Proof-of-Stake (PoS).

Here's how it works in simple terms:

1. **You "Stake" Your Coins:** You take a certain amount of a blockchain's native cryptocurrency (e.g., Ethereum's ETH) and lock it in a smart contract. This acts as a security deposit or collateral.
2. **You Help the Network:** By staking your coins, you become a validator (or delegate your coins to one).

Validators are responsible for essential network tasks like confirming the legitimacy of new transactions and adding them to new blocks.

3. **You Earn Rewards:** In exchange for your service and your staked collateral, the network automatically pays you rewards, usually in the form of more of the same cryptocurrency.

Think of it as being paid for performing a valuable service. It's like earning interest in a savings account, but instead of a bank paying you, the blockchain protocol itself is rewarding you for your contribution to its security. It is a very popular way for investors to earn passive income on their holdings.

Case Study: Ethereum's "Merge"

For years, the Ethereum network was secured by Proof-of-Work, an energy-intensive process. However, the community planned for years to transition to the more efficient Proof-of-Stake model. This monumental event, known as "The Merge," finally happened in September 2022.

Overnight, the second-largest blockchain in the world changed its fundamental consensus mechanism. This was one of the most significant and ambitious software upgrades in history. The immediate effect for investors was that Ethereum's native asset, ETH, became a productive asset. For the first time, regular holders could stake their ETH to help secure the network and earn a yield on their holdings, transforming it from just a speculative asset into something akin to a digital bond or a dividend-paying stock.

Practical Application: Researching Staking Yields

Different blockchains offer different reward rates for staking, based on their specific economic models.

- **Try This How-To:**

1. Go to a data website like StakingRewards.com. This site aggregates staking data from across the crypto ecosystem.
2. In the search bar, look up a major Proof-of-Stake cryptocurrency like Ethereum (ETH), Cardano (ADA), or Solana (SOL).
3. The site will show you the current estimated "reward rate" or Annual Percentage Rate (APR) for staking that asset.

This allows you to see the real-time potential returns for participating in network security and compare the yields offered by different blockchains.

Key Takeaways

- **Staking is Participation:** It involves locking up your crypto assets to actively participate in and help secure a blockchain network.
- **Earn Rewards for Your Service:** In return for helping to secure the network, you earn passive income, typically in the form of more of the same cryptocurrency.
- **A Core Feature of Proof-of-Stake:** Staking is the central economic mechanism for blockchains that use the energy-efficient Proof-of-Stake consensus model.

Bridge to the Next Lesson

Staking is a powerful way to earn yield on Layer-1

blockchains. But to participate more deeply in DeFi and trade a wider variety of assets, you'll need to use a new kind of marketplace. In our next lesson, we'll explore the engine of DeFi trading: the Decentralized Exchange (DEX).

Lesson 04 - What is a DEX (Decentralized Exchange)?

An Introduction to Peer-to-Peer Trading

In the last module, you learned how to buy crypto on a Centralized Exchange (CEX) like Coinbase—a familiar, company-run marketplace. But the world of DeFi operates on a different philosophy, one that removes the middleman entirely. A Decentralized Exchange, or DEX, is a marketplace with no company, no CEO, and no central operator. It's a radical new model for trading that puts you in complete control. This lesson will explain how these revolutionary platforms work.

The Core Explanation: A Marketplace Run by Code

A DEX is a peer-to-peer marketplace where users can trade cryptocurrencies directly with each other without needing a trusted intermediary to manage their funds. Unlike a CEX, which is run by a corporation, a DEX is run by self-executing smart contracts on the blockchain.

The key differences are profound:

- **No Central Operator:** There is no single company that can be shut down, hacked, or can freeze your account. The marketplace is a public utility that runs autonomously on the blockchain.
- **Permissionless:** Anyone can list a token for trading on a

DEX, and anyone can trade it. This fosters a massive and diverse market for new and emerging assets that aren't yet available on centralized platforms.

- **Self-Custody:** This is the most important difference. When you use a DEX, you trade directly from your own non-custodial wallet (like MetaMask). Your funds are never deposited into an exchange-controlled account. You always maintain full custody and control of your assets. The smart contract only facilitates the "swap" between the tokens.

This model removes the counterparty risk associated with centralized exchanges and embodies the core crypto principle of self-sovereignty.

Case Study: The FTX Collapse

The catastrophic failure of the centralized exchange FTX in November 2022 provided the most powerful argument for the value of DEXs. FTX was one of the largest and seemingly most trustworthy exchanges in the world. However, it was revealed that the company had been mismanaging customer funds on a massive scale.

When the company collapsed, it froze all user withdrawals. Hundreds of thousands of customers who had trusted FTX to hold their assets lost everything, with their funds trapped in bankruptcy proceedings.

During this exact same period, DEXs like Uniswap and dYdX operated without any issue. Users of these platforms were completely unaffected because their funds were not held by a company; they were safe in their own self-custody wallets. This event drove a massive wave of users and trading volume towards DEXs as people sought a more transparent and trustworthy alternative.

Practical Application: Exploring a DEX Interface

You can see the difference between a CEX and a DEX just by looking at their user interfaces.

- **Try This How-To:**

1. Go to the website of a major DEX like Uniswap.
2. You don't need to connect a wallet. Just observe the main interface. You won't see a complex order book with buy and sell orders like on a stock trading platform.
3. Instead, you'll see a very simple interface with two fields: one for the token you have and one for the token you want. This is called a "swap" interface.

This simple user experience is a direct result of the underlying AMM technology that powers most DEXs, which we will explore in the next level.

Key Takeaways

- **A DEX is a Peer-to-Peer Marketplace:** It allows users to trade crypto directly with each other without a central intermediary.
- **Powered by Smart Contracts:** A DEX is not a company; it is an autonomous application that runs on the blockchain.
- **You Are Always in Control:** The defining feature of a DEX is that you trade from your own wallet and never give up custody of your funds.

Bridge to the Next Lesson

Seeing a DEX interface is one thing; using it is another. In our next lesson, we'll walk through the conceptual steps of making your very first trade, or "swap," on a decentralized exchange.

Lesson 05 - Your First Swap on a DEX (e.g., Uniswap)

An Introduction to On-Chain Trading

It's time to put theory into practice. The single most common and fundamental action in all of DeFi is the "swap"—trading one token for another on a Decentralized Exchange. It is your gateway to thousands of assets and the entire ecosystem of Web3 applications. This lesson will be your practical guide, walking you through the steps of making your first swap so you can navigate the world of on-chain trading safely and with confidence.

The Core Explanation: A Step-by-Step Guide

Making a "swap" is the term for trading one cryptocurrency for another on a DEX. The process involves interacting with the DEX's smart contracts directly from your non-custodial wallet. Let's walk through the steps using a popular DEX like Uniswap as our example.

1. **Navigate to the DEX and Connect:** First, you go to the official website of the DEX. Then, you click the "Connect Wallet" button, which will prompt your browser wallet (like MetaMask) to ask for permission to connect to the site. This connection allows the website to see your wallet's address and the tokens you hold.

2. **Select Your Tokens:** The swap interface will have two fields. In the "From" field, you select the token you currently have in your wallet and want to trade away. In the "To" field, you select the token you wish to receive.
3. **Approve the Token (A One-Time Step):** If this is the first time you've ever traded this specific token on this DEX, you must first grant the DEX's smart contract permission to access it. You'll click an "Approve" button and sign a transaction in your wallet. This is like giving the vending machine permission to take a specific type of coin from you.
4. **Execute the Swap:** Once the token is approved, you can enter the amount you wish to trade. The interface will show you an estimated amount of the other token you'll receive. You will then click the "Swap" button.
5. **Confirm in Your Wallet:** Your wallet will pop up one last time, showing you the final details of the trade and the estimated gas fee. You must click "Confirm" in your wallet to sign and broadcast the transaction to the blockchain.

Once confirmed, the smart contract handles the rest, and the new tokens will appear directly in your wallet a few moments later.

Case Study: Discovering a New Project

Imagine a new and innovative project has just launched. Its token is not yet listed on any major centralized exchanges, as that process can take months. The only place to acquire the token is on a DEX like Uniswap, where the project's founders have created a liquidity pool.

An investor who has done their research and wants to invest

early must use a DEX. By following the swap process, they can connect their wallet and trade their ETH for this new token, becoming an early supporter of the project. This highlights the permissionless and open nature of DEXs—they are often the very first place where innovation becomes accessible to the public.

Practical Application: A Safe Rehearsal

The first time you connect your wallet and sign a transaction can be daunting. You can practice the first step without any risk.

- **Try This How-To:**

1. Make sure you have a non-custodial wallet like MetaMask installed in your browser.
2. Go to the official Uniswap website (app.uniswap.org).
3. Click the "Connect" button in the top-right corner.
4. Your MetaMask wallet will pop up, asking you to select an account and grant permission for the site to *view* your address. This is not a transaction and costs no gas.
5. Once connected, you will see your wallet address displayed on the site.

This simple exercise helps you get comfortable with the fundamental step of connecting your personal wallet to a dApp, which is the gateway to all Web3 interactions. You can disconnect your wallet from the site's settings at any time.

Key Takeaways

- **A "Swap" is a DEX Trade:** Swapping is the common term

for exchanging one token for another using a DEX's smart contracts.

- **It's a Wallet-Based Process:** All actions on a DEX, from connecting to swapping, must be initiated and approved from your personal non-custodial wallet.
- **Two Steps: Approve then Swap:** For many tokens, you must first complete a one-time "Approve" transaction before you can execute the "Swap" transaction.

Bridge to the Next Lesson

You've learned how to trade in a decentralized way. But who governs these protocols and makes decisions about their future? In our next lesson, we'll explore the revolutionary new way of organizing people and capital on the internet: the Decentralized Autonomous Organization, or DAO.

Lesson 06 - What is a DAO (Decentralized Autonomous Organization)?

An Introduction to Internet-Native Companies

What if a company could run itself, without a CEO, a board of directors, or a traditional management hierarchy? What if its rules were public, its treasury was transparent, and its decisions were made by a global community of members? This is the radical idea behind a DAO, or Decentralized Autonomous Organization. It's a new, internet-native way to organize people and capital around a shared mission, and it could fundamentally change how we govern everything from financial protocols to social clubs.

The Core Explanation: A Company Run by a Community

A DAO is a community-led organization where the rules are encoded as transparent smart contracts on the blockchain, and decisions are made through votes by its members. It's a bottom-up structure that contrasts sharply with the top-down hierarchy of a traditional company.

Here's how it generally works:

1. **Mission and Rules:** A DAO is founded with a specific mission and a set of rules that are programmed into its smart contracts. These rules govern things like how votes are cast and how treasury funds can be spent.
2. **Membership via Tokens:** To become a member and gain voting rights, you typically need to hold the DAO's specific governance token. In most cases, one token equals one vote, meaning those with more tokens have a greater say in the organization's direction.
3. **Proposals and Voting:** Any member can submit a proposal for the DAO to consider—for example, "We should invest treasury funds into a new marketing campaign" or "We should change this feature of our protocol." The community then discusses the proposal and votes on it using their tokens.
4. **Execution:** If a proposal passes, it can often be executed automatically by the DAO's smart contracts, ensuring the will of the community is carried out in a trust less manner.

Case Study: ConstitutionDAO

In November 2021, the world witnessed a stunning demonstration of a DAO's power to coordinate collective action.

A rare, original copy of the U.S. Constitution was set to be auctioned by Sotheby's. In response, a group of people on the internet spontaneously formed ConstitutionDAO with a single, clear goal: to pool their money and buy the document on behalf of the people.

In less than a week, the DAO raised over $40 million in Ethereum from thousands of contributors around the globe. It was a historic and viral moment, showing the unprecedented speed and scale at which a DAO could coordinate and deploy capital. Although the DAO was ultimately outbid at the auction, it became a powerful case study for how these new internet-native organizations could mobilize communities around a shared purpose.

Practical Application: Observing Live Governance

You can watch the decision-making process of DAOs happen in real-time.

- **Try This How-To:**

1. Go to a DAO voting platform website like **Snapshot.org**.
2. This is a hub where thousands of DAOs host their governance proposals and conduct votes.
3. Browse the list of DAOs or search for a well-known one like "Uniswap" or "Aave."
4. You can view active and past proposals. Read the details of a proposal and look at the voting results. You will see public wallet addresses voting "Yes" or "No."

This provides a transparent, live look into the democratic (or token-cratic) process that governs some of the largest protocols in DeFi.

Key Takeaways

- **A DAO is a Community-Led Organization:** It operates without a central leader, using smart contracts for its rules and token-based voting for its decisions.
- **Bottom-Up Governance:** Unlike a traditional company, DAOs are governed from the bottom-up, with the community of token holders proposing and voting on its future direction.
- **Powerful Coordination Tools:** DAOs are a new and powerful structure for organizing people and capital on the internet around a common goal.

Bridge to the Next Lesson

DAOs and NFTs are often bought, sold, and explored on specialized platforms. In our next lesson, we will explore the "digital art galleries" and "decentralized eBays" of the Web3 world: NFT marketplaces.

Lesson 07 - Exploring NFT Marketplaces (e.g., OpenSea)

An Introduction to the Digital Town Square

Where do you go to buy, sell, and discover unique digital assets? The answer is an NFT marketplace. These platforms are the vibrant commercial hubs of the NFT economy, functioning like a blend of a digital art gallery, a collectibles fair, and a decentralized eBay. Understanding how to navigate these marketplaces is the key to participating in the world of digital ownership, whether you're a collector, an artist, or just curious.

The Core Explanation: The Amazon for NFTs

An NFT marketplace is an online platform where users can browse, buy, sell, and "mint" (create) Non-Fungible Tokens. While the NFTs themselves are secured on the blockchain, these marketplaces provide a user-friendly interface to interact with them. **OpenSea** is one of the oldest and most well-known examples.

The core functions of a typical NFT marketplace are:

1. **Discovery:** You can browse millions of NFTs, searching by name, collection, or category. The platform organizes the vast world of NFTs, making it discoverable.
2. **Trading:** You can buy and sell NFTs in several ways. You can buy one at a fixed "Buy Now" price, or you can place a bid and participate in an auction.
3. **Minting:** Many platforms offer tools that allow creators to upload their work (like an image or a song) and "mint" it as a new NFT on the blockchain, ready to be sold.
4. **Wallet Integration:** To use any of these features, you must **connect your non-custodial wallet** (like MetaMask). This is how the marketplace verifies which NFTs you own and how you authorize purchases and sales. The platform never takes custody of your assets; it simply facilitates the transactions between users' wallets.

Case Study: The Rise of OpenSea

During the NFT boom of 2021, OpenSea became the undisputed giant of the space. As the first platform to offer a simple, open, and user-friendly experience, it captured a massive first-mover advantage.

At its peak, OpenSea was processing billions of dollars in trading volume per month. Its success was a powerful lesson in user experience. While the underlying technology of NFTs was decentralized, the market strongly favoured a centralized, easy-to-use "front-end" to browse and trade them. OpenSea became the default "town square" for the entire NFT ecosystem, demonstrating the power of network effects—buyers went where the sellers were, and sellers went where the buyers were, creating a powerful feedback loop that solidified its dominance.

Practical Application: Gauging a Collection's Health

You can learn a lot about an NFT project without spending any money, simply by analysing its data on a marketplace.

- **Try This How-To:**

1. Go to an NFT marketplace like OpenSea or Blur.
2. Find a well-known collection, like the Bored Ape Yacht Club or CryptoPunks.
3. Look for these key metrics on the collection's main page:

Floor Price: This is the lowest "Buy Now" price for any NFT in the collection. It's the cheapest price of entry.

Total Volume: This shows the total amount of money that has been spent trading the collection over its lifetime. It's a measure of its historical significance.

Owners: This shows how many unique wallets own an NFT from the collection. A high number of owners suggests a wide and decentralized community.

Analysing these data points is the first step that collectors take to gauge the health and popularity of an NFT project.

Key Takeaways

- **Marketplaces are the Hub for NFTs:** They are the primary platforms for discovering, buying, selling, and creating unique digital assets.
- **Interaction is via Your Own Wallet:** To participate in a marketplace, you must connect your non-custodial wallet, ensuring you always maintain control of your assets.
- **Data is Transparent:** Marketplaces provide a wealth of public data, like floor price and trading volume, that you can use to research and analyse projects.

Bridge to the Next Lesson

NFTs and the concept of true digital ownership are a key component of a futuristic idea that has captured the world's imagination. In our next lesson, we'll introduce the ambitious and exciting vision of the Metaverse.

Lesson 08 - Introduction to the Metaverse

An Introduction to the Next Generation of the Internet

For decades, science fiction has dreamed of immersive, shared virtual worlds where people can work, play, and connect. Today, that science fiction vision is slowly starting to become a technological reality under the banner of the **Metaverse**. It's an ambitious concept that aims to evolve the internet from a flat network of 2D pages we look at, into a persistent, 3D universe we can step inside of. This lesson will introduce you to this futuristic vision and explain the crucial role that crypto plays in building it.

The Core Explanation: A Persistent, Shared 3D World

The Metaverse refers to a future vision of the internet as a single, shared, and immersive 3D virtual space. It's not a single game or application, but a network of interconnected virtual worlds.

Key characteristics of the Metaverse vision include:

- **Immersion and Presence:** Users will interact with this world through avatars, feeling a sense of true presence as if they are physically there, often using technologies like virtual and augmented reality (VR/AR).
- **Persistence:** The world exists and continues to evolve even when you are not logged in, just like the real world.
- **Social and Economic:** It will be a space for rich social interaction, but also a fully-functioning economy where people can work, create, own property, and trade goods and services.

This is where blockchain technology becomes essential. For a true Metaverse to exist, it needs a neutral and open foundation for property rights. Blockchains and NFTs are the key technologies that will allow users to truly own their digital assets (like virtual land, avatar clothing, or digital art) and carry them across different virtual worlds, a concept known as interoperability. Without this, every "metaverse" is just another walled garden owned by a single company.

Case Study: The Virtual Land Boom

In 2021, as the Metaverse concept captured mainstream attention, a speculative boom occurred around "virtual land" in leading blockchain-based worlds like Decentraland and The Sandbox.

These platforms are early versions of the Metaverse, with maps made up of thousands of individual parcels of land, each represented by an NFT. During the hype cycle, plots of this digital real estate were selling for hundreds of thousands, and in some cases, millions of dollars. Major brands like Adidas, Atari, and Samsung purchased virtual land to build digital headquarters and experiences. Even a "virtual yacht" was sold in The Sandbox for $650,000. This boom, while highly speculative, was a tangible demonstration that major brands and investors were willing to place significant capital behind the idea of persistent virtual worlds with real digital property rights.

Practical Application: Exploring a Virtual World Map

You can get a sense of how these virtual worlds are structured without ever putting on a VR headset.

- **Try This How-To:**

1. Go to the website for Decentraland and find its "Marketplace" or "Map" section.
2. You will see an interactive 2D map of the entire virtual world. Each coloured square represents a parcel of land, which is an NFT.
3. You can click on different parcels to see who owns them (represented by their public wallet address) and if they are for sale.

This gives you a concrete idea of how a virtual world can be built on a foundation of blockchain-based property, where every piece of the world is a unique, ownable asset.

Key Takeaways

- **The Metaverse is an Immersive Internet:** It's a vision for a persistent, shared, 3D virtual space where users interact through avatars.
- **Blockchain Provides the Foundation for Ownership:** NFTs and blockchain technology are crucial for enabling true, provable ownership of digital assets like virtual land and items.
- **An Emerging, Speculative Frontier:** While the full vision of the Metaverse is still many years away, early versions are being built, and they are creating new and highly speculative markets.

Bridge to the Next Lesson

The Metaverse is just one of many ecosystems being built in the crypto space. Most of the thousands of cryptocurrencies that exist are not Bitcoin. In our next lesson, we'll explore the wild and diverse universe of "Altcoins."

Lesson 09 - What are Altcoins? (Layer-1s, Memecoins)

An Introduction to the Crypto Universe Beyond Bitcoin

The crypto world is far more than just Bitcoin. While Bitcoin was the pioneering invention that started it all, its success spawned a universe of thousands of other cryptocurrencies. These are collectively known as **"Altcoins,"** and they range from serious technological projects aiming to reinvent the internet, to speculative assets based on internet jokes. Understanding the broad categories of altcoins is key to navigating the wider market and its vast spectrum of risk and opportunity.

The Core Explanation: A Universe of Alternatives

The term 'Altcoin' is short for "alternative coin," and it refers to any cryptocurrency other than Bitcoin. Since Bitcoin was the first, every one of the thousands of coins that came after it is considered an "alternative." While it's impossible to track them all, they can be grouped into several major categories:

1. **Layer-1 Blockchains (L1s):** These are the foundational blockchains that, like Ethereum, are designed to be platforms for building decentralized applications. They are often called "ETH competitors" because they have their own unique technology and are trying to solve the Blockchain Trilemma with a different approach. Major examples include Solana (SOL), Avalanche (AVAX), and Cardano (ADA).
2. **Memecoins:** These are cryptocurrencies that were created based on an internet meme or a joke. Their value is typically driven almost entirely by community hype, social media attention, and viral marketing rather than any underlying technology or utility. The most famous examples are Dogecoin (DOGE) and Shiba Inu (SHIB).
3. **DeFi Tokens, GameFi Tokens, and more:** Many altcoins are the native governance or utility tokens for a specific decentralized application. For example, the UNI token governs the Uniswap DEX, and the SAND token is the

currency of The Sandbox metaverse.

As a rule, it is crucial to understand that **altcoins are considered higher-risk and more volatile investments** than the two established market leaders, Bitcoin and Ethereum.

Case Study: Dogecoin - The Joke that Became a Giant

Dogecoin is the ultimate case study of a memecoin. It was created in 2013 by two software engineers, primarily as a joke to satirize the wild speculation they saw in the crypto space. They forked Bitcoin's code, changed a few parameters, and famously put the face of the Shiba Inu dog from the "Doge" meme on the coin.

For years, it was a small, niche community coin, used mostly for tipping creators online. However, in 2021, a perfect storm of retail investor enthusiasm, social media trends on platforms like TikTok and Reddit, and high-profile endorsements from figures like Elon Musk caused its price to soar by over 10,000%. A coin that was created as a joke became a multi-billion-dollar asset, demonstrating the raw power of narrative and community attention in the crypto market. It is a classic example of a memecoin's value being completely detached from any technological fundamentals.

Practical Application: Navigating the Altcoin Market

Learning to categorize altcoins helps you to better assess their potential purpose and risk profile.

- **Try This How-To:**

1. Go to the homepage of a crypto data site like CoinGecko.
2. Scroll past Bitcoin (#1) and Ethereum (#2). The rest of the list, from #3 downwards, is the world of altcoins.

3. Pick a coin in the top 20 that you haven't heard of. Click on it.
4. Read its description and look at the "tags" associated with it. See if you can identify what category it falls into (e.g., is it a "Layer-1," "Gaming," "DeFi," or "Meme" token?).

This exercise trains you to quickly classify new assets and apply the right mental model for understanding their potential role in the market.

Key Takeaways

- **An "Altcoin" is Any Crypto Besides Bitcoin:** The term covers a vast universe of thousands of different projects.
- **A Spectrum of Seriousness:** Altcoins range from serious technology projects designed to be the foundation of the new internet (Layer-1s) to purely speculative, hype-driven assets (Memecoins).
- **Higher Risk, Higher Volatility:** The altcoin market is generally considered to be much higher on the risk-reward spectrum than Bitcoin or Ethereum.

Bridge to the Next Lesson

Investing in any crypto asset, especially altcoins, comes with an important real-world consequence that many beginners overlook. In our next lesson, we'll cover the essential basics of cryptocurrency taxes.

Lesson 10 - Understanding Crypto Taxes (The Basics)

An Introduction to Your Real-World Obligations

In the fast-moving, digital world of crypto, it can be easy to forget that your activities have real-world consequences. One of the most important and often overlooked of these is taxes. While the regulations are still evolving, tax authorities around the world have made it clear that profits from crypto are taxable. Understanding your basic obligations isn't just good practice; it's a legal requirement for being a responsible investor.

The Core Explanation: Crypto as Property

In most countries, including Australia, cryptocurrencies are not treated as currency for tax purposes. Instead, they are treated as an asset, or property, like how you would treat stocks, investment properties, or other collectibles. This means that when you make a profit from your crypto, you are generally liable for Capital Gains Tax **(CGT)**.

A capital gain (or loss) occurs when you have a "disposal event." It's crucial to understand that a disposal is not just when you sell for cash. A disposal event includes:

1. **Selling crypto for fiat currency** (e.g., selling your Bitcoin for Australian Dollars).
2. **Trading one cryptocurrency for another** (e.g., swapping your Ethereum for Solana). This is a taxable event, and you must calculate the capital gain or loss in AUD at the time of the trade.
3. **Using crypto to pay for goods and services** (e.g., buying a coffee with crypto).
4. **Gifting crypto** to someone else.

Because every single one of these actions is a taxable event, the single most important habit you must build is **meticulous record-keeping**. For every transaction, you need to record the date, the type of crypto, the amount, and its value in Australian Dollars at the time of the transaction.

Disclaimer: This is general information, not professional tax advice. The rules can be complex and change over time. You should always consult with a qualified tax professional regarding your personal situation.

Case Study: The Active Trader's Nightmare

Let's consider a hypothetical investor, "Jane." During the 2021 bull run, Jane got heavily into DeFi and altcoin trading. Over the course of the financial year, she made hundreds of trades on multiple decentralized exchanges, swapping dozens of different tokens. She made some great profits but also had some losses.

The problem? She didn't keep any records. At the end of the year, she was faced with an impossible task: trying to go back and reconstruct the exact date, time, and, most difficultly, the Australian Dollar value of every single one of those hundreds of trades to calculate her capital gains. She ended up having to pay a specialized crypto accountant a significant fee to help her sort through the mess, and she still risked penalties for inaccurate reporting. Jane's story is a powerful cautionary tale: record-keeping is not something you can do later; it must be done from day one.

Practical Application: Using a Crypto Tax Tool

Manually tracking hundreds of transactions is nearly impossible. Fortunately, there is software designed specifically for this purpose.

- **Try This How-To:**

1. Do a web search for "crypto tax software Australia." You will find several reputable services.
2. Explore the features of one of these platforms. You will see that they allow you to connect your exchange accounts (via API keys) and your public blockchain addresses.
3. The software will then automatically import your entire transaction history and calculate the capital gains for you, generating reports that you can provide to your accountant or use for your tax return.

Familiarizing yourself with these tools is the first step to becoming a compliant and organized crypto investor.

Key Takeaways

- **Crypto is Treated as Property:** For tax purposes, crypto is generally viewed as an asset, and profits are subject to Capital Gains Tax.
- **Many Actions are Taxable Events:** Selling, swapping one crypto for another, and spending are all "disposal events" that can trigger a capital gain or loss.
- **Meticulous Record-Keeping is Essential:** You must keep detailed records of all your transactions. Using specialized crypto tax software is the most effective way to do this.

Bridge to the Next Lesson

Keeping track of your own transactions can be difficult. Luckily, the blockchain itself is a transparent and public ledger where every transaction is recorded forever. In our next lesson, we'll learn how to use a powerful tool called a "block explorer" to see every transaction for ourselves.

Lesson 11 - Using a Block Explorer (e.g., Etherscan)

An Introduction to "Don't Trust, Verify"

One of the most powerful features of blockchain technology is its radical transparency. Unlike the traditional financial system, where ledgers are private and hidden within banks, the blockchain is an open, public book for all to see. A block explorer is your window into that book. It is a tool that lets you independently verify any transaction, check any wallet, and explore the network without needing to trust anyone. This lesson will teach you how to use this essential tool to become a more informed and sovereign crypto user.

The Core Explanation: The Google for Blockchains

A block explorer is a website that acts like a search engine for a specific blockchain. It downloads and indexes all the data on the blockchain, presenting it in a simple, human-readable format. For the Ethereum blockchain, the most popular and widely used block explorer is **Etherscan**.

Using a block explorer, you can:

1. **Track Transactions:** You can enter any transaction ID (TxID or Hash) to see its full details: the sender's address, the recipient's address, the amount, the gas fee paid, and its current status (pending, successful, or

failed).

2. **Inspect Wallet Addresses:** You can enter any public wallet address to view its entire transaction history, its current balance of the native coin (like ETH), and a list of all the other tokens it holds.
3. **Analyse Smart Contracts:** You can view the code of verified smart contracts, see all the transactions going in and out of them, and even interact with their functions directly.

A block explorer is the ultimate tool for transparency. It allows you to verify information for yourself, embodying the crypto ethos of "don't trust, verify."

Case Study: Verifying a Payment

Imagine you are a freelancer who has just completed a project for a new client, and they have agreed to pay you in the stablecoin USDC on the Ethereum network. The client sends you an email saying, "Payment sent!" but you don't see it in your wallet yet.

Instead of waiting anxiously or repeatedly asking the client, you can take control of the situation. You simply ask them for the transaction ID **(TxID)**.

1. You copy the TxID they provide.
2. You go to Etherscan.io and paste the TxID into the search bar.
3. The block explorer will instantly show you the live status of the transaction. You can confirm that it was sent from their wallet, that the recipient address is correctly yours, and that the transaction is being confirmed by the network.

This provides you with absolute certainty and removes the need to blindly trust the other party.

Practical Application: Tracking a "Whale"

"Whales" are wallets that hold a very large amount of a cryptocurrency. Their actions can sometimes give clues about the market. Let's look at a famous one.

- **Try This How-To:**

1. Go to the Etherscan.io website.
2. The Ethereum Foundation, a key organization in the Ethereum ecosystem, uses the ENS (Ethereum Name Service) address ens.eth. Type ens.eth into the search bar and press Enter.
3. You will be taken to the public page for this address. You can see its ETH balance, the value of all the tokens it holds, and a complete, time-stamped list of every transaction it has ever made.

This is the radical transparency of the blockchain in action. Every financial action is a public record.

Key Takeaways

- **A Block Explorer is a Blockchain Search Engine:** It's a website that allows you to look up and verify any transaction, address, or smart contract on a public blockchain.
- **It Enables "Trustless" Verification:** You can confirm information for yourself without needing to rely on or trust another person or entity.
- **Etherscan is the Standard for Ethereum:** It is the most

popular and feature-rich block explorer for the Ethereum network and its related tokens.

Bridge to the Next Lesson

Block explorers are a powerful tool, but sometimes you might use one to find unexpected tokens in your wallet that you don't recognize. In our next lesson, we'll discuss the phenomenon of "Airdrops" and how projects distribute tokens for free.

Lesson 12 - What are Airdrops?

An Introduction to Free Token Distributions

Imagine a new software company, instead of spending millions on advertising, decided to give free shares of its stock to all of its most loyal, early users. In the world of Web3, this happens all the time. It's called an **airdrop**, and it's a unique marketing and distribution strategy where a new crypto project sends its tokens directly to the wallets of community members, often for free. This lesson will explain why projects do this and what you need to know to navigate them safely.

The Core Explanation: A Web3 Marketing Strategy

An airdrop is a marketing method used by crypto projects to distribute their tokens to the public. The goal is to rapidly bootstrap a community and generate widespread awareness.

There are two primary reasons why a project conducts an airdrop:

1. **Marketing and Community Building:** By giving away tokens to thousands of people, a project can instantly create a large base of token holders who have a vested interest in the project's success. It's a powerful tool for generating grassroots buzz.
2. **Rewarding Early Adopters & Decentralizing Governance:** This is the most common reason for major projects. A protocol might launch without a token and operate for months or years. When they are ready to decentralize their governance, they will take a "snapshot" of all the wallets that have used their protocol up to that point. They then "airdrop" their new governance token to these early users as a reward for their loyalty and to hand over control of the protocol to its community.

While some airdrops can be valuable, you must be very cautious of "scam" airdrops that require you to connect your wallet to a malicious website or sign a transaction to "claim" your tokens. A legitimate airdrop will often just appear in your wallet.

Case Study: The Uniswap (UNI) Airdrop

In September 2020, Uniswap, the leading Decentralized Exchange, decided to transition to a community-governed model by launching its UNI governance token. To do this, it conducted the most famous and influential airdrop in crypto history.

Uniswap airdropped 400 UNI tokens to every single wallet address that had ever made a swap on its platform, even if the swap had failed. On the day of the airdrop, this was worth approximately $1,200 USD. For many users, this was a completely unexpected and substantial reward simply for having used the protocol. The UNI airdrop became a legendary event that rewarded early users, instantly created one of the largest DAOs, and set the standard for the "retroactive airdrop" model that hundreds of other projects have since followed.

Practical Application: Being Cautious and Curious

You will often see random, unknown tokens appear in your wallet. The vast majority of these are worthless spam or scams. It's important to know how to investigate them safely.

- **Try This How-To:**

1. If you see an unknown token in your wallet, your first action should be to do nothing. Do not visit its website or try to trade it immediately.
2. Copy the token's contract address (not your wallet address) from your wallet interface.
3. Go to a block explorer like Etherscan and paste the token's contract address into the search bar. This will show you how many people hold the token and other key details.
4. A healthy, legitimate token will usually have an active community on Twitter and a clear website. A scam token will often have very few holders and a suspicious website.

This cautious research process protects you from interacting with malicious smart contracts.

Key Takeaways

- **Airdrops are a Free Token Distribution:** They are used by new projects as a marketing tool and to reward early community members.
- **A Tool for Decentralization:** Major protocols often use retroactive airdrops to distribute governance power to their most loyal users.
- **Proceed with Extreme Caution:** While some airdrops are valuable, the space is filled with scams. Never connect your wallet or sign a transaction to claim an unknown airdrop without extensive research.

Bridge to the Next Lesson

Airdrops are part of the unique culture of crypto, a culture that has even developed its own language and slang. To better understand the conversations happening online, our next lesson will cover some of the most common crypto slang.

Lesson 13 - Glossary of Common Crypto Slang

An Introduction to the Language of the Culture

Every community has its own language, and the fast-paced, online world of crypto is no exception. It's a culture filled with memes, inside jokes, and unique terminology that can be confusing to newcomers. Understanding this slang isn't just for fun; it's a practical skill that helps you read the mood of the market, understand the sentiment on social media, and navigate the culture like an insider. This lesson will be your dictionary for some of the most common crypto terms.

The Core Explanation: Speaking Crypto

Here are some of the essential terms you will encounter as you explore the crypto community on platforms like X (Twitter), Discord, and Reddit.

- **HODL:** This is arguably the most famous piece of crypto slang. It originated from a 2013 forum post where a user, in a drunken and emotional rant during a market crash, misspelled the word "holding." It has since been adopted by the community to mean holding onto your cryptocurrency for the long term, refusing to sell regardless of price volatility. It represents a deep, long-term conviction in an asset.
- **WAGMI / NGMI:** These are acronyms that represent the powerful emotions of optimism and pessimism in the community.
- **WAGMI:** Stands for **"We're All Gonna Make It."** It's a powerful rallying cry used to express shared belief and optimism in the future of a project or the market.
- **NGMI:** Stands for **"Not Gonna Make It."** It's used to describe a bad decision, a flawed project, or someone who is destined to fail because they lack conviction or understanding.
- **Shilling:** This is the act of enthusiastically promoting a cryptocurrency, often for one's own personal benefit. Someone who is "shilling" a coin is trying to create hype to get others to buy it, which would in turn drive up the price of their own holdings. It usually implies a promotion that is not objective or fully transparent.
- **FUD/FOMO:** While we've covered these as psychological concepts, they are also used as active slang. People will accuse others of spreading "FUD" if they are being critical

of a project, or they might admit to "FOMO-ing in" when they buy an asset that is rising quickly.

Case Study: The "WAGMI" Culture

During the 2021 bull market, the term "WAGMI" became more than just a piece of slang; it became the cultural glue for many NFT communities and crypto projects. On Discord servers and Twitter threads, you would see it used constantly as a way to build camaraderie and reinforce a collective belief in the project's success.

When prices were up, "WAGMI" was a celebration. When prices dipped, "WAGMI" was a tool to encourage everyone to "HODL" and maintain their conviction. This shows how a simple piece of slang can encapsulate a powerful collective belief system, fostering a sense of shared purpose and optimism that can, in itself, become a powerful driver of a project's narrative and momentum.

Practical Application: Reading the Digital Room

Understanding slang is about understanding sentiment.

- **Try This How-To:**

1. Go to X (Twitter) and search for the "cashtag" of a cryptocurrency that is currently experiencing a lot of price volatility (e.g., $BTC or $SOL).
2. Spend 10 minutes browsing the "Latest" tab to see the real-time conversation.
3. Look for the terms we've discussed. Are people posting

"WAGMI" and celebrating, or are they accusing others of spreading "FUD" and panicking?

This exercise is a fantastic way to start getting a feel for the "vibe" of the market and to understand how these cultural terms are used to express the raw emotions of greed and fear.

Key Takeaways

- **Crypto Has a Unique Culture and Language:** Understanding the slang helps you interpret the sentiment and conversations happening within the community.
- **HODL is a Strategy of Conviction:** It means holding an asset for the long term, through all market ups and downs.
- **WAGMI and NGMI are Expressions of Sentiment:** They are used as shorthand for community optimism or pessimism.

Bridge to the Next Lesson

As you start to acquire different assets, from Bitcoin you've bought to tokens you've received in airdrops, keeping track of everything can become a real challenge. In our next lesson, we'll look at the essential tools for organizing your portfolio.

Lesson 14 - Portfolio Tracking Tools

An Introduction to Your Financial Dashboard

You buy some Bitcoin on one exchange. You buy some Ethereum on another. You hold some NFTs in a MetaMask wallet and an airdropped token in another. Suddenly, your assets are scattered across the digital landscape. Answering the simple question, "How are my investments doing?" becomes a complex and time-consuming task. Portfolio trackers are the solution. They are the essential dashboards that consolidate all your holdings into one place, giving you a clear and accurate picture of your financial position.

The Core Explanation: Consolidating Your Holdings

A portfolio tracker is a website or mobile application that helps you monitor all of your crypto holdings in a single, unified view. Instead of logging into multiple exchanges and wallets, you can see everything at once.

There are two primary ways that these trackers work:

1. **Connecting Exchange Accounts:** For assets you hold on a centralized exchange, you can create a **"read-only" API key** in your exchange's settings. This is a special key that you can give to the tracker that allows it to *view* your balances without having the permission to make trades or withdrawals. The tracker uses this to automatically sync your exchange holdings.
2. **Adding Public Wallet Addresses:** For assets you hold in your own non-custodial wallets, you simply need to add your public wallet address to the tracker. Since all wallet data is public on the blockchain, the tracker can automatically see all the assets held at that address.

Once connected, a good portfolio tracker will give you a real-time overview of your total net worth, your profit and loss over time, and a breakdown of your best and worst performing assets. The most popular and feature-rich portfolio trackers are offered for free by the major crypto data sites, **CoinGecko** and **CoinMarketCap**.

Case Study: Jane, the Organized Investor

Let's consider a hypothetical investor, Jane. She has a well-diversified portfolio:

- Bitcoin and Ethereum held in a secure, cold storage wallet.
- A small amount of Solana on the Binance exchange, which she uses for trading.
- Some NFTs and DeFi tokens in a MetaMask hot wallet.

Without a portfolio tracker, to check her net worth, Jane would need to:

1. Plug in her hardware wallet and check its balance.
2. Log in to her Binance account.
3. Connect her MetaMask wallet to a portfolio app.
4. Manually add up the values in Australian Dollars.

With a portfolio tracker, she sets it up once by adding her public addresses and the Binance API key. Now, she can just open one app on her phone and see the total, real-time value of all her assets combined. When it's time to do her taxes, she has a much clearer picture of her holdings.

Practical Application: Building a Dummy Portfolio

You can experience the power of a portfolio tracker without

connecting any of your real accounts.

- **Try This How-To:**

1. Go to **CoinGecko** or **CoinMarketCap** and create a free account.
2. Find the "Portfolio" section.
3. Instead of connecting an exchange or wallet, choose the option to "Add New" transaction manually.
4. Create a dummy portfolio. Pretend you bought 0.1 Bitcoin, 1 Ethereum, and 100 Cardano on different dates.
5. Once you've added these, watch how the dashboard tracks their value in real-time. It will show you your total portfolio value and your "unrealized" profit or loss.

This exercise is the best way to understand the features and benefits of these essential tools.

Key Takeaways

- **Trackers Consolidate Your Portfolio:** They are essential tools that bring all your crypto holdings from various wallets and exchanges into a single dashboard.
- **They Provide a Clear Financial Overview:** Portfolio trackers help you monitor your overall net worth and investment performance in real-time.
- **Major Data Sites Offer Them for Free:** Reputable platforms like CoinGecko and CoinMarketCap provide powerful and easy-to-use portfolio tracking tools.

Bridge to the Next Lesson

Now that you have all the foundational knowledge and the tools to track your performance, it's time to put it all together. How should you structure your very first portfolio? In our final lesson of the Beginner Level, we'll discuss a sensible and prudent approach to building a beginner's crypto portfolio.

Lesson 15 - Building a Beginner's Portfolio

An Introduction to Your Starting Lineup

You've reached the starting line. You understand the fundamentals of money, the technology of the blockchain, and the tools of the ecosystem. You are ready to build your first portfolio. This is an exciting moment, but it's also one that requires discipline and prudence. A beginner's first portfolio should not be about hitting a home run; it should be about getting on base safely. This final lesson will provide a sensible and time-tested framework for constructing a foundational portfolio designed for learning and long-term success.

The Core Explanation: A Foundation of Blue-Chips

When you are just starting out, the primary goal is to gain experience and learn the market without taking on excessive risk. The wisest way to do this is to build your portfolio around the most established, liquid, and technologically significant assets in the space. In crypto, these are known as the "blue-chips."

A sensible and widely recommended approach for a beginner's portfolio is to allocate a large percentage of your capital **(e.g., 60-80%)** to the two undisputed market leaders: Bitcoin

(BTC) and Ethereum (ETH).

- **Bitcoin (BTC):** As the original and most decentralized cryptocurrency, it acts as the "digital gold" or risk-off reserve asset of the crypto world. It is the most secure and established network.
- **Ethereum (ETH):** As the leading smart contract platform, it is the foundation for the vast majority of the DeFi and NFT ecosystems. It represents a bet on the growth of the entire Web3 economy.

By making these two assets the cornerstone of your portfolio, you are building a solid foundation. The remaining, smaller percentage of your portfolio (20-40%) can then be allocated to other promising but higher-risk altcoins that you have thoroughly researched, such as other Layer-1 blockchains or established DeFi projects. It is strongly advised to avoid highly speculative assets like memecoins and new, unproven projects until you have much more experience.

Case Study: The Tale of Two Beginners

Let's consider two hypothetical beginners, Alex and Ben, who both start their crypto journey at the same time with $1,000.

- **Alex** gets caught up in the hype on social media. He ignores the established assets and puts his entire $1,000 into a new, highly speculative memecoin that is being shilled by influencers. The coin briefly pumps, but the hype dies down, and its price crashes by 95%. Alex loses almost all his money, becomes disillusioned, and quits crypto forever.

- **Ben** follows a more prudent strategy. He allocates $700 to Bitcoin and Ethereum (70%) and uses the remaining $300 to buy small positions in three other well-regarded altcoin projects (10% each). Even if one of his altcoin picks performs poorly, his core holdings in the market leaders provide stability. His portfolio is much more resilient and has a significantly higher probability of appreciating over the long term.

Ben's approach allows him to learn and stay in the game, while Alex's high-risk gamble ends his journey before it even begins.

Practical Application: Architecting Your Personal Portfolio

Now it's time to apply what you've learned about your own goals and risk tolerance to design a sample portfolio.

- **Try This How-To:**

1. Based on the risk tolerance questions you answered in Module 1, decide on your ideal "blue-chip" percentage. Are you a conservative 80% BTC/ETH person, or a more aggressive 60%?
2. On a piece of paper, sketch out your ideal beginner's portfolio. Write down the percentages.
3. For your "altcoin" allocation, go to CoinGecko and look at the projects ranked from #3 to #20. Read their descriptions and pick two or three that you would be interested in researching further.

This exercise solidifies your personal strategy and gives you a clear, actionable plan for when you are ready to invest.

Key Takeaways

- **Start with a Strong Foundation:** A beginner's portfolio should be heavily weighted towards the "blue-chip" assets of the crypto world, Bitcoin and Ethereum.
- **Allocate to Altcoins with Caution:** Only a smaller, manageable portion of your portfolio should be dedicated to higher-risk altcoins, and only after you have done your own research.
- **Align with Your Risk Tolerance:** Your portfolio allocation should always be a direct reflection of your personal financial goals and your comfort level with risk.

6

Module 3 Recap

Congratulations! You have now completed the final module of the Beginner Level. You have moved beyond theory and into the world of practical application.

- You've learned about the key pillars of the Web3 economy: NFTs (digital ownership), DeFi (open finance), and **DAOs (community governance)**.
- You have the practical skills to navigate this world, from making your first swap on a DEX to exploring NFT marketplaces.
- You understand the importance of real-world obligations like taxes and the cultural norms of the space, including its unique slang.
- Finally, you have a prudent framework for building your very first beginner's portfolio.

You have successfully completed your journey from zero knowledge to a point of confidence, safety, and understand-

ing. You are no longer a spectator; you are an active and informed participant in the digital asset ecosystem. You are now ready to advance to the Intermediate Level.

7

Level 2: Intermediate

Goal: To move from "what it is" to "how it works." The user can now interact with the ecosystem confidently and wants to understand the mechanics and basic strategies to make more informed decisions.

Module 1: Advanced Investing & Market Analysis

Module Introduction: You've mastered the basics; now it's time to learn the craft. This module will equip you with the tools and mental models used by experienced investors to analyse markets. We'll move beyond simple buying and holding to explore the art of reading charts (Technical Analysis), the science of evaluating network health (On-Chain Analysis), and the discipline required to execute proven investment strategies. This is where you transition from a passive participant to an active and informed analyst.

Lesson 01 - Support, Resistance, and Trends

An Introduction to the Language of Charts

Technical Analysis (TA) is the art and science of reading the market's collective psychology as it is expressed through price charts. It's a visual language that can help you identify key moments of decision. The fundamental grammar of this language is built on three simple but powerful concepts:

Support, Resistance, and Trends. Mastering these will allow you to look at any chart and immediately understand the key battlegrounds where buyers and sellers are fighting for control.

The Core Explanation: The Battle for Price

Technical Analysis (TA) is a method of evaluating investments by analysing statistical trends gathered from trading activity, such as price movement and volume. The core assumption is that past price action and market psychology can provide clues about future movements.

The foundational concepts are:

Support: This is a price level where an asset has historically shown a tendency to stop falling. Think of it as a price floor. When the price hits this level, a significant number of market participants believe it is "cheap" and begin to buy, supporting the price.

Resistance: This is a price level where an asset has historically shown a tendency to stop rising. Think of it as a price ceiling. When the price hits this level, a significant number of participants believe it is "expensive" and begin to sell, providing resistance against further upward movement.

Trend: This is the general direction the price is heading. An asset can be in an uptrend (making a series of higher highs and higher lows), a downtrend (making a series of lower highs and lower lows), or moving sideways (ranging between a clear support and resistance level).

Case Study: Bitcoin's 2021 Tug-of-War

The Bitcoin price chart from 2021 provides a perfect, large-scale example of these concepts in action.

Support: After an initial surge to over $60,000, Bitcoin's price crashed in May 2021. For the next two months, it repeatedly fell to the $30,000 level but failed to break below it. Each time it hit this price, a massive amount of buying pressure stepped in. The $30,000 level became a clear and powerful support zone.

Resistance: After rallying from the $30,000 support, Bitcoin's price surged to a new all-time high of around $69,000 in November 2021. It hit this level and was immediately rejected. This peak became the ultimate resistance level, marking the top of the bull market.

Traders who identified the $30k level as strong support had a clear area of opportunity to buy, while those who recognized the weakness at the $69k resistance level had a clear signal to sell.

Practical Application: Drawing Your First Lines

The first step in all technical analysis is simply drawing lines on a chart to identify these key levels.

Try This How-To:

1. Go to a free charting website like TradingView.
2. Bring up the chart for BTCUSD (Bitcoin / US Dollar) and set the timeframe to "1D" (Daily).
3. Look at the price action over the last 1-2 years.

Using the line drawing tool, try to draw a horizontal line at a price where the market has repeatedly bounced up from (a support level).

Now, try to draw a horizontal line where the price has repeatedly been rejected from (a resistance level).

This simple act of drawing lines on a chart is the foundational skill of a technical analyst. It transforms a chaotic chart into a strategic map of key price zones.

Key Takeaways

- Technical Analysis uses historical price and volume data to forecast future prices.
- Support is a price floor where an asset tends to stop falling, while Resistance is a price ceiling where it tends to stop rising.
- Identifying the primary trend (uptrend, downtrend, or sideways) is a core goal of TA.

Bridge to the Next Lesson

These key levels are the landmarks on our map. But to get more specific signals about market momentum and potential turning points, traders use specialized tools called indicators. In our next lesson, we'll explore two of the most popular and powerful indicators in the technical analyst's toolkit: the RSI and the MACD.

Lesson 02 - RSI, MACD

An Introduction to the Market's Dashboard

If support and resistance levels are the landmarks on your financial map, then

indicators are the gauges on your dashboard. They are tools that take raw price and volume data and transform it into visual, actionable insights about the market's momentum, trend strength, and potential turning points. While there are hundreds of indicators, understanding two of the most famous—the RSI and the MACD—will give you a powerful new lens through which to analyze any price chart.

The Core Explanation: Measuring Momentum and Trend

Indicators are calculations based on price and volume that add another layer to chart analysis. They are not crystal balls, but rather tools that help to confirm your analysis and provide signals that might not be obvious from looking at price alone.

Relative Strength Index (RSI):

What it is: The RSI is a momentum indicator that measures the speed and change of price movements on a scale of 0 to 100. It doesn't tell you the price; it tells you how fast the price is moving up or down.

How to use it: The RSI is primarily used to identify "overbought" and "oversold" conditions.

A reading above 70 is generally considered overbought. This suggests that an asset has risen very quickly and might be due for a pause or a price correction downwards.

A reading below 30 is generally considered oversold. This suggests an asset has fallen very quickly and might be due for a bounce or a price reversal upwards.

Moving Average Convergence Divergence (MACD):

What it is: The MACD is a trend-following momentum indicator. It is composed of two lines (the MACD line and the Signal line) that track the relationship between two different moving averages of an asset's price.

How to use it: The most common signal is the "crossover."

- When the MACD line crosses above the Signal line, it is considered a bullish signal, suggesting that upward momentum is increasing.
- When the MACD line crosses below the Signal line, it is considered a bearish signal, suggesting that downward momentum is increasing.

Case Study: Bitcoin's 2021 Bull Market Top

Let's look at the final peak of the Bitcoin bull market in November 2021. The price made a new all-time high, slightly higher than the previous peak in April 2021. To many, this looked like a sign of strength. However, traders who were looking at indicators saw a very different story.

This is a classic example of "bearish divergence." The price was making a higher high, but the RSI indicator was making a lower high. This showed that even though the price was ticking up, the underlying momentum of the move was significantly weaker than before. This divergence was a major warning sign that the trend was exhausted. Shortly after, the MACD had a bearish crossover, confirming the shift in momentum. For traders who understood these indicators, these were powerful signals to exit the market before the major crash that followed.

Practical Application: Adding Indicators to Your Chart

The best way to understand indicators is to see them in action.

Try This How-To:

1. Go back to your chart on TradingView.
2. At the top of the chart, find and click the "Indicators" button.
3. In the search box, type "Relative Strength Index" and click on it to add it to your chart. You will see the RSI appear in a new panel below your price chart.
4. Go back and add the "Moving Average Convergence Divergence" (MACD) as well.

Now, look at the historical price chart. Can you spot the major peaks and bottoms? Look down at your indicators. Do you see how major price peaks often coincide with the RSI being above 70, and major bottoms with it being below 30? Can you spot the major MACD crossovers that happened near significant trend changes?

Key Takeaways

- Indicators help confirm trends and identify potential buy or sell signals.
- The RSI is a momentum indicator that helps gauge if an asset is overbought (above 70) or oversold (below 30).
- The MACD is a trend-following indicator used to identify trend direction and momentum.

Bridge to the Next Lesson

While charts tell us about market psychology, they don't tell us about the fundamental health of the network itself. For that, we need a different kind of analysis that is completely unique to crypto. In our next lesson, we will dive into the powerful world of "On-Chain Metrics."

Lesson 03 - On-Chain Metrics

An Introduction to Crypto's Superpower

In traditional finance, the most important data—company financials, trading volumes, order books—is often hidden, delayed, or accessible only to a privileged few. Crypto is fundamentally different. Because blockchains are public, transparent ledgers, they offer a superpower to the average investor: the ability to analyse the real-time economic activity of the network itself. This is on-chain analysis, and it's like having a perfect, live satellite view of a country's economy. This lesson will introduce you to this unique and powerful form of fundamental analysis.

The Core Explanation: Analysing the Digital Economy

While Technical Analysis focuses on price charts, Fundamental Analysis (FA) is the practice of evaluating an asset's intrinsic value to determine if it is currently overvalued or undervalued. In crypto, this goes beyond just reading a whitepaper; it means analysing 'on-chain' metrics—data extracted directly from the blockchain.

This data provides an unprecedented, real-time, and transparent view into a network's health, growth, and user activity. Here are some of the most important on-chain metrics:

Active Wallet Addresses: This metric tracks the number of unique wallet addresses that are active on the network over a certain period. A sustained increase in the number of active addresses is a powerful indicator of a growing user base and increasing adoption. It's a fundamental measure of network growth.

Transaction Volume: This measures the total value of assets being moved across the blockchain. It shows how much economic activity the network is actually facilitating. A high and rising transaction volume indicates that the network is being used for meaningful commerce and value transfer.

Hash Rate (for Proof-of-Work chains): Hash rate measures the total computational power that miners are dedicating to securing the network. A high and rising hash rate means the network is extremely secure and that miners find it profitable to expend significant resources to protect it. It is a direct measure of the network's security.

Case Study: The Growth of Ethereum

In the early years of Ethereum (2016-2018), the price of its native asset, ETH, was extremely volatile, experiencing massive booms and busts. For a trader looking only at the price chart, the future of the network might have seemed highly uncertain.

However, on-chain analysts saw a different, much clearer story. Even during the brutal bear market of 2018 when the price of ETH fell by over 90%, the on-chain metrics told a story of relentless growth. The number of active Ethereum addresses continued to climb steadily month after month. The number of smart contracts deployed on the network was exploding. This on-chain data showed that, regardless of the short-term market speculation, developers and users were flocking to the network and building on it.

This strong fundamental growth, visible only through on-chain analysis, provided a powerful long-term bullish signal that the network was healthy and here to stay.

Practical Application: Exploring On-Chain Charts

Many specialized websites now provide easy-to-understand charts for this on-chain data.

Try This How-To:

1. Go to a data site like Glassnode or IntoTheBlock (many have free charts).
2. Search for a major asset like Bitcoin or Ethereum.
3. Find and click on a chart for "Active Addresses" or "Transaction Count."
4. Set the time frame to "All-Time." You will see a chart showing the growth of the network's user base over its entire history.

Compare this long-term growth chart to a long-term price chart. You can often see how the fundamental growth of the network underpins its long-term value appreciation.

Key Takeaways

- Fundamental Analysis in crypto aims to determine if a project is over or undervalued.
- On-chain data provides a unique, transparent look into a network's real-time usage and health.
- Metrics like a rising number of active addresses can be a powerful signal of growing adoption.

Bridge to the Next Lesson

On-chain data tells us about a network's health, but what about the health of the token itself? The economic design of a token is a crucial factor in its long-term success. In our next lesson, we'll explore the fascinating science of "Tokenomics."

Lesson 04 - What is Tokenomics?

An Introduction to the Science of a Token's Value

Why is Bitcoin considered a store of value while other tokens are not? Why are some cryptocurrencies designed to increase in value as their network grows, while others seem destined to fail? The answer lies in Tokenomics. It is the science of a token's economic properties, a blueprint that defines its rules, its purpose, and its potential for value accrual. Understanding the basics of tokenomics is one of the most crucial skills in fundamental analysis, as it allows you to look past the hype and evaluate a project's long-term economic viability.

The Core Explanation: The Blueprint for a Digital Economy

'Tokenomics' is a blend of the words **"token" and "economics."** It covers everything that makes a token valuable. Strong, well-designed tokenomics are crucial for a project's long-term success.

Here are the three key pillars of tokenomic analysis:

1. **Supply:** This examines the rules governing how many

tokens will ever exist.

- Is the supply capped or inflationary? A token with a hard, fixed supply, like Bitcoin's, is deflationary by nature. This provable scarcity can be a powerful driver of value. A token with an uncapped, inflationary supply may struggle to hold its value unless the demand for it consistently outpaces the creation of new tokens.
- What is the emission schedule? How quickly are new tokens released into the market? A rapid release can create significant selling pressure.

1. **Distribution:** This looks at how the tokens were initially allocated.

- Was it a fair launch, where everyone had an equal opportunity to acquire the tokens from the start?
- Or was a large percentage allocated to the team and early VC investors? If so, you must look at their "vesting schedules"—the timeline over which their tokens unlock. A large upcoming unlock can signal major potential sell pressure.

1. **Utility:** This is the most important question: What is the token's purpose? What can you use it for?

- Does it grant governance rights, allowing holders to vote on the future of the protocol?
- Is it used to pay transaction fees within its ecosystem?
- Can it be staked to earn a share of the protocol's revenue?

A token with strong, clear utility has an organic reason for people to buy and hold it, creating sustainable demand.

Case Study: Bitcoin (BTC) vs. Dogecoin (DOGE)

Let's compare the tokenomics of two famous assets:

- **Bitcoin (BTC):**
- **Supply:** Hard-capped at 21 million. Highly deflationary.
- **Distribution:** A perfectly fair launch. No pre-mine, no insider allocation.
- **Utility:** The native asset for paying fees on the world's most secure blockchain; widely considered the ultimate decentralized store of value.
- **Result:** Extremely strong tokenomics that reinforce its value proposition as "digital gold."
- **Dogecoin (DOGE):**
- **Supply:** Uncapped, inflationary supply. A fixed number of new coins are created every year, forever.
- **Distribution:** Created as a joke, it also had a fair launch with no pre-mine.
- **Utility:** Primarily used for tipping and small payments; its value is almost entirely driven by community sentiment and memes.
- **Result:** Weak tokenomics from a scarcity perspective. Its value is not tied to a strong use case or a deflationary model, making it a highly speculative asset.

This comparison shows how crucial a project's economic design is to its long-term investment thesis.

Practical Application: Your First Tokenomic Check

You can perform a quick, high-level tokenomic analysis on any project in just a few minutes.

- **Try This How-To:**

1. Go to a data site like CoinGecko or CoinMarketCap.
2. Search for a project you are interested in (ideally one outside the top 10).
3. On its main page, find the section with the market data. Look for three key numbers:

- **Circulating Supply:** How many tokens are currently on the market.
- **Total Supply:** How many tokens have been created so far.
- **Max Supply:** The absolute maximum number of tokens that will ever exist.

Ask yourself: Is the Circulating Supply very close to the Max Supply? (This is a good sign, meaning less future inflation). Or is the Circulating Supply a very small fraction of an uncapped Total Supply? (This can be a red flag for high future inflation).

This simple check on a token's supply dynamics is the first and most important step in any tokenomic evaluation.

Key Takeaways

- Tokenomics analyses the economic factors that impact a token's value.
- A limited supply (like Bitcoin's) can create scarcity and drive value.
- A token's utility (its use case) is a primary driver of demand.
- Strong tokenomics are crucial for a project's long-term

success.

Bridge to the Next Lesson

A project's tokenomics are its logical foundation. But markets are not always logical; they are driven by powerful and predictable human emotions that play out in repeating cycles. In our next lesson, we will examine the psychological cycles that govern all financial markets.

Lesson 05 - Market Cycles and Investor Psychology

An Introduction to the Market's Rhythm

"This time is different." These are famously the four most expensive words in investing. While technology, assets, and news headlines are constantly changing, there is one thing that remains stubbornly consistent: human psychology. Because markets are driven by the collective emotions of greed and fear, they tend to move in predictable, repeating cycles of boom and bust. Understanding the rhythm of these cycles is one of the most powerful mental models an investor can possess, helping you to maintain perspective and avoid becoming a victim of emotional decision-making.

The Core Explanation: The Four Phases of a Cycle

Financial markets, and especially the volatile crypto market, move in waves. A typical market cycle can be broken down into four distinct phases, each characterized by a different prevailing emotion:

1. **Accumulation (The Bottom):** This phase occurs after

a major market crash. The news is terrible, prices are low, and the general public has lost interest. The dominant emotion is despair or boredom. This is when patient, long-term investors ("smart money") begin to accumulate assets at a discount.

2. **Markup (The Bull Run):** Prices begin to rise, slowly at first, and then with increasing momentum. Public interest returns, and the news becomes positive. The dominant emotions shift from hope to optimism, and eventually to euphoria as prices go parabolic. This is when the public, driven by FOMO, piles into the market.
3. **Distribution (The Top):** The market reaches a point of "maximum financial risk." Prices are at all-time highs, and every headline is euphoric. This is when the smart money that bought during the accumulation phase begins to sell their holdings to the euphoric public.
4. **Markdown (The Bear Market):** The buying pressure is finally exhausted, and prices begin to fall. The initial drop causes anxiety, which turns to denial. As prices continue to collapse, this gives way to fear, panic, and finally, capitulation, as the last of the public who bought at the top sell their assets at a massive loss to "make the pain stop".

This completes the cycle and sets the stage for the next accumulation phase to begin. Understanding this cycle helps investors avoid buying at the peak of euphoria and selling at the bottom of despair.

Case Study: The "Wall Street Cheat Sheet" and Bitcoin's History

The "Wall Street Cheat Sheet: Psychology of a Market

Cycle" is a famous and enduring infographic that perfectly maps these emotional states onto a classic market bubble chart. This exact pattern has played out in Bitcoin's history multiple times.

Let's look at the 2017-2018 cycle:

- **Markup:** During 2017, Bitcoin's price surged from under $1,000 to nearly $20,000. The public excitement was immense, a clear phase of euphoria.
- **Distribution:** The price peaked in December 2017, marking the point of maximum financial risk.
- **Markdown:** Throughout 2018, the price crashed by over 80%, wiping out a huge amount of value. This was the bear market, filled with fear and panic.
- **Accumulation:** For much of 2019 and early 2020, the price of Bitcoin moved sideways in a range, and public interest waned. This was the long and boring accumulation phase, or "crypto winter," where patient investors built their positions before the next major bull run.

This demonstrates that this psychological pattern is not just a theory; it is a recurring historical reality.

Practical Application: Taking Your Emotional Temperature

The first step to mastering market psychology is to become aware of your own emotional state.

- **Try This How-To:**

1. The next time there is a major market event—either a

huge price surge or a sudden crash—take a moment to pause before you act.

2. Ask yourself: "What emotion am I feeling right now? Is it greed (FOMO)? Is it fear?"
3. Look at the "Psychology of a Market Cycle" chart. Try to pinpoint where your current feeling sits on that emotional spectrum.
4. Then, ask: "Is acting on this emotion right now consistent with my long-term financial plan?"

This simple act of self-awareness creates a crucial gap between feeling and action, allowing your logical mind to take back control from your emotional instincts.

Key Takeaways

- Crypto markets move in predictable cycles of boom and bust.
- These cycles are heavily influenced by collective investor emotions like greed and fear.
- Recognizing the current phase of the cycle is a key investment skill.
- The goal is to avoid buying in euphoria (the top) and selling in despair (the bottom).

Bridge to the Next Lesson

These broad market cycles are the overarching rhythm of the market. But within these cycles, capital often flows in smaller waves between specific hot trends or stories. In our next lesson, we'll look at the powerful and risky strategy of

"Narrative-Driven Investing."

Lesson 06 - Narrative-Driven Investing

An Introduction to Investing in Stories

In crypto, a good story can be more powerful than good technology.

'Narratives' are powerful, simplified stories that capture the market's attention and drive enormous investment trends. These themes can cause entire sectors of the crypto market to surge in value, sometimes with little regard for the underlying fundamentals of the projects themselves. Understanding narratives isn't about abandoning research; it's about recognizing the powerful role that storytelling and hype play in a market driven by social media and rapid innovation.

The Core Explanation: Following the Flow of Capital

In the crypto market, capital is constantly moving, seeking the next big opportunity. This movement often consolidates around a compelling narrative. One month, the hot story might be 'Layer-1 Blockchains,' with projects like Solana and Avalanche seeing huge interest. A few months later, the narrative might shift to 'GameFi' (Game Finance) or 'AI Tokens'.

This creates a phenomenon known as capital rotation. As a narrative gains momentum, money flows into that sector, pushing up the prices of all related tokens. Eventually, the narrative becomes overheated, and investors begin to take profits and look for the *next* emerging story.

Identifying a strong, emerging narrative early can be a

highly profitable, albeit risky, investment strategy. It requires staying constantly up-to-date with market trends and conversations on platforms like X (Twitter) and Discord, trying to spot the next big theme before the crowd does.

Case Study: The "Metaverse" Narrative of Late 2021

In October 2021, Facebook announced it was rebranding its entire company to "Meta," signalling a massive corporate push into the Metaverse. This single news event acted as a powerful catalyst, igniting a market-wide "Metaverse" narrative.

Suddenly, a huge wave of hype and capital flooded into any existing crypto project related to gaming and virtual worlds. The prices of tokens like Decentraland (MANA), The Sandbox (SAND), and Axie Infinity (AXS) exploded, in some cases rising by hundreds of percent in just a few weeks. This surge was not driven by any sudden technological breakthrough in the projects themselves, but almost entirely by the power of this new, compelling story that had captured the world's imagination. It's a perfect example of a narrative driving market prices.

Practical Application: Identifying Current Narratives

You can learn to spot narratives by observing how the market groups different assets together.

- **Try This How-To:**

1. Go to a crypto data site with a "Categories" section, like CoinGecko.
2. Look at the list of categories. You will see dozens of themes, such as 'AI Tokens,' 'Layer 2,' 'DeFi,' 'GameFi,' etc. These are the market's established narratives.

3. Click on one of the top-performing categories for the day or week.
4. Notice how many of the tokens within that single category are all moving in the same direction (e.g., all are green or all are red). This synchronized movement is a clear sign of capital flowing into or out of a specific narrative.

Key Takeaways

- A narrative is a dominant story or theme driving a crypto market sector.
- Investment capital in crypto tends to rotate between different narratives.
- Identifying emerging narratives can be profitable but is a high-risk strategy that requires staying very active and informed.

Bridge to the Next Lesson

Narrative investing is a very active strategy that requires you to time the market. For most long-term investors, a more disciplined and less stressful approach is needed to build a position over time. In our next lesson, we'll compare the two primary strategies for deploying capital: Dollar-Cost Averaging (DCA) and Lump Sum investing.

Lesson 07 - Dollar-Cost Averaging (DCA) vs. Lump Sum

An Introduction to Your Investment Strategy

You've done your research, you have your financial goals, and you have capital ready to invest. Now you face a crucial strategic decision: what's the best way to actually deploy that capital into the market? Do you invest it all at once to get maximum exposure, or do you ease in over time to reduce risk? This is the core debate between Lump Sum investing and Dollar-Cost Averaging (DCA). The choice you make will have a significant impact on both your financial returns and your psychological well-being.

The Core Explanation: Two Paths to Investing

There are two primary strategies for how to put your money to work:

1. **Lump Sum Investing:**

- **What it is:** This strategy involves investing all of your available capital into an asset at one single point in time. If you have $1,200 to invest, you invest the full $1,200 today.
- **Pros:** Historically, in markets that tend to go up over time (like stock markets), lump sum investing has often produced better returns. It gives your money the maximum amount of time in the market to compound.
- **Cons:** It carries a significant timing risk. If you happen to invest your entire lump sum at the very peak of a market cycle, you will suffer the maximum possible drawdown and may have to wait years to recover.

1. **Dollar-Cost Averaging (DCA):**

- **What it is:** This is the strategy of investing a fixed amount of money at regular intervals, regardless of the asset's price. For example, you might decide to invest $100 every Friday.
- **Pros:** The main benefit of DCA is that it reduces the risk of bad timing and smooths out your average purchase price over time. When the price is high, your $100 buys fewer units; when the price is low, your $100 buys more units. It is a disciplined and psychologically easier approach for most investors, as it removes the emotion and stress of trying to perfectly "time the market".
- **Cons:** In a relentlessly rising market, DCA may underperform a perfectly timed lump sum investment, as some of your capital remains on the sidelines for longer.

Case Study: Two Investors in a Volatile Year

Let's consider two investors, Alex and Ben, who both have $1,200 to invest in Bitcoin at the start of a volatile year.

- **Alex (Lump Sum):** He invests the full $1,200 on January 1st when the price of Bitcoin is $40,000. He gets 0.03 BTC.
- **Ben (DCA):** He invests $100 on the first day of every month for 12 months. Imagine the price of Bitcoin is volatile: it drops to $30,000 for a few months, then rises to $50,000, and ends the year at $45,000. Because Ben's fixed $100 monthly purchase bought *more* BTC when the price was low, his average purchase price for the year might be closer to $38,000. He might end up with, for example, 0.0315 BTC. Even though Alex invested earlier,

Ben's DCA strategy allowed him to take advantage of the volatility, resulting in a lower average cost and more total BTC for the same amount of money invested.

Practical Application: Automating Your Discipline

The easiest way to execute a DCA strategy is to put it on autopilot.

- **Try This How-To:**

1. Log in to a major centralized exchange that you have an account with.
2. Look for a feature called "Recurring Buy" or "Auto-Invest."
3. Explore the interface (you don't need to set it up). You'll see that you can choose a cryptocurrency, a dollar amount, and a frequency (daily, weekly, or monthly).
4. This tool allows you to automatically execute a DCA strategy, taking the emotion and effort out of the process completely. This is the most practical way to build a long-term position in an asset.

Key Takeaways

- Lump Sum is investing everything at once; DCA is investing in smaller, regular increments.
- DCA reduces the impact of volatility and lowers the risk of bad timing by averaging out your purchase price.
- Historically, Lump Sum performs better if the market only goes up, but DCA is psychologically easier and a more

disciplined approach for most investors.

Bridge to the Next Lesson

DCA is a powerful strategy for accumulating assets and building your portfolio. But what do you do once your portfolio is established and some of your assets have grown much more than others, throwing your original plan out of balance? In our next lesson, we'll cover the essential discipline of portfolio rebalancing.

Lesson 08 - Portfolio Rebalancing Strategies

An Introduction to a Winning Discipline

As your portfolio grows, you'll inevitably face a wonderful problem: some of your investments will perform much better than others. While this is great, it can silently unbalance your entire strategy, concentrating your risk in a few winners and leaving you overexposed. Portfolio rebalancing is the essential discipline of trimming your winners and adding to your laggards to return your portfolio to its original, intended state. It's a counter-intuitive but powerful technique that forces you to sell high and buy low systematically.

The Core Explanation: Realignment and Risk Management

Portfolio rebalancing is the process of realigning the weightings of the assets in your portfolio back to their original target allocations. Your initial asset allocation (e.g., 70% Bitcoin, 30% Altcoins) is a reflection of your risk tolerance and financial goals. Over time, as markets move, this allocation will drift. Rebalancing is the act of restoring that original balance.

The process is simple:

1. **Set Your Targets:** Define your ideal long-term asset allocation (e.g., 80% BTC, 20% ETH).
2. **Monitor Your Portfolio:** At regular intervals (e.g., quarterly or annually), review your portfolio's current weightings.
3. **Realign:** If the weightings have drifted significantly, you sell a portion of the outperforming assets and use the proceeds to buy more of the underperforming assets to bring your portfolio back to its target.

This disciplined process is one of the keys to managing risk over the long term. It prevents your portfolio from becoming too concentrated in a single asset that has experienced a massive price run-up. More importantly, it enforces a 'buy low, sell high' discipline in a systematic, unemotional way.

Case Study: The Overexposed ETH Investor

Let's imagine an investor, Sarah, who decided on a target allocation of 80% BTC and 20% ETH at the start of the year. She invests $10,000 ($8,000 in BTC, $2,000 in ETH).

During the year, Ethereum has a massive rally and its value triples, while Bitcoin's value stays flat. At the end of the year, her portfolio looks like this:

- Bitcoin: $8,000
- Ethereum: $6,000
- Total Portfolio Value: $14,000

Her new allocation is now approximately 57% BTC and 43% ETH. While she's happy with the profit, her portfolio is now far riskier and much more dependent on the performance of ETH than she originally intended. To rebalance, she would sell a portion of her ETH to lock in some profits and use that money to buy more BTC, bringing the portfolio back to her original 80/20 risk profile. She has systematically sold a winner and bought a laggard.

Practical Application: A Rebalancing Calculation

Let's make the concept of rebalancing tangible with a simple exercise.

- **Try This How-To**:

1. Imagine you have a simple two-asset portfolio with a target of 60% BTC and 40% ETH, starting with $10,000 ($6,000 in BTC, $4,000 in ETH).
2. Now, imagine the price of ETH doubles, while BTC stays the same. Your portfolio is now worth $14,000 ($6,000 in BTC, $8,000 in ETH).
3. Calculate your new target positions: 60% of $14,000 is $8,400 for BTC, and 40% of $14,000 is $5,600 for ETH.
4. Determine the trade you need to make: You need to sell $2,400 worth of ETH ($8,000 - $5,600) and use that money to buy $2,400 worth of BTC ($8,400 - $6,000).

This exercise shows the exact mechanics of a rebalancing trade, transforming it from a concept into a clear, calculated action.

Key Takeaways

- Rebalancing brings your portfolio back to its target asset allocation.
- It is a key discipline for managing risk over the long term.
- The process forces you to systematically sell assets that have performed well and buy assets that have underperformed, enforcing a "sell high, buy low" strategy.

Bridge to the Next Lesson

Rebalancing is a key part of managing a portfolio. But when you execute those trades, especially with less common assets, you might encounter issues like "slippage." In our next lesson, we'll explore the crucial market concepts of liquidity and slippage.

Lesson 09 - Understanding Liquidity and Slippage

An Introduction to the Cost of Trading

Why can you sell a million dollars' worth of Bitcoin in seconds with almost no issue, but trying to sell a rare collectible might take months? The answer is liquidity. Liquidity is the lifeblood of any financial market, determining how quickly and easily you can buy or sell an asset without the price moving against you. Understanding this concept is crucial, as its opposite—illiquidity—can lead to hidden trading costs in the form of "slippage."

The Core Explanation: The Ease of Entry and Exit In financial markets,

'Liquidity' refers to the ease with which an asset can be bought or sold without affecting its market price.

- **High Liquidity:** An asset like Bitcoin is highly liquid because there is a deep market with a huge number of buyers and sellers at any given moment. You can execute large trades without significantly impacting the price.
- **Low Liquidity:** A new, small-cap altcoin is often illiquid. There are very few buyers and sellers, so even a moderately sized trade can cause a massive price swing.

This leads directly to the concept of 'Slippage'. Slippage occurs when a trader must accept a different price than expected between the time, they place an order and the time it's executed. This is a common problem in low-liquidity markets because your own trade can "move the market". When you buy, you push the price up; when you sell, you push the price down. The difference between the price you expected and the less favourable price you got is the slippage.

Case Study: The Illiquid Altcoin Trader

A trader wants to invest $10,000 into a new, small-cap altcoin currently trading at $1.00. They go to a DEX and place a large "market buy" order for 10,000 tokens.

However, because the market is illiquid, there aren't 10,000 tokens for sale at $1.00. The smart contract works through the available orders:

- The first 2,000 tokens are filled at $1.00.
- The next 3,000 tokens are filled at $1.02, as the initial sellers are bought up.
- The final 5,000 tokens are filled at an average price of $1.05.

The trader's final average price for their 10,000 tokens is not

$1.00, but closer to $1.03. They paid an extra $300 (or 3%) more than they expected. This 3% difference is the slippage they incurred due to the low liquidity of the market. For a seller, the effect would be the same but in the opposite direction, receiving a lower price than expected.

Practical Application: Observing Slippage on a DEX

Decentralized exchanges make it very easy to see the potential impact of slippage before you trade.

- **Try This How-To:**

1. Go to a major DEX like Uniswap or PancakeSwap.
2. In the swap interface, set up a trade between two highly liquid assets, like ETH and the stablecoin USDC. Enter a reasonable amount, like 0.1 ETH. You will likely see a "Price Impact" or "Slippage" warning that is very low (e.g., less than 0.1%).
3. Now, keep the ETH amount the same, but change the token you want to receive to a very obscure, small-cap altcoin.
4. Notice how the estimated slippage for the exact same trade amount is now much, much higher, perhaps several percent.

This is a live, real-world demonstration of how an asset's liquidity directly impacts your trading costs.

Key Takeaways

- Liquidity is the ability to buy or sell an asset quickly without impacting its price.

- Slippage is the difference between the expected trade price and the actual execution price.
- Low liquidity leads to high slippage, especially for large orders, effectively acting as a hidden cost of trading.

Bridge to the Next Lesson

Understanding market mechanics like liquidity is part of managing risk. But the most important part is having a personal framework to protect your capital from devastating losses. In our final lesson of this module, we'll cover the essentials of building your own risk management framework.

Lesson 10 - Risk Management Frameworks

An Introduction to Staying in the Game

Warren Buffett famously has two rules for investing: "Rule No. 1: Never lose money. Rule No. 2: Never forget Rule No. 1." While never losing money is impossible, the wisdom behind this quote is that capital preservation is the most important skill for long-term survival. In the highly volatile crypto markets, this is doubly true. A risk management framework is your personal set of rules designed to protect your capital and ensure you can stay in the game long enough to succeed.

The Core Explanation: Your Personal Rulebook

Effective risk management is crucial for survival in volatile crypto markets. It's not about avoiding risk entirely, but about managing it intelligently so that no single event can cause a catastrophic loss. A framework includes several key rules you set for yourself *before* you invest:

1. **Position Sizing:** This is the most important rule. It dictates that you should never allocate too much of your portfolio to a single, high-risk asset. For example, you might set a personal rule that no single altcoin investment can ever exceed 5% of your total portfolio value. This ensures that if that one investment goes to zero, it's a painful loss, but not a portfolio-destroying one.
2. **Stop-Losses:** A stop-loss is a predetermined price at which you will sell an asset to cut your losses. By setting this price in advance, you take the emotion out of the decision. You are defining the exact maximum loss you are willing to accept on a trade before you enter it.
3. **Asymmetric Bets:** This is a mindset where you focus on investments where the potential upside is many times larger than the potential downside. If you are risking $100 on a trade (your maximum loss), you should only do so if you have a reasonable belief that the potential gain is $300, $500, or more.

Underpinning all of this is the golden rule you must never forget: never invest more than you can afford to lose completely.

Case Study: The Disciplined vs. the Emotional Trader

Let's consider two traders who both want to invest in the same high-risk altcoin at a price of $1.00.

- The Emotional Trader: Believing the coin will "go to the moon," they invest 50% of their entire portfolio into it. They have no exit plan. The coin's price drops to $0.50. Now in a state of panic (FUD), they sell everything, realizing a massive 50% loss on half their portfolio.

- The Disciplined Trader: They use a risk management framework.
- **Position Size:** They decide to allocate only 3% of their portfolio to this trade.
- **Stop-Loss:** They immediately set a stop-loss order at $0.80 (a 20% loss).
- **Asymmetry:** Their research suggests the coin has the potential to go to $4.00, so the potential reward is much larger than their defined risk.

The coin's price drops. The disciplined trader's stop-loss order automatically triggers at $0.80. They lose 20% on a 3% position, resulting in a tiny, manageable loss to their overall portfolio. They have preserved their capital and can move on to the next opportunity, while the emotional trader has suffered a devastating blow.

Practical Application: Defining Your Own Rule

The act of writing down your rules makes them real and harder to break in a moment of emotional pressure.

- **Try This How-To:**

1. Take out a piece of paper or open a new document.
2. Title it "My Risk Management Rules."
3. Write down your own personal "Golden Rule" for a single investment. Be specific.

- **Example 1:** "I will never allocate more than 5% of my total crypto portfolio to any single altcoin."
- **Example 2:** "For any trade I make, I will always pre-

define a price at which I will sell for a loss (my stop-loss) and a price at which I will sell for a profit (my take-profit)."

Creating and committing to your own simple rules is the first step toward becoming a disciplined and resilient investor.

Key Takeaways

- Risk management is about preserving your capital so you can stay in the game.
- Position sizing and stop-losses are critical tools to limit potential losses on any single investment.
- Focus on asymmetric bets where the potential upside is significantly greater than the amount you are willing to risk.
- Always remember the #1 rule: never invest more than you are willing to lose completely.

8

Module 1 Recap

Congratulations, you've completed the first module of the Intermediate Level and have equipped yourself with a powerful new toolkit for analysing the market.

- You've learned the language of Technical Analysis, understanding how to identify Support, Resistance, and Trends, and how to use indicators like the RSI and MACD to gauge market momentum.
- You've explored the unique superpower of crypto investing—On-Chain Analysis—and the importance of evaluating a project's fundamental economic design through Tokenomics.
- Most importantly, you now understand the disciplined strategies for navigating the market, from recognizing psychological cycles and implementing DCA to the crucial practice of creating your own risk management framework.

You are now thinking less like a beginner and more like a seasoned analyst.

Module 2 - Blockchain Technology Deep Dive

Module Introduction: In the Beginner Level, we used simple analogies to understand what a blockchain is. Now, we go under the hood. This module is designed to give you a deeper understanding of the core technological concepts that differentiate blockchains and drive innovation in the space. You'll learn how these networks agree on the truth without a leader, the fundamental challenges they face in trying to scale, and the clever solutions being developed to overcome them. This is where you learn the "how" and "why" behind the technology.

Lesson 01 - Proof-of-Work vs. Proof-of-Stake

An Introduction to the Engine of a Blockchain

How does a global network of computers, with no central leader, agree on which transactions are valid? This is the fundamental question of decentralized consensus, and the answer is the "engine" of the blockchain: its

consensus mechanism. These mechanisms are the rulebooks that ensure everyone agrees on the state of the ledger. The two most important and influential engines in the crypto world are Proof-of-Work and Proof-of-Stake. Understanding their differences is key to understanding the technology's evolution.

The Core Explanation: Energy vs. Capital

Consensus mechanisms are the rules that allow a decentralized network to agree on the truth. The two dominant systems achieve this in fundamentally different ways:

1. **Proof-of-Work (PoW):**

- **What it is:** This is the original mechanism, pioneered by Bitcoin. It requires network participants, called "miners," to use powerful computers to solve complex mathematical puzzles. The first miner to solve the puzzle gets to validate the latest block of transactions and is rewarded with new coins.
- **Security Model:** PoW secures the network with real-world energy. To attack the network, you would need to control most of the computational power, which is incredibly expensive and difficult to acquire. This makes the system very secure but also very energy-intensive.

1. **Proof-of-Stake (PoS):**

- **What it is:** This is a newer and more energy-efficient mechanism used by blockchains like Ethereum. Instead of computational power, it relies on economic incentives. Participants, called "validators," lock up or "stake" their own crypto as collateral to get the chance to validate a new block.
- **Security Model:** PoS secures the network with capital. If a validator acts honestly, they receive a reward. If they act maliciously, they risk having their staked collateral

destroyed ("slashed"). To attack the network, you would need to acquire most of the staked capital, making it economically irrational. PoS is far more energy-efficient than PoW.

Case Study: The Ethereum "Merge"

For years, the biggest criticism of Ethereum was its reliance on the energy-intensive Proof-of-Work mechanism. After years of complex research and engineering, in September 2022, the Ethereum network underwent a historic upgrade known as "The Merge."

In a seamless transition, the network's engine was swapped out in real-time from PoW to PoS. The immediate and most dramatic effect was a reduction in Ethereum's energy consumption by over 99%. The event was a massive technological achievement and a powerful validation of the Proof-of-Stake model's viability at a global scale, fundamentally changing the narrative around the environmental impact of blockchains.

Practical Application: Visualizing the Security Models

You can see the scale of these two different security models in real-time.

- **Try This How-To:**

1. Go to a data website like Blockchain.com or Glassnode. Search for the Bitcoin "hash rate" chart. You will see a graph representing the immense and constantly growing computational power (energy) being expended to secure the PoW network.
2. Now, go to a site like StakingRewards.com or search for

an "Ethereum staking dashboard." You will see charts showing the millions of ETH (capital) that are currently staked to secure the PoS network.

This visually contrasts the two security models: one is secured by a "wall of energy," the other by a "wall of capital."

Key Takeaways

- Consensus Mechanisms are Rules for Agreement: They are the core engines that allow a decentralized network to stay secure and agree on the truth.
- Proof-of-Work (PoW) Uses Energy: It relies on computational power ("mining") to secure the network, as seen in Bitcoin.
- Proof-of-Stake (PoS) Uses Capital: It relies on economic incentives ("staking") to secure the network, making it far more energy-efficient.

Bridge to the Next Lesson

These consensus mechanisms are designed to solve a fundamental challenge in blockchain architecture. In our next lesson, we will explore the famous "Blockchain Trilemma," which explains the difficult trade-offs that every network must make.

Lesson 02 - The Blockchain Trilemma

An Introduction to "Fast, Cheap, Good - Pick Two"

In the world of engineering, there's a common saying: "Fast, cheap, or good: you can only pick two." You can have a product made quickly and cheaply, but the quality won't be good. You can have it fast and good, but it won't be cheap. This concept of unavoidable trade-offs applies directly to the world of blockchains. The "Blockchain Trilemma" is the most famous framework for understanding the difficult choices and compromises that every blockchain developer faces.

The Core Explanation: The Three Competing Goals

The Blockchain Trilemma is a concept, widely discussed by Ethereum's founder Vitalik Buterin, which states that it is incredibly difficult for a blockchain to achieve all three of its core properties simultaneously. These three competing properties are:

1. **Security:** How strong is the network's defence against attacks? Can it prevent fraudulent transactions and resist being taken over by a malicious actor?
2. **Scalability:** How well can the network handle a large volume of transactions? Can it process thousands of transactions per second at a low cost for its users, or does it become slow and expensive when it gets busy?
3. **Decentralization:** How distributed is the power and control of the network? Is it run by thousands of independent participants around the world, making it censorship-resistant (high decentralization), or is it run by a small, easily identifiable group of powerful computers (low decentralization)?

The trilemma suggests that most blockchains are forced to make a trade-off. They can typically excel in two of these areas, but only by sacrificing the third.

Case Study: Ethereum vs. Solana

The different design philosophies of Ethereum and Solana provide a perfect real-world example of the trilemma in action.

- Ethereum has historically prioritized decentralization and security. It is designed so that a regular person can run a node on a consumer-grade computer, leading to a massive and highly decentralized network of validators. The trade-off has been scalability. This focus on decentralization has made the base layer slow and expensive during times of high demand.
- Solana, on the other hand, was designed from the ground up to prioritize scalability. It can process thousands of transactions per second at a very low cost. However, it achieves this high performance by requiring its validators to run extremely powerful and expensive hardware. This high barrier to entry results in a smaller and more centralized group of validators, thus making a clear trade-off on the decentralization front.

Neither approach is "right" or "wrong"—they are simply different sets of engineering trade-offs designed to appeal to different users and applications.

Practical Application: Analysing a New Blockchain

You can use the trilemma as a mental model to quickly analyse any new blockchain project you encounter.

- **Try This How-To:**

1. The next time you read about a new Layer 1 blockchain that claims to be "the fastest ever."
2. Ask yourself the critical question: "What trade-off are they likely making to achieve that speed?"
3. Look into their technology. Do they have a very small number of validators? Do they have very high hardware requirements to run a node?
4. By asking this question, you are using the trilemma framework to think critically about a project's claims, moving beyond marketing hype to understand its fundamental design choices.

Key Takeaways

- **The Trilemma Consists of Three Competing Goals:** Security, scalability, and decentralization.
- **It is Very Difficult to Maximize All Three**: Most blockchains are forced to make trade-offs, prioritizing two properties at the expense of the third.
- **It is a Framework for Analysis:** The trilemma is a powerful mental model for understanding the design choices and compromises of different blockchain networks.

Bridge to the Next Lesson

The Blockchain Trilemma is the core problem that all developers are trying to solve. The two most popular approaches to solving the "scalability" part of the trilemma are by improving the base layer or by building on top of it. In our next lesson, we will explore Layer 1 vs. Layer 2 scaling solutions.

Lesson 03 - Layer 1 vs. Layer 2 Scaling Solutions

An Introduction to the Scalability Problem

For a blockchain to achieve global adoption, it needs to be able to handle thousands of transactions per second, just like a major payment network like Visa. However, as we learned in the "Blockchain Trilemma," achieving this level of scalability without sacrificing security or decentralization is incredibly difficult. This challenge, known as the "scalability problem," is the holy grail of blockchain development. This lesson will explore the two competing philosophies for how to solve it: building a better base layer (L1) versus building on top of the existing one (L2).

The Core Explanation: Widening the Highway vs. Building a High-Speed Train

There are two primary approaches to making a blockchain faster and cheaper to use:

1. **Layer 1 (L1) Scaling:**

- A Layer 1 (L1) is the base blockchain itself, like Bitcoin or Ethereum.
- L1 scaling involves making changes *directly to the main blockchain's protocol* to try and improve its performance.
- This is like trying to solve a traffic jam by widening the main highway—for example, by increasing the block

size to fit more transactions or changing the consensus mechanism to be faster. The goal is to increase the native capacity of the main chain.

1. **Layer 2 (L2) Scaling:**

- A Layer 2 (L2) is a separate protocol or framework that is built *on top of* a Layer 1 blockchain.
- L2 scaling aims to improve performance without changing the secure, decentralized base layer. It's like building a high-speed rail network alongside the main highway to offload traffic.
- The core mechanism is to handle transactions 'off-chain' in a faster, cheaper environment. It then bundles hundreds or thousands of these transactions together and posts a single, compressed summary back to the secure Layer 1. This drastically reduces fees and increases transaction speed for users, while still inheriting the powerful security guarantees of the main chain.

For Ethereum, the community has firmly decided that the Layer 2 scaling approach is the primary path forward.

Case Study: The Real-World Cost of a Congested L1

During the peak of the 2021 bull market, the Ethereum network was overwhelmed with demand. The "highway" was completely congested. A simple token swap on a DEX on the Ethereum Layer 1 could cost anywhere from $50 to $200 in gas fees. While this was acceptable for large transactions, it priced out the average user completely, making the network unusable for small-scale activities.

In contrast, the rise of Layer 2 solutions like Arbitrum and

Optimism provided a solution. By moving their activity to these L2s, users could perform the exact same token swap for a fraction of the cost, often for less than $1. This tangible, real-world difference in user experience was a powerful demonstration of the necessity and effectiveness of L2 scaling solutions.

Practical Application: Measuring the L2 Ecosystem

You can see the massive scale of the L2 ecosystem in real-time.

- **Try This How-To:**

1. Go to the analytics website L2BEAT.com. This site is the leading tracker for the health and scale of the Ethereum Layer 2 ecosystem.
2. On the homepage, you will see a list of the top Layer 2 networks ranked by "Total Value Locked (TVL)," which represents the amount of capital users have bridged to these networks.
3. Look at the combined TVL of all the L2s. This multi-billion-dollar figure gives you a clear sense of how much economic activity has already migrated from the congested Layer 1 to these more efficient scaling solutions.

Key Takeaways

- Layer 1 is the main, underlying blockchain network.
- Layer 2 is a separate protocol built on top of an L1 to improve performance.

- L2s increase scalability by processing transactions off the main chain and posting a summary back, offering lower fees and faster speeds.

Bridge to the Next Lesson

Most of the Layer 2 ecosystem is designed to enhance one specific Layer 1: Ethereum. Ethereum's immense power and influence come from its "brain," a core component that allows it to function as a world computer. In our next lesson, we will explore the Ethereum Virtual Machine, or EVM.

Lesson 04 - Ethereum and the EVM

An Introduction to the Blockchain's Brain

What truly separates Ethereum from Bitcoin? While Bitcoin is a masterful ledger for a single asset, Ethereum is a full-fledged computing platform. The innovation that makes this possible is the Ethereum Virtual Machine (EVM). The EVM is the heart of the Ethereum network; it is the "brain" that executes code and transformed the blockchain from a simple data store into a dynamic, programmable "world computer." Understanding the EVM is key to understanding the entire smart contract ecosystem.

The Core Explanation: A Global, Decentralized Computer

The Ethereum Virtual Machine (EVM) is the computation engine of the Ethereum network that is responsible for running all smart contracts.

- **What it is:** Think of the EVM as a single, global, and decentralized computer. It is a sandboxed virtual machine, meaning the code it runs is isolated from the rest of the network, which ensures security. This "computer" is run simultaneously on thousands of independent nodes around the world.

- **How it works:** Developers write smart contracts in high-level languages like Solidity. This code is then "compiled" down into low-level instructions called bytecode. The EVM is the part of every Ethereum node that reads and executes this bytecode, changing the state of the blockchain according to the smart contract's logic.
- **Why it matters:** Because the EVM runs on thousands of computers, it guarantees that a deployed application will run exactly as programmed, without any possibility of downtime, censorship, or interference. It is a trustless execution environment.

The design of the EVM was so successful that it has become the de facto standard for smart contract platforms. Many new blockchains, like Polygon, Avalanche, and BNB Chain, are "EVM-compatible," meaning they have implemented their own version of the EVM. This makes it incredibly easy for developers to take their applications and tools built for Ethereum and deploy them on these other chains with minimal changes, creating powerful network effects.

Case Study: The Autonomy of Uniswap

The decentralized exchange Uniswap is a perfect illustration of the EVM's power. The entire protocol, which has facilitated trillions of dollars in trading volume, is simply a set of smart contracts deployed on the Ethereum blockchain.

- There is no CEO who can shut it down.
- There are no corporate servers that can be hacked.
- The smart contracts will continue to execute trades according to their code, 24/7, as long as the Ethereum network exists.

Uniswap is an autonomous financial machine that exists only on the EVM. It is a powerful example of the kind of unstoppable applications that can be built on this "world computer."

Practical Application: Viewing EVM Bytecode

You can see the raw language of the EVM for yourself on a block explorer.

- **Try This How-To:**

1. Go to Etherscan and look up the contract address for a popular dApp, for example, the Uniswap V3 Router (0x68b3465833fb72A70ecDF485E0e4C7bD8665Fc45).
2. Navigate to the "Contract" tab.
3. Scroll down past the Solidity source code until you see a section for "Contract Creation Code" or "Bytecode."
4. This long string of numbers and letters is the low-level language that the EVM actually reads and executes.

This makes the abstract concept of a "program running on the blockchain" tangible. You are looking at the raw instructions for one of the world's most important financial applications.

Key Takeaways

- The EVM is the computation engine of Ethereum that runs smart contracts.
- It acts like a decentralized computer that anyone can deploy applications on.
- EVM-compatibility allows developers to easily port their Ethereum apps to other chains, making it the dominant standard in Web3.

Bridge to the Next Lesson

The EVM became the dominant standard, but it is not the only design. In the quest for greater scalability, many new blockchains have emerged, trying to solve the Blockchain Trilemma with entirely different architectures. In our next lesson, we'll explore the competitive and innovative world of alternative Layer 1s.

Lesson 05 - Exploring Alternative Layer 1s

An Introduction to the Multi-Chain World

While Ethereum is the dominant smart contract platform, it is not the only one. A whole ecosystem of

alternative Layer 1 blockchains has emerged, each with its own unique design and approach to solving the Blockchain Trilemma. These are often called "ETH Killers," though a more accurate term is "ETH competitors." They create a vibrant and innovative multi-chain world, giving users and developers a choice of platforms with different trade-offs in speed, cost, and decentralization.

The Core Explanation: Different Designs, Different Trade-

offs

Alternative Layer 1s are base-layer blockchains that compete with Ethereum, usually by focusing on higher scalability and lower fees. They achieve this by using different consensus mechanisms and network architectures. Let's look at two prominent examples to understand these different designs:

1. **Solana (SOL):**

- **Design:** Solana is a "monolithic" blockchain, designed for extremely high performance. It uses a unique consensus mechanism called Proof-of-History (PoH) in conjunction with Proof-of-Stake. PoH acts as a cryptographic clock, time-stamping transactions before they are bundled into blocks, which allows for very fast parallel processing.
- **Trade-off:** This design allows Solana to achieve incredibly high transaction speeds (thousands of TPS) and very low costs, making it popular for applications that need high throughput, like certain types of trading. However, the hardware requirements to run a Solana validator are very high, which leads to a smaller number of validators and makes it generally less decentralized than Ethereum.

1. **Avalanche (AVAX):**

- **Design:** Avalanche uses a novel architecture with "subnets" (sub-networks). This allows individual applications or groups of applications to have their own dedicated, sovereign blockchains that are customized for their specific needs.

- **Trade-off:** This "app-chain" model prevents applications from having to compete for blockspace with every other app on the network, avoiding the network-wide congestion issues that can happen on Ethereum. The trade-off is the complexity of bootstrapping and securing these individual subnets.

These are just two of many "ETH Killers" that create a competitive and innovative multi-chain landscape.

Case Study: The Rise of Solana in 2021

During the 2021 bull run, Ethereum's high gas fees made the network unusable for many small-scale users and applications. This created a massive opportunity for a high-speed, low-cost alternative.

Solana, with its promise of near-instant finality and sub-cent transaction fees, seized this opportunity. It attracted a massive wave of users, developers, and venture capital. A vibrant ecosystem of dApps, particularly in the NFT and high-frequency trading spaces, exploded on the network. The price of its native token, SOL, surged dramatically. This was a clear case study demonstrating the immense market demand for alternative Layer 1s with different performance characteristics, proving that the future of crypto would likely be a multi-chain one, not a winner-take-all market.

Practical Application: Exploring a Multi-Chain Ecosystem

You can see the diversity of the multi-chain world using analytics tools.

- **Try This How-To:**

1. Go to a dApp analytics site like DappRadar.
2. On the homepage, you can view the rankings of dApps across all chains. Find the filter option for "Chains."
3. First, select "Ethereum" to see the applications in its ecosystem.
4. Then, clear the filter and select "Solana" or "Avalanche."
5. You will see that while Ethereum is dominant, these other chains have their own unique and thriving ecosystems of applications, often with a different focus (e.g., more games or NFT projects on one vs. more DeFi on another).

Key Takeaways

- Alternative L1s compete with Ethereum, usually by focusing on higher scalability.
- They use different consensus mechanisms and architectures to achieve their goals, each with its own set of trade-offs.
- The rise of successful alternative L1s like Solana and Avalanche suggests that the future of Web3 will be a multi-chain one.

Bridge to the Next Lesson

These alternative L1s represent a "monolithic" approach to scaling, where the base layer itself is designed to be highly performant. But as we've learned, the dominant scaling strategy for Ethereum is via Layer 2s. In our next lesson, we will take a closer look at the leading L2 technologies and the different types of rollups.

Lesson 06 - Introduction to Layer 2s

An Introduction to the High-Speed Rail of Blockchains

If scaling a Layer 1 blockchain is like trying to widen a congested highway, then Layer 2s are like building a parallel, high-speed rail network. They are designed to offload traffic from the main chain, offering users a dramatically faster and cheaper experience without leaving the security of the main network. This lesson will dive into "Rollups," the most popular and important type of Layer 2 technology that is making Ethereum accessible to everyone.

The Core Explanation: The Two Flavors of Rollups

'Rollups' are the most popular type of Layer 2 scaling solution. Their core function is to execute transactions outside the L1, then post the compressed transaction data back to the L1. This allows them to inherit Ethereum's security while offering much higher throughput. There are two main types of rollups, distinguished by how they prove to the L1 that their transactions are valid:

1. **Optimistic Rollups (e.g., Arbitrum, Optimism):**

- **How they work:** These rollups "optimistically" assume that all the transactions they process and post to Ethereum are valid. They don't provide an upfront proof.
- **Security Model:** To catch any potential fraud, there is a "challenge period" (typically 7 days). During this time, anyone can submit a "fraud proof" to the mainnet if

they spot an invalid transaction. If the proof is valid, the fraudulent transaction is reverted, and the fraudster is penalized. It's a system of "innocent until proven guilty."

1. **ZK-Rollups (e.g., Polygon zkEVM, zkSync):**

- **How they work:** These rollups use advanced cryptography called zero-knowledge proofs. For every batch of transactions, they generate a compact, cryptographic proof (a SNARK or STARK) that mathematically guarantees the validity of those transactions.
- **Security Model:** This validity proof is posted to the L1 along with the transaction data. The L1 smart contract just needs to verify this single proof to know that all the transactions in the batch are correct. There is no challenge period needed. It's a system of "guilty until proven innocent with mathematical proof."

ZK-Rollups are generally considered the more secure and efficient long-term solution, but the technology is more complex to build.

Case Study: The Arbitrum Airdrop

In March 2023, Arbitrum, a leading optimistic rollup, launched its ARB governance token. To distribute the token and decentralize its governance, it conducted a massive airdrop to its early users and builders.

The scale of the event was a powerful testament to the success of Layer 2s. Over 625,000 wallets were eligible for the airdrop, based on their historical activity on the Arbitrum network. This demonstrated that hundreds of thousands of users had already migrated their activity from the expensive

Ethereum mainnet to this L2 to take advantage of its low fees and fast transaction speeds. The airdrop was a landmark event that cemented the "rollup-centric" roadmap as a real, successful, and heavily adopted scaling strategy for Ethereum.

Practical Application: Comparing L2 Costs

The cost savings of using an L2 are not theoretical; they are real and dramatic.

- **Try This How-To:**

1. Go to the website L2Fees.info.
2. This site provides a live comparison of the cost to perform various transactions (like sending ETH or swapping tokens) on the Ethereum L1 versus the leading Layer 2 networks.
3. You will immediately see the stark difference. A transaction that costs several dollars on the Ethereum mainnet will often cost only a few cents on an L2 like Arbitrum or Optimism.

This simple dashboard provides the most compelling, real-time argument for the value and necessity of Layer 2 scaling solutions.

Key Takeaways

- Rollups are a leading type of L2 scaling solution.
- Optimistic Rollups assume transactions are valid and use a fraud-proof system with a challenge period.
- ZK-Rollups use cryptographic proofs to mathematically

guarantee transaction validity, allowing for faster finality.

Bridge to the Next Lesson

As a multi-chain and multi-layer world emerges, with assets living on Ethereum, Solana, Arbitrum, and more, the need to move assets between these different networks becomes critical. In our next lesson, we will explore the vital (and often risky) infrastructure that makes this possible: cross-chain bridges.

Lesson 07 - Cross-Chain Bridges and Interoperability

An Introduction to Connecting Blockchain Islands

Imagine each blockchain is an isolated island, with its own economy and its own currency. You might have ETH on Ethereum Island and SOL on Solana Island, but you can't spend your ETH on Solana, and you can't use your SOL on Ethereum. For these separate economies to thrive and interact, they need a way to connect. Cross-chain bridges are the vital infrastructure that connects these blockchain islands, allowing for the free flow of assets and data and creating a truly interconnected ecosystem.

The Core Explanation: The Lock and Mint Mechanism

'Cross-chain bridges' are protocols that allow users to transfer tokens from one blockchain to another (e.g., from Ethereum to Arbitrum). They are the critical piece of the puzzle for achieving interoperability—the ability of different blockchains to communicate and exchange value with each other.

While there are many different bridge designs, the most common one works on a 'lock and mint' mechanism:

1. **Lock:** A user deposits an asset (e.g., 1 ETH) into a smart contract on the source chain (Ethereum). This asset is now locked.
2. **Verify:** A network of validators watches the source chain, sees the lock transaction, and verifies it.
3. **Mint:** Once verified, the validators authorize the creation of a new, "wrapped" version of the asset on the destination chain (e.g., 1 "Wrapped ETH" or WETH). This wrapped asset is a synthetic token that is fully backed by the original, locked asset.
4. **Use:** The user can now use this Wrapped ETH on the destination chain to interact with its dApps. When they want to move back, the process is reversed: the wrapped asset is "burned" (destroyed), and the original asset is unlocked on the source chain.

While bridges are essential for a multi-chain world, they are also technologically complex and have historically been major targets for hackers, representing one of the biggest security risks in the crypto space.

Case Study: The Wormhole Bridge Hack (2022)

The Wormhole bridge, which connects Ethereum to Solana and other chains, suffered one of the largest hacks in DeFi history in February 2022. A hacker found a vulnerability in the bridge's smart contract code. They exploited this flaw to trick the validators into authorizing the creation of 120,000 Wrapped ETH on the Solana blockchain *without* actually locking the corresponding 120,000 ETH on the Ethereum side.

The hacker essentially minted over $320 million worth of unbacked assets out of thin air. The event was a catastrophic failure of the bridge's security and served as a stark, industry-wide warning about the immense security challenges involved in building secure cross-chain infrastructure.

Practical Application: Exploring Bridge Aggregators

There are hundreds of different bridges connecting various chains, each with different speeds, costs, and security assumptions. Bridge aggregators are tools that help users find the best route.

- **Try This How-To:**

1. Go to a bridge aggregator website like Bungee or LI.FI (Lifi).
2. These sites act like search engines for bridges.
3. In the interface, select a "From Chain" (e.g., Ethereum) and a "To Chain" (e.g., Polygon). Select a token you want to move (e.g., USDC) and an amount.
4. The site will then show you multiple different bridge "routes" you could take to complete your transfer, comparing them on factors like estimated fees, speed, and security.

This demonstrates the variety and complexity of the bridge ecosystem and the tools being built to make it easier to navigate.

Key Takeaways

- Bridges enable the transfer of assets and data between different blockchains.
- They are crucial for creating an interconnected, multi-chain ecosystem.
- Bridge security is a major challenge in the cryptocurrency space, and they have been the target of some of the largest hacks.

Bridge to the Next Lesson

Bridges help move assets between chains, but how do smart contracts on one chain get reliable information about the real world, like the current price of the Australian Dollar? In our next lesson, we will tackle the fundamental challenge of bringing external data onto the blockchain: "The Oracle Problem."

Lesson 08 - Oracles and The Oracle Problem

An Introduction to a Blockchain's Senses

By design, blockchains are powerful, secure, and self-contained systems. They are experts at knowing the state of their own digital world. However, this security creates a limitation: they are fundamentally deaf and blind to anything happening outside of it. A smart contract has no way of knowing the current price of Bitcoin, the weather in Sydney, or the winner of a football match. This fundamental challenge is known as "The Oracle Problem," and solving it is mission-critical for connecting blockchains to the real world.

The Core Explanation: Bridging the Digital and Physical

Worlds

The 'Oracle Problem' is the challenge of getting external, off-chain data onto the blockchain in a secure and trustworthy manner. If a smart contract needs real-world information to execute, how can it trust that the information is accurate and hasn't been tampered with?

The solution is a service called an 'oracle'. An oracle is a third-party service that acts as a secure data bridge between the blockchain (on-chain) and the real world (off-chain). It fetches, verifies, and delivers external data to smart contracts so they can execute based on real-world inputs and outputs.

However, using a single, centralized oracle creates a massive security risk. If that one oracle is hacked or provides bad data, the entire smart contract that relies on it can be exploited. This is why decentralized oracle networks are the industry standard.

The most well-known of these is Chainlink. Instead of relying on a single source of truth, Chainlink uses a large, decentralized network of independent oracle nodes. These nodes all fetch the same piece of data from multiple sources. The network then aggregates their responses to arrive at a highly reliable and tamper-proof consensus value, which it then posts on-chain for smart contracts to use. This decentralized approach eliminates any single point of failure.

Case Study: The DeFi Lending Protocol

A DeFi lending protocol like Aave or Compound is perhaps the best example of why oracles are essential.

- A user wants to deposit 10 ETH as collateral to borrow $10,000 worth of USDC.
- The protocol's smart contract needs to know the real-

time price of ETH/USD to determine if the user's collateral is sufficient.

- This price data must come from an oracle.
- Furthermore, the smart contract must continuously monitor this price feed. If the price of ETH drops and the user's collateral value falls below a certain threshold, the oracle's price feed will trigger the smart contract to automatically liquidate the position to protect the lenders.

Without a secure, reliable, and constantly updating price feed from a decentralized oracle network like Chainlink, the entire multi-billion-dollar DeFi lending industry could not exist.

Practical Application: Viewing a Decentralized Price Feed

You can see how a decentralized oracle network functions in real-time.

- **Try This How-To:**

1. Go to the official Chainlink Data Feeds page.
2. You will see a list of dozens of different price feeds available on various blockchains (e.g., ETH/USD, BTC/USD).
3. Click on a major feed like ETH/USD for the Ethereum network.
4. You will see the current, aggregated price. More importantly, you can often see a list of the individual, independent oracle nodes that are all reporting that price. Each node has its own address and reputation.

This visually demonstrates how a decentralized network of sources is used to create a single, highly trustworthy data point for smart contracts.

Key Takeaways

- Blockchains cannot access real-world, off-chain data by themselves.
- Oracles are services that provide this external data to smart contracts.
- Decentralized oracles like Chainlink are crucial for DeFi applications because they provide secure and reliable real-world data without a single point of failure.

Bridge to the Next Lesson

Oracles provide the critical data that powers smart contracts. But what exactly can these smart contracts do with that data? In our next lesson, we will take a deeper look at the capabilities and functions of these fundamental building blocks of Web3.

Lesson 09 - What Can Smart Contracts Do?

An Introduction to the Building Blocks of Web3

We've talked a lot about smart contracts as the engine of Ethereum and the backbone of DeFi. But what are they, really? At their core, they are just code. However, because this code runs on a decentralized blockchain, it becomes something much more powerful: an unstoppable, unchangeable, and transparent digital agreement. This lesson will explore what these fundamental building blocks of Web3 can actually do, from simple transfers to creating entire autonomous economies.

The Core Explanation: Unstoppable "If-Then" Logic

At their most basic level, smart contracts are 'if-then' statements written in code and stored on a blockchain. Because they run on a decentralized network, they have two incredibly powerful properties:

1. **Immutability:** Once a smart contract is deployed to the blockchain, its code cannot be changed. It will execute exactly as programmed, forever.
2. **Unstoppability:** A smart contract runs on a global network of thousands of computers. As long as the blockchain itself is running, the smart contract cannot be stopped or censored.

These properties allow smart contracts to perform a wide range of functions without the need for a traditional intermediary. Their use cases range from simple to highly complex:

- Custody and Transfer of Value: A smart contract can hold and manage digital assets, releasing them only when specific, pre-defined conditions are met. This is the foundation of digital escrow services.
- Managing Agreements: They can manage complex agreements between multiple users automatically. Think of a multi-signature wallet that requires 3 out of 5 people to approve a transaction before funds can be moved.
- Powering dApps: They can act as the complete backend logic for a decentralized application. The entire functionality of a protocol like Uniswap is just a collection

of smart contracts working together.

Case Study: A Decentralized Crowdfunding Campaign

Imagine a creator wants to fund a new project using a smart contract instead of a traditional platform like Kickstarter.

- **The smart contract is programmed with two simple rules:**

1. A funding goal (e.g., 100 ETH).
2. A deadline (e.g., 30 days).

- **The "IF-THEN" Logic:**
- IF the funding goal of 100 ETH is reached before the 30-day deadline, THEN the smart contract will automatically transfer the full 100 ETH to the creator's wallet.
- IF the funding goal is *not* reached by the deadline, THEN the smart contract will automatically and instantly refund all the deposited ETH back to the original contributors.

In this example, the smart contract acts as a perfectly trustworthy and automated escrow agent. It removes the need to trust the creator to manage the funds or issue refunds correctly. The rules are code, and the execution is guaranteed by the blockchain.

Practical Application: Thinking in Smart Contract Logic

You can start to see the world through the lens of smart contract logic by breaking down real-world agreements.

- **Try This How-To:**

1. Think of a simple real-world agreement, like a bet between two friends on a football game.
2. On a piece of paper, try to define the "IF-THEN" logic that would be needed to turn this into a smart contract.

You would need:

- A way for both friends to deposit their wager (ETH) into the contract.
- A trusted data source (an oracle!) to tell the contract the final score of the game.
- Logic in the contract that says: IF the oracle reports Team A won, THEN send all the funds to Friend A's address; otherwise, send them to Friend B.

This thought exercise helps you understand the clear, unambiguous, and automated logic that is at the heart of every smart contract.

Key Takeaways

- Smart contracts are automated, self-executing agreements on a blockchain.
- They are immutable and will always execute exactly as programmed.
- They are the fundamental components used to build dApps, NFTs, and DAOs, acting as everything from simple token managers to the logic for complex financial products.

Bridge to the Next Lesson

Every serious crypto project starts with an idea, which is then formalized into a foundational document that explains its purpose, technology, and goals. In our next lesson, we will learn how to read and analyse a project's most important document: its "whitepaper."

Lesson 10 - Anatomy of a Whitepaper

An Introduction to a Project's Blueprint

Before a single line of code is written for a new crypto project, there is the whitepaper. This is the foundational, authoritative document that introduces the project to the world. It is part mission statement, part technical blueprint, and part economic plan. For an investor, learning how to read and analyse a whitepaper is the most critical first step in fundamental analysis (DYOR). It is your opportunity to look past the marketing hype and evaluate the project on the substance of its own ideas.

The Core Explanation: Deconstructing the Document

A whitepaper is a foundational document released by a crypto project that explains its purpose, technology, and goals. While some can be highly technical, a good whitepaper should clearly communicate its core vision to a reasonably informed audience. A well-structured whitepaper is a sign of a well-structured project.

When analysing a whitepaper, you should look for several key sections:

1. **The Problem:** The introduction should clearly and

concisely define the problem that the project is trying to solve. Is it a real, significant problem that needs a blockchain-based solution?
2. **The Solution:** This section should detail the project's proposed solution. How does it work? What is its unique value proposition?
3. **The Technology:** This is often the most technical part. It should explain the underlying technology, such as the blockchain architecture, consensus mechanism, or smart contract design that makes the solution possible.
4. **The Tokenomics:** This crucial section should explain the role and design of the project's native cryptocurrency. It should cover its utility, supply mechanics, and distribution plan.
5. **The Team:** A good whitepaper will introduce the core team behind the project, highlighting their experience and expertise.
6. **The Roadmap:** This section outlines the project's planned stages of development and future goals, providing a timeline for its execution.

It is important to remember that a good whitepaper is a detailed and technical document, not just a glossy marketing brochure.

Case Study: The Bitcoin Whitepaper

The most famous and influential whitepaper in history is Satoshi Nakamoto's 2008 paper, "Bitcoin: A Peer-to-Peer Electronic Cash System." It is the perfect model of a great whitepaper.

- It is only nine pages long, yet it is incredibly dense with

information.
- The introduction perfectly defines the problem: the need for an electronic payment system based on cryptographic proof instead of trust in a third-party financial institution.
- It then systematically lays out the solution, introducing concepts like the distributed timestamp server (the blockchain), Proof-of-Work, and the rules for network operation.
- It contains no marketing hype, no price predictions, and no mention of "investment." It is a purely academic and technical document that presents a solution to a problem. Its clarity and elegance single-handedly launched the entire cryptocurrency industry.

Practical Application: Reading the Original

Every serious student of crypto should read the introduction to the Bitcoin whitepaper.

- **Try This How-To**:

1. Go to the website bitcoin.org.
2. Find the link to the original whitepaper (it's available in many languages).
3. You don't need to understand all the technical details. Just read the one-page "Introduction" section.
4. Notice how clearly and powerfully Satoshi defines the problem with the traditional financial model ("the inherent weaknesses of the trust based model") and proposes a solution. This is the hallmark of a whitepaper with a clear and compelling vision.

Key Takeaways

- A whitepaper is an authoritative report outlining a new crypto project.
- It should clearly define the problem, solution, technology, and tokenomics.
- Analysing the whitepaper is a critical step in fundamental analysis (DYOR).

Bridge to the Next Lesson

Whitepapers outline the initial rules of a blockchain protocol. But software is not set in stone; it needs to be upgraded over time. How do you upgrade a decentralized network with no central administrator? In our next lesson, we will explore the mechanisms for changing a blockchain's protocol: hard forks and soft forks.

Lesson 11 - Hard Forks vs. Soft Forks

An Introduction to Upgrading a Decentralized Network

Like any piece of software, a blockchain's protocol needs to be updated over time to add new features, fix bugs, or improve performance. But how do you upgrade a global, decentralized network with thousands of independent participants and no central authority to push the "update" button? The process is called a "fork," and it's the mechanism by which a blockchain community agrees to change its own rules. Understanding the two types of forks is key to understanding how blockchains evolve.

The Core Explanation: Backwards-Compatible vs. Non-Backwards-Compatible

A 'fork' is a change to a blockchain's protocol or rules. When this happens, the chain splits into two, and the network participants must choose which set of rules to follow. The key difference lies in whether the change is backwards-compatible.

1. **Soft Fork:**

- A soft fork is a backwards-compatible upgrade. This means that nodes (the computers running the blockchain software) that have *not* upgraded to the new rules can still participate in the network and validate transactions.
- **Analogy:** This is like a new version of Microsoft Word that saves documents in a new format, but the older version of Word can still open them. The new features are available to those who upgrade, but it doesn't break the system for those who don't.

1. **Hard Fork:**

- A hard fork is a non-backwards-compatible upgrade. This means that all nodes on the network must upgrade to the new rules to continue participating. Any node that does not upgrade will be left on a separate, older version of the chain, following the old rules.
- **Analogy:** This is like a major new version of a video game console. Games made for the new console will not work on the old one. You must upgrade your hardware to participate in the new ecosystem.

Hard forks can be contentious if there is a disagreement within the community about the proposed change. If a significant portion of the community refuses to upgrade, the blockchain can permanently split into two separate chains, each with its own community and currency.

Case Study: The Ethereum vs. Ethereum Classic Split

As we discussed in a previous lesson, the 2016 hack of "The DAO" created a massive crisis on Ethereum. The community was faced with a difficult choice: should they reverse the theft, which would violate the principle of immutability, or should they let the hacker keep the funds?

A proposal was made to execute a hard fork that would rewrite the blockchain's history to return the stolen funds.

- **The Majority:** The vast majority of the community, including the Ethereum Foundation, supported the hard fork and upgraded their software to the new rules. This new chain is the one we know today as Ethereum (ETH).
- **The Minority:** A smaller group of users, who believed in absolute immutability ("code is law"), rejected the hard fork. They refused to upgrade and continued to run the original, unaltered version of the protocol.

Because the change was a non-backwards-compatible hard fork, this disagreement resulted in a permanent chain split. The original chain continued to exist and is now known as

Ethereum Classic (ETC). This is the most famous example of a contentious hard fork in crypto history.

Practical Application: Observing an Upgrade

You can see the results of these forks on any major crypto data site.

- **Try This How-To:**

1. Go to a site like CoinGecko or CoinMarketCap.
2. In the search bar, type "Ethereum" (ETH). Look at its price and market cap.
3. Now, search for "Ethereum Classic" (ETC).
4. You will see that it is a completely separate cryptocurrency with its own, much lower, price and market cap.

You are looking at the live, economic result of the contentious hard fork that happened in 2016.

Key Takeaways

- A fork is an update to a blockchain's software.
- Soft forks are like optional, backwards-compatible software updates.
- Hard forks are mandatory, non-backwards-compatible updates; failure to upgrade results in a split from the network.

Bridge to the Next Lesson

Forks are one way to decide on major, often contentious, changes to a protocol. But for more routine decision-making, a more formalized, built-in process is becoming the standard. In our next lesson, we will look at how DAOs and other protocols use on-chain governance models.

Lesson 12 - On-Chain Governance Models

An Introduction to Decentralized Decision-Making

In a traditional company, the board of directors and the CEO make the big decisions. In a nation-state, the government does. But in a decentralized network with no leader, who decides? Who gets to propose changes, and how does the community agree to adopt them? On-chain governance is the answer. It is a formalized, often democratic, process for managing and upgrading a blockchain protocol, with the rules and votes happening directly on the blockchain itself.

The Core Explanation: Voting with Your Tokens

On-chain governance is the process by which changes to a blockchain protocol are proposed, voted on, and implemented by its users, typically the holders of the protocol's native governance token.

In this model, the rules for making decisions are coded directly into the blockchain's protocol, making the process transparent and auditable. While the specifics can vary, the process generally follows these steps:

1. **Proposal:** A token holder (or a group of them) who meets a certain threshold can submit a formal proposal for a change to the protocol. This could be anything from changing a transaction fee, to funding a new development initiative, or upgrading a smart contract.
2. **Voting:** The proposal enters a voting period. During this time, other token holders can cast their vote ("Yes," "No," or "Abstain") on the proposal. In most models, a user's voting power is proportional to the number of tokens they hold.

3. **Implementation:** If the proposal receives enough votes to pass the quorum and approval thresholds defined in the protocol's rules, the change can often be implemented automatically by the smart contracts.

This model is a core feature of most DAOs and aims to make protocol management more transparent and decentralized than traditional "off-chain" governance, where a small group of core developers often makes the final decisions.

Case Study: Uniswap's Governance Process

The Uniswap protocol, a leading DEX, is governed by the holders of its UNI token. Its on-chain governance process is a clear example of this model in action.

- To submit a proposal, a user must hold at least 2.5 million UNI tokens (this high threshold prevents spam).
- A recent major proposal was to implement a "fee switch," a change that would redirect a small portion of the protocol's trading fees to UNI token holders.
- This proposal was heavily debated by the community on public forums for months.
- It then went to a formal on-chain vote, where millions of UNI tokens were used to vote.
- The proposal passed, and the community is now in the process of implementing this significant economic change to the protocol.

This is a perfect example of on-chain governance being used by a community of token holders to make a critical, multi-billion-dollar decision about the protocol's future.

Practical Application: Observing Decentralized Democ-

racy

You can watch the debates and votes of these decentralized governments happen in public.

- **Try This How-To:**

1. Go to the official governance forum for a major DeFi protocol, such as gov.uniswap.org or governance.aave.com.
2. You can read the actual proposals being discussed by the community right now. You'll see detailed arguments for and against different changes to the protocol.
3. Then, go to a voting platform like Snapshot or Tally and find that same protocol. You can see the results of past on-chain votes, including which addresses voted and how much voting power they had.

This is the "parliamentary debate" and the "ballot box" of a DAO, happening transparently in public.

Key Takeaways

- On-chain governance allows token holders to propose and vote on protocol changes.
- It is a formalized and transparent process for managing a decentralized network.
- This model is central to the operation of DAOs and represents a new form of digital democracy.

Bridge to the Next Lesson

Governance, voting, and all blockchain security ultimately

rely on one thing: cryptography. It's the "crypto" in cryptocurrency. In our next lesson, we will touch on the basics of hashing, the fundamental cryptographic concept that makes a blockchain secure.

Lesson 13 - Hashing and Cryptography Basics

An Introduction to the "Crypto" in Cryptocurrency

What makes a blockchain secure? What prevents someone from simply changing a transaction in a past block? The answer lies in the "crypto" part of cryptocurrency: cryptography. This is the mathematical magic that underpins the entire system, providing the security and integrity that allows a decentralized network to function without a central authority. This lesson will introduce you to hashing, the single most important cryptographic concept that makes a blockchain's immutability possible.

The Core Explanation: The Digital Fingerprint

Cryptography is the foundation of blockchain security. The most important concept to understand is hashing.

A hash function is a mathematical algorithm that takes an input of any size and produces a fixed-size, unique string of characters known as the hash. Think of it as a machine that can create a perfect, unique "digital fingerprint" for any piece of data.

Hash functions have two crucial properties:

1. **They are a One-Way Function:** It is incredibly easy to take an input and create a hash. However, it is practically impossible to take the hash (the output) and reverse-

engineer it to figure out the original input. This one-way nature is critical for security.

2. **They are Deterministic and Sensitive:** The same input will *always* produce the exact same output hash. However, if you change even a single, tiny part of the input (like changing one letter from lowercase to uppercase), the resulting hash will change completely and unpredictably. This is known as the "avalanche effect."

In blockchains, groups of transactions are hashed together to create the unique fingerprint for each block. Crucially, this block hash is then included in the data of the *next* block, which is then hashed itself. This is what creates the secure, cryptographic "chain." If a hacker tried to alter a transaction in a past block, it would change that block's hash, which would break the link to the next block, and so on, making the tampering instantly obvious to the entire network.

Case Study: Password Security

A perfect real-world analogy for a one-way hash function is how modern websites store your passwords. When you create an account and choose a password, a secure website does not store your actual password in its database.

- Instead, it takes your password, runs it through a hash function, and stores the resulting hash.
- When you log in later, it takes the password you enter, hashes it again, and compares it to the stored hash.
- If the two hashes match, the system knows you entered the correct password and lets you in.

This way, even if the website's database is hacked, the attackers only get a list of meaningless hashes, not your actual passwords. They cannot reverse the hashes to find the original inputs. This is the power of a one-way function.

Practical Application: Creating Your Own Hash

You can experience the power of hashing for yourself with a simple online tool.

- **Try This How-To:**

1. Do a web search for an "online SHA-256 hash generator." (SHA-256 is the specific hashing algorithm used by Bitcoin).
2. In the input box, type your name. You will see the unique, fixed-length hash that it produces.
3. Now, change just one tiny detail. For example, change one letter in your name from lowercase to uppercase.
4. Notice how the resulting hash changes completely and unpredictably. This demonstrates the "avalanche effect" and is the key to why hashing is so effective at detecting tampering.

Key Takeaways

- Hashing creates a unique, fixed-length digital fingerprint of data.
- Hash functions are one-way, making them practically impossible to reverse.
- Hashing is used to link blocks together securely in a blockchain, ensuring the integrity and immutability of

the ledger.

Bridge to the Next Lesson

Hashing is the key to creating secure blocks. But what happens to your transaction *before* it gets put into a block? In our next lesson, we will explore the blockchain's chaotic but crucial "waiting room": the mempool.

Lesson 14 - Introduction to Mempools

An Introduction to the Blockchain's Waiting Room

When you send a crypto transaction, it doesn't appear on the blockchain instantly. It first enters a kind of digital purgatory, a chaotic waiting area where it competes with thousands of other transactions for a coveted spot in the next block. This waiting room is called the mempool. Understanding the mempool is key to understanding why some transactions confirm faster than others and why fees fluctuate so much during busy periods.

The Core Explanation: The Pool of Pending Transactions

The 'mempool' (a contraction of "memory pool") is the holding area for all unconfirmed transactions on a blockchain network. Each node (computer) running the blockchain software maintains its own version of the mempool.

The process works like this:

1. **Broadcast:** When you send a transaction from your wallet, it is first broadcast out to the nodes on the network.

2. **Enter the Mempool:** Each node that receives your valid transaction holds it in its mempool, a temporary queue of pending transactions.
3. **Selection:** Miners or validators (the block producers) then look into their mempool to select which transactions to include in the next block they are trying to build.
4. **Prioritization by Fee:** Because block space is limited, validators cannot include every transaction. To maximize their own profit, they will almost always prioritize the transactions that are offering the highest fee.

If the network is very busy (congested), the mempool can grow very large, filled with thousands of pending transactions. This creates a bidding war, leading to longer wait times and higher fees for everyone. Your transaction is essentially waiting in line, and you can pay a higher fee to jump to the front.

Case Study: The Urgent Transaction

Imagine a user is trying to make an urgent transaction during a period of high network congestion, like a popular NFT mint.

- They send their transaction with a standard, average fee.
- They go to a block explorer and see that their transaction's status is "Pending."
- This is because their transaction is sitting in the mempool, but thousands of other users are paying higher fees to mint the NFT, so the validators are picking those more profitable transactions first.

To get their transaction included, the user would need to use a "Speed Up" or "Accelerate" function in their wallet. This action essentially replaces their original, pending transaction in the mempool with a new one that has the exact same details but offers a higher fee, making it more attractive for a validator to include it in the next block.

Practical Application: Visualizing the Mempool

You can watch this real-time auction for block space happen live.

- **Try This How-To:**

1. Go to a mempool visualization website like mempool.space.
2. This site provides a live, visual representation of the Bitcoin mempool and the blocks being built.
3. You will see a large pool of pending transactions, often color-coded by the fee rate (higher fees are brighter colours). You will also see the "template" for the next block, showing how the validator is packing it with the highest-fee transactions from the top of the pool.

This provides a fascinating, real-time look at the on-chain transaction market in action.

Key Takeaways

- The mempool is a 'waiting room' for pending transactions.
- Miners/validators pick transactions from the mempool to build the next block, typically prioritizing those with the highest fees.

- A large mempool indicates high network congestion, leading to higher fees and longer confirmation times.

Bridge to the Next Lesson

The mempool is a key part of how the network functions for those who are running a full copy of the blockchain software. But you don't need to do that to participate. In our final lesson of this module, we will look at a more lightweight and accessible way to connect to the network: running a light node.

Lesson 15 - Running a Light Node

An Introduction to Sovereign Connectivity

To interact with a blockchain, your wallet needs to connect to it. By default, most wallets like MetaMask connect to the network through a third-party company's server. While convenient, this introduces an element of trust. But what if you could connect directly to the network yourself, without needing a massive hard drive to store its entire history? This is the promise of a light node. It is a powerful step towards becoming a more secure, private, and sovereign crypto user.

The Core Explanation: Full vs. Light Nodes

To understand a light node, you first have to understand a full node.

- A 'full node' is a computer that runs the full blockchain software. It downloads, verifies, and stores the entire history of the blockchain, which for a network like Ethereum can require terabytes of data storage. Full nodes are the bedrock of the network's decentralization and security, as they independently enforce all the rules.

- A 'light node' is a much more lightweight and accessible alternative. It is designed for users who want a direct connection to the network without the massive resource requirements of a full node.
- **How it works:** A light node does not store the full blockchain history. Instead, it only downloads the block headers. A block header is a small piece of summary information for each block. By using these headers, a light node can still independently verify transactions that are relevant to it, without needing to process every single transaction on the network.

The main benefit of running your own light node is that it increases your security and privacy. You are broadcasting your transactions directly to the network, not sending them through a centralized third-party service provider (like Infura or Alchemy, which MetaMask uses by default) that could potentially log your IP address and transaction data.

Case Study: The Infura Outage

In November 2020, a major third-party node provider called Infura experienced a service outage. Because many of the most popular dApps and wallets in the Ethereum ecosystem, including MetaMask, rely on Infura's servers by default to connect to the blockchain, this outage had a massive cascading effect.

For a period of several hours, many users found that their MetaMask wallets were not showing the correct balances and that they could not send transactions or interact with

DeFi protocols. The "decentralized" network effectively felt "down" for a huge number of its users.

Crucially, users who were running their own full or light nodes were completely unaffected by this outage. Because they had a direct, sovereign connection to the network, their experience was uninterrupted. This event was a powerful lesson on the hidden centralization risks of relying on a few dominant third-party service providers.

Practical Application: Exploring Your Wallet's Connection

You can see this reliance on third-party providers directly in your MetaMask wallet.

- **Try This How-To:**

1. Open your MetaMask browser extension.
2. Click on the network selector at the top-left (it will likely say "Ethereum Mainnet").
3. A list of networks will appear. Click "Add network."
4. You will be taken to a settings page where you can add custom networks. Look at the details required: Network Name, RPC URL, Chain ID.
5. The "RPC URL" is the address of the node your wallet connects to. By default, MetaMask uses a URL provided by Infura. Running your own node means you would be able to put http://localhost:8545 in this field, telling your wallet to connect to the node running on your own computer.

This shows you the specific connection point that can be switched from a trusted third party to your own sovereign node.

Key Takeaways

- Full nodes store the entire blockchain; light nodes store only block headers.
- Light nodes offer a good balance between security and resource requirements for regular users.
- Running your own node reduces reliance on third-party services, increasing your security, privacy, and censorship resistance.

9

Module 2 Recap

You have now completed a deep dive into the core technology that makes blockchains work.

- You understand the different "engines" of a blockchain, the trade-offs between Proof-of-Work and Proof-of-Stake, and the fundamental design challenge of the Blockchain Trilemma.
- You can differentiate between Layer 1 and Layer 2 scaling solutions, understand the critical role of the EVM, and appreciate the competitive landscape of alternative L1s.
- You've explored the crucial infrastructure that connects the ecosystem, like bridges and oracles, and the technical foundations of forks, governance, and cryptography.

You are now equipped with a much deeper technical understanding of how these networks operate, preparing you to explore the complex and innovative applications built on top of them.

Module 3 - DeFi Mechanics & Strategies

Module Introduction: You've learned what DeFi is; now it's time to understand how its most important protocols actually work. This module will take you deep into the mechanics of decentralized exchanges, lending markets, and yield farming. You'll learn the key concepts, from automated market makers to impermanent loss, and the associated risks. This knowledge will equip you to navigate this innovative landscape safely and effectively, transforming you from a passive user into a confident DeFi participant.

Lesson 01 - How Automated Market Makers (AMMs) Work

An Introduction to the Engine of a DEX

How can a decentralized exchange, with no central company or order book, possibly function as a marketplace? The magic is in its engine: the Automated Market Maker (AMM). An AMM is a revolutionary concept that replaces the traditional matchmaking system of buyers and sellers with a simple, elegant mathematical formula. Understanding this engine is the key to understanding how the vast majority of decentralized trading actually works.

The Core Explanation: Trading Against a Formula

Automated Market Makers (AMMs) are the smart contracts that power most decentralized exchanges (DEXs). They are a radical departure from the traditional "order books" that power stock exchanges and centralized crypto exchanges.

- An order book matches individual buyers with individual sellers. If you want to buy at $10, you have to wait for someone who wants to sell at $10.
- An AMM uses a pool of tokens locked in a smart contract, known as a "liquidity pool". Instead of trading against another person, you trade directly against the assets in this pool.

The price of the tokens in the pool isn't set by buy and sell orders, but rather by a mathematical formula. The most common is the constant product formula: x * y = k.

- x is the amount of Token A in the pool.
- y is the amount of Token B in the pool.
- k is a constant that must remain unchanged by the trade.

When a trader wants to swap Token A for Token B, they add Token A to the pool (increasing x). To keep k constant, the smart contract must remove a proportional amount of Token B from the pool (decreasing y). The ratio of tokens removed determines the price. This process automatically adjusts the price based on the new ratio of tokens in the pool after every trade.

Case Study: The Uniswap Breakthrough

In the early days of DeFi, DEXs tried to replicate traditional order books on the blockchain. They were incredibly slow, expensive, and inefficient because every single order had to be submitted as a costly on-chain transaction.

The launch of Uniswap in 2018 was a breakthrough because it introduced the simple but brilliant x * y = k AMM model to Ethereum. This model was far more gas-efficient and, crucially, it allowed for passive liquidity provision. Any user could deposit their assets into a pool and start earning fees, without needing to be an active market maker. This elegant design unlocked the massive growth of DeFi and established the AMM as the dominant model for on-chain trading.

Practical Application: The AMM as a Calculator

The interface of a DEX is essentially a user-friendly calculator for its underlying AMM formula.

- **Try This How-To:**

1. Go to a DEX like Uniswap.
2. Select a major trading pool, like ETH/USDC. On an analytics page for the pool, you can see the total liquidity—the exact amount of ETH (x) and USDC (y) in the smart contract.
3. In the swap interface, enter a small amount to trade (e.g., sell 0.1 ETH). The interface calculates and shows you how much USDC you will receive.
4. Now, enter a very large amount (e.g., sell 1,000 ETH). Notice how the "price" per ETH gets worse. This is the AMM formula in action; a large trade significantly shifts the ratio of assets in the pool, resulting in a less favourable price (this is also known as slippage).

Key Takeaways

- AMMs replace traditional order books with algorithmically managed liquidity pools.
- The price is determined by a constant product formula (x

  * y = k), and users trade against the smart contract, not against other specific users.
- This model is more efficient for on-chain environments and enables anyone to become a liquidity provider.

Bridge to the Next Lesson

This AMM engine is powered by capital provided by users. But why would someone lock up their valuable tokens in one of these pools? In our next lesson, we will explore the role of Liquidity Providers and the unique, often misunderstood risk that comes with it: Impermanent Loss.

Lesson 02 - Liquidity Pools and Impermanent Loss Explained

An Introduction to "Being the House"

In a casino, the "house always wins" because it takes a small cut of every game played. In the world of DeFi, liquidity pools allow *you* to be the house. By depositing your assets into an AMM, you can earn a share of the trading fees from every swap that happens. This is called providing liquidity, and it's one of the most fundamental ways to earn a yield in DeFi. However, this reward comes with a unique and complex risk that every potential liquidity provider must understand.

The Core Explanation: Earning Fees, Facing Risks

A 'liquidity pool' is a collection of two or more different crypto tokens that are locked in a smart contract, enabling trades on an AMM. These pools are crowdsourced by users known as Liquidity Providers (LPs). To become an LP, you must supply an equal *value* of both tokens to the pool (e.g., $500 of ETH and $500 of USDC). In return for providing your capital, you receive a share of the trading fees generated by the pool, proportional to your share of the pool.

However, being an LP exposes you to a unique risk called 'Impermanent Loss' (IL).

- **Definition:** Impermanent Loss is the difference in value between depositing your tokens in a liquidity pool versus simply holding those same tokens in your wallet.
- **How it works:** When the price of one token in the pool changes significantly relative to the other, arbitrage traders will buy the underpriced asset and sell the over-priced asset to the pool to bring it back in line with the global market price. This process automatically rebalances the number of tokens you hold. You will be left with more of the token that went down in price and less of the token that went up. This can result in you having less total value than if you had just held the two assets separately.
- **Why "Impermanent"?** It's called "impermanent" because if the prices of the two tokens return to the exact ratio they were at when you deposited, the loss disappears. However, if you withdraw your funds while there's a price divergence, the loss becomes very permanent.

For your LP position to be profitable, the trading fees you earn must be greater than the Impermanent Loss you incur.

Case Study: A Practical Example of IL

Let's walk through a simplified example:

- An LP provides liquidity to an ETH/USDC pool when 1 ETH = $2,000. They deposit 1 ETH and 2,000 USDC (a total value of $4,000).
- The price of ETH then doubles to $4,000 on external markets.
- Arbitrageurs rebalance the pool, leaving the LP with approximately 0.707 ETH and 2,828 USDC. The total value of their position is now $5,656 (0.707 * $4000 + $2828).
- However, if they had simply held their original 1 ETH and 2,000 USDC, their portfolio would be worth $6,000 (1 * $4000 + $2000).

The difference of $344 is their Impermanent Loss. They are still in profit, but they would have made more money by simply holding the assets.

Practical Application: Calculating Potential IL

You can get an intuitive feel for this risk using online tools.

- **Try This How-To**:

1. Do a web search for an "Impermanent Loss Calculator".
2. These free tools allow you to input a starting price for two assets and then use a slider to see how the value of your LP position changes as the price of one asset moves up or down.
3. Notice how the IL is minimal for small price changes but grows exponentially the further the prices diverge. This shows that providing liquidity to a pool with two very volatile assets is much riskier than providing liquidity to a pool with a more stable pair (like USDC/DAI).

Key Takeaways

- Liquidity pools are crowdsourced collections of tokens that enable trading on DEXs.
- Liquidity Providers (LPs) earn fees for supplying tokens to these pools.
- Impermanent Loss is the risk that the value of your deposited assets decreases compared to simply holding them, and it is most significant during periods of high volatility.

Bridge to the Next Lesson

Providing liquidity is just one way to generate a return in DeFi. Some advanced users chain multiple strategies together—lending, borrowing, and providing liquidity—to maximize their returns. In our next lesson, we will explore the high-risk, high-reward world of "Yield Farming."

Lesson 03 - Yield Farming: Strategies and Risks

An Introduction to DeFi's High-Stakes Game

If providing liquidity is like being the house at the casino, then yield farming is like being a professional card sharp, moving from table to table, chasing the hottest game with the biggest payout. It is the aggressive and often complex practice of strategically moving your crypto assets between various DeFi protocols to generate the highest possible return, or "yield." It represents the cutting edge of DeFi strategy—a high-risk, high-reward activity that pushes the limits of programmable money.

The Core Explanation: Chasing the Highest APY

Yield farming is the practice of strategically moving your crypto assets between different DeFi protocols to generate the highest possible return, or 'yield'. This can involve a single action, like staking, or much more complex combinations of lending, borrowing, and providing liquidity.

A common yield farming strategy, often called "leveraged farming," might look like this:

1. **Deposit Collateral:** A user deposits a volatile asset like ETH into a lending protocol (e.g., Aave).
2. **Borrow Stablecoins:** They then borrow a stablecoin, like USDC, against that ETH collateral.
3. **Provide Liquidity:** They take that borrowed USDC and pair it with another token to become a Liquidity Provider (LP) on a DEX, allowing them to earn trading fees.
4. **Stake for Rewards:** Many DEXs offer extra incentives. The LP token the user receives can often be staked in another smart contract to earn additional rewards in the form of the DEX's native governance token.

This layering of strategies can lead to very high returns, but it also compounds the risks at every step. These include smart contract vulnerabilities, impermanent loss, and market volatility that could cause your initial loan to be liquidated.

Case Study: "DeFi Summer" of 2020

The summer of 2020 is famously known as "DeFi Summer," and it was the period when yield farming exploded into the mainstream. The catalyst was the launch of the Compound protocol's governance token, COMP. Compound began distributing its COMP token as an additional reward to users who were lending or borrowing on its platform.

This kicked off a frenzy. Users would deposit assets, borrow other assets, and redeposit them to maximize their share of the COMP rewards. Other protocols quickly copied this "liquidity mining" model, offering their own governance tokens as incentives. A new class of "yield farmers" was born, actively moving millions of dollars from protocol to protocol, chasing the highest Annual Percentage Yield (APY), which sometimes reached into the thousands of percent. It was a chaotic, innovative, and highly profitable period for sophisticated users but also resulted in many losing funds to unaudited, risky "food-coin" protocols that popped up overnight.

Practical Application: Exploring a Yield Aggregator

Manually executing complex yield farming strategies is difficult and costly. Yield aggregators are protocols designed to automate this process.

- **Try This How-To:**

1. Go to a yield aggregator platform like Yearn Finance or Beefy Finance.
2. Navigate to their "Vaults" or "Strategies" section.
3. You will see a list of different investment vaults with their corresponding APYs. Click on one to read its strategy description.
4. You will often see that the vault is automatically performing a complex yield farming strategy on behalf of its users (e.g., "This vault provides liquidity to a Curve pool, stakes the LP token, and automatically harvests

and compounds the rewards").

Exploring these vaults gives you a direct glimpse into the types of automated strategies that exist in the world of yield farming.

Key Takeaways

- Yield farming is an advanced strategy to maximize returns from DeFi protocols.
- It often involves a complex chain of lending, borrowing, and liquidity providing.
- The risks are significant, including smart contract bugs, impermanent loss, and the risk of liquidation.

Bridge to the Next Lesson

The foundation of many yield farming strategies, and of DeFi itself, is the ability to lend and borrow assets in a decentralized way. In our next lesson, we will explore the mechanics of DeFi's core infrastructure: the decentralized money markets.

Lesson 04 - DeFi Lending & Borrowing Protocols

An Introduction to Decentralized Money Markets

What if you could take out a loan against your assets instantly, at any time of day, without filling out a single piece of paperwork or speaking to a loan officer? What if you could earn a competitive interest rate on your savings without trusting a bank? This is the reality of DeFi lending protocols. These protocols act as autonomous, decentralized money markets, allowing anyone in the world to lend or borrow assets in a permissionless and transparent way.

The Core Explanation: The Two Sides of the Market

DeFi lending protocols like Aave and Compound function as decentralized money markets, using smart contracts to connect lenders and borrowers.

The system has two sides:

1. **Lenders (Suppliers):** Users can deposit their crypto assets into the protocol's various pools to act as lenders. Their deposited funds are added to a large pool of liquidity that is available for others to borrow. In return for supplying this capital, they earn a variable interest rate on their assets, which is paid out by the borrowers.
2. **Borrowers:** Other users can borrow assets from these pools. To do so, they must first supply their own crypto as collateral. A key safety mechanism of these protocols is that all loans are 'overcollateralized,' meaning you must deposit collateral that is worth significantly more than the amount you are borrowing (e.g., deposit $1,500 of ETH to borrow $1,000 of USDC). This overcollatera lization protects the lenders and ensures the protocol remains solvent.

A critical component of these protocols is the automated liquidation process. If the value of a borrower's collateral falls below a certain threshold (due to market volatility), the smart contract will automatically allow other users (liquidators) to sell a portion of that collateral on the open market to repay the loan. This prevents the protocol from accumulating bad debt.

Case Study: The Strategic Borrower

Consider a long-term Bitcoin holder who believes the price of BTC will appreciate significantly over the next few years. She needs access to $10,000 for a real-world expense, but she does not want to sell her Bitcoin because: a) She would miss out on the potential future gains. b) Selling would trigger a Capital Gains Tax event.

Instead of selling, she can use a DeFi lending protocol. She deposits, for example, $20,000 worth of Wrapped Bitcoin (WBTC) into a protocol like Aave as collateral. She then borrows $10,000 worth of the stablecoin USDC against it. She can now sell that USDC for cash to cover her expense.

As long as she maintains her healthy collateralization ratio and the price of Bitcoin doesn't crash dramatically, she gets the liquidity she needs without having to sell her long-term investment. She has effectively used her crypto as productive collateral.

Practical Application: Exploring the Markets

You can see the live interest rates for lending and borrowing on these platforms at any time.

- **Try This How-To:**

1. Go to the official website for Aave or Compound.
2. Navigate to their main "Market" page. You will see a list of all the assets available to be supplied or borrowed.
3. Notice that each asset has two different interest rates: a 'Supply APY' (the interest you earn for lending that asset) and a 'Borrow APY' (the interest you pay for

borrowing it).

4. Observe how these rates are different for different assets. Volatile assets often have higher borrow rates than stablecoins, reflecting their higher risk.

Key Takeaways

- DeFi lending protocols allow users to earn interest by lending their crypto or to borrow crypto by providing collateral.
- To ensure safety for lenders, all loans are overcollateralized.
- Liquidation is an automated process that sells a borrower's collateral if its value falls too low, protecting the protocol from bad debt.

Bridge to the Next Lesson

These protocols allow you to borrow existing assets from a pool. But what if you could use your collateral to create a brand-new asset out of thin air? In our next lesson, we will look at protocols like MakerDAO that allow you to mint decentralized stablecoins.

Lesson 05 - Collateralized Debt Positions (CDPs) and Minting Stablecoins

An Introduction to Decentralized Stablecoins

We've learned about centralized stablecoins like USDC, which are backed by real dollars held in a bank account. But this model relies on trusting a central company. Can we create a stablecoin that is decentralized and backed by crypto assets instead? The answer is yes, and the mechanism that makes it possible is the Collateralized Debt Position (CDP). This powerful DeFi primitive, pioneered by the MakerDAO protocol, allows users to mint a stablecoin that is born on the blockchain.

The Core Explanation: Minting Your Own Money

Protocols like MakerDAO allow users to generate or "mint" their own decentralized stablecoins. The most famous of these is DAI. Instead of being backed by dollars in a bank, DAI is backed by an overcollateralized and diversified portfolio of crypto assets locked in MakerDAO's smart contracts.

The process works through a Collateralized Debt Position (CDP), now more commonly called a "Vault":

1. **Open a Vault:** A user opens a Vault by depositing a volatile crypto asset, like ETH, into the MakerDAO smart contract. This ETH now serves as collateral.
2. **Mint DAI:** Based on the value of their deposited collateral, the user is now allowed to mint a certain amount of new DAI tokens. This DAI is essentially a loan that the user has taken out against their own collateral. The user must maintain a healthy collateralization ratio (e.g., 150%), meaning for every $1 of DAI they mint, they must

have at least $1.50 worth of ETH locked as collateral.

3. **Use DAI:** The newly minted DAI is a fully functional stablecoin, pegged to $1, that the user can now spend or use in other DeFi protocols.
4. **Repay and Reclaim:** To get their original ETH collateral back, the user must repay the DAI they minted, plus a small stability fee (interest). When the DAI is repaid, it is "burned" (destroyed), and the user can withdraw their ETH.

If the value of the user's ETH collateral falls too low and threatens the collateralization ratio, the Vault is automatically liquidated, and the ETH is sold to repay the DAI debt.

Case Study: The Resilience of DAI

DAI is one of the oldest and most respected decentralized stablecoins in the entire crypto ecosystem. It has survived multiple extreme market crashes (known as "black swan" events) and has successfully maintained its peg to the US Dollar.

Its resilience is a testament to the strength of its underlying model. Unlike algorithmic stablecoins that have failed, DAI's value is not based on an algorithm but on the real, transparent, and overcollateralized value of the assets locked in the MakerDAO protocol. Its success has proven that it is possible to create a truly decentralized stablecoin that is not reliant on a company, a CEO, or the traditional banking system for its stability and value. It is a cornerstone of the DeFi ecosystem.

Practical Application: Verifying the Collateral

The beauty of this system is its transparency. You can verify the health of the DAI stablecoin for yourself at any time.

- **Try This How-To:**

1. Go to a DeFi dashboard or analytics site that tracks the MakerDAO protocol (like daistats.com or the protocol's page on Zapper).
2. You will be able to see a real-time, detailed breakdown of all the assets that are currently locked in MakerDAO's vaults backing all the DAI in circulation.
3. You can see exactly how much ETH, Wrapped BTC, and other assets are serving as collateral, and you can see the overall collateralization ratio of the entire system.

This provides a level of transparency that is impossible with centralized stablecoins, whose reserves are often opaque.

Key Takeaways

- CDPs allow users to mint stablecoins using their volatile crypto as collateral.
- MakerDAO is a primary example, where users lock assets like ETH to mint the DAI stablecoin.
- This creates a decentralized stablecoin backed by a transparent and overcollateralized portfolio of crypto assets instead of fiat currency in a bank.

Bridge to the Next Lesson

Locking up assets to mint stablecoins is one powerful way to use your capital. Another very popular activity is staking, which also involves locking up assets. But what if you could earn staking rewards while keeping your capital liquid and usable in DeFi? In our next lesson, we'll explore the popular and innovative world of liquid staking.

Lesson 06 - Liquid Staking

An Introduction to Unlocking Your Staked Capital

Traditional staking presents a classic financial dilemma: you can lock up your assets to earn a steady yield, but in doing so, you lose the ability to use that capital for other opportunities. Your assets become illiquid. What if you could have it both ways? Liquid staking is the innovative DeFi solution that solves this problem, allowing you to earn staking rewards while simultaneously keeping your capital liquid and usable in the broader DeFi ecosystem. It's a powerful concept that supercharges the efficiency of your assets.

The Core Explanation: Staking Without the Lock-up

Liquid staking protocols like Lido and Rocket Pool solve the illiquidity problem of traditional staking. They allow you to earn staking rewards while keeping your capital liquid and productive.

The mechanism is simple but brilliant:

1. **Deposit Your Asset:** You take an asset like ETH and deposit it into the liquid staking protocol's smart contract. The protocol then stakes this ETH on your behalf.
2. **Receive a Receipt Token:** In return for your deposit, the protocol instantly gives you a new token, known as a 'Liquid Staking Token' (LST). For example, if you deposit ETH into Lido, you receive stETH.

3. **Earn and Use:** This LST (stETH) is a receipt that represents your claim on the underlying staked ETH. It automatically accrues the staking rewards, so its value increases over time relative to the original asset. Crucially, this LST is a fully liquid ERC-20 token that you can use in other DeFi protocols.

This unlocks the value of your staked assets, allowing you to earn two sources of yield at once: the underlying staking yield plus any yield you can earn by using your LST in other DeFi applications.

Case Study: The Rise of Lido's stETH

Following Ethereum's move to Proof-of-Stake, Lido's stETH became one of the most important and integrated assets in all of DeFi. Its utility demonstrated the immense demand for capital efficiency.

- A user could hold stETH, earning the base Ethereum staking yield.
- They could then deposit that same stETH as collateral into a lending protocol like Aave to borrow stablecoins.
- They could even take that stETH and provide liquidity for it on a DEX like Curve, earning trading fees.

This ability to "stack" yields on top of the base staking reward made liquid staking a dominant, multi-billion-dollar sector in DeFi. The stETH token became a core "money lego" used as a building block in countless other financial applications across the ecosystem.

Practical Application: Seeing LSTs in the Wild

You can see the deep integration of Liquid Staking Tokens

across the DeFi landscape.

- **Try This How-To:**

1. Go to the website of a major DeFi lending protocol like Aave or a DEX like Curve.
2. Browse the list of assets that you can supply as collateral (on Aave) or provide as liquidity (on Curve).
3. You will almost certainly see one or more Liquid Staking Tokens listed, such as stETH (Lido Staked Ether) or rETH (Rocket Pool ETH).

This shows you the real-world "composability" of DeFi, where the token generated by one protocol (Lido) can be seamlessly used as a core building block in a completely separate protocol (Aave).

Key Takeaways

- Liquid staking allows you to earn staking rewards while keeping your capital liquid.
- You receive a Liquid Staking Token (LST) that represents your staked position and accrues rewards.
- This LST can be used in other DeFi applications, enabling greater capital efficiency.

Bridge to the Next Lesson

Liquid staking is a powerful way to make your capital more efficient. But as DeFi strategies get more complex, managing them can feel like a full-time job. In our next lesson, we will look at "Yield Aggregators," protocols that are designed to automate this complex process for you.

Lesson 07 - Yield Aggregators

An Introduction to Automated DeFi Strategies

The world of yield farming is complex, time-consuming, and expensive due to gas fees. Constantly moving your funds to chase the best returns is simply not feasible for the average user. This is where yield aggregators come in. Think of them as the "robot advisors" of DeFi. They are protocols designed to automatically deploy your capital into the most optimal yield-generating strategies, saving you time, gas fees, and the headache of constant management.

The Core Explanation: "Set-and-Forget" Yield Farming

Yield aggregators are protocols that automate complex yield farming strategies. The most famous example is Yearn Finance.

The model is built around 'Vaults':

1. **Deposit:** A user finds a vault for an asset they hold (e.g., a vault for a stablecoin like USDC). They deposit their funds into the vault's smart contract.
2. **Automated Strategy:** The protocol's smart contracts then automatically deploy that capital using the best and most efficient yield farming strategies available. The strategy for a USDC vault might involve depositing the funds into various lending protocols, moving them to whichever one is currently offering the highest interest rate.

3. **Auto-Compounding:** The aggregator automatically harvests the rewards generated by the strategy, sells them, and redeposits them back into the vault, automatically compounding the returns for all users.

By pooling the funds of thousands of users, these protocols also socialize the costs of transactions. The gas fees for executing these complex strategies are shared across all users in the pool, making it far more efficient than if each user were to try and do it themselves. It is a 'set-and-forget' approach to yield farming.

Case Study: The Fair Launch of Yearn Finance (YFI)

Yearn Finance, created by the influential developer Andre Cronje, exploded in popularity during the "DeFi Summer" of 2020. Its ability to automate yield farming was revolutionary. But what made it legendary was the launch of its governance token, YFI.

In a move that defined the "fair launch" ethos, Cronje announced that the entire supply of YFI tokens would be distributed for free to the early users who provided liquidity to the protocol's first set of pools. There was no pre-mine for the team and no allocation for VCs. This act of pure decentralization, combined with the protocol's powerful utility, caused Yearn to attract billions in TVL and made the YFI token one of the most famous and successful stories of the DeFi era.

Practical Application: Exploring Vault Strategies

You can browse the menu of automated investment strategies offered by these aggregators.

- **Try This How-To:**

1. Go to the website of a yield aggregator like Yearn Finance, Beefy Finance, or PancakeSwap (which has its own "Syrup Pools").
2. Navigate to their "Vaults" or "Pools" section.
3. You will see dozens of different vaults for different assets, each displaying its current estimated APY (Annual Percentage Yield).
4. Click on one of the vaults and read its strategy description. You will often see a detailed explanation of the automated strategy the smart contract is running (e.g., "This vault supplies USDC to the Aave lending protocol and automatically compounds the interest earned").

This gives you a direct look at the "menu" of automated investment options available in DeFi.

Key Takeaways

- Yield aggregators automate complex yield farming strategies.
- Users deposit funds into vaults, and the protocol's smart contracts manage the investment to maximize returns.
- They save users time and gas fees by socializing the costs of transactions and auto-compounding the rewards.

Bridge to the Next Lesson

Aggregators automate yield strategies. But DeFi offers more than just earning a yield on your assets; it also provides access to advanced trading tools, like the ability to use leverage and speculate on price movements. In our next lesson, we will explore the world of decentralized derivatives and perpetuals.

Lesson 08 - Decentralized Derivatives and Perpetuals

An Introduction to Advanced On-Chain Trading

In traditional finance, the market for derivatives—financial contracts that derive their value from an underlying asset—is orders of magnitude larger than the market for the assets themselves. These tools allow traders to hedge risk, speculate on future price movements, and use leverage. Decentralized derivatives are bringing this high-stakes world of trading to the blockchain, offering a non-custodial and transparent alternative to centralized exchanges.

The Core Explanation: Futures, Options, and Perps

Derivatives are financial contracts that derive their value from an underlying asset, like a stock, commodity, or cryptocurrency. The most common types now available in DeFi are:

1. **Decentralized Options:** An options contract gives the buyer the right, but not the obligation, to buy or sell an asset at a predetermined price on a future date. They are used for hedging and complex speculation.
2. **Decentralized Futures:** A futures contract is an agreement to buy or sell an asset at a predetermined price on a specific date in the future.
3. **Perpetual Swaps ("Perps"):** This is the most popular type of derivative in the crypto world.

Perps are a type of futures contract that never expires. They allow traders to speculate on the future price of an asset with leverage, meaning they can control a large position with a small amount of capital.

Platforms like GMX and dYdX are leading decentralized exchanges that allow users to trade these instruments directly from their self-custody wallets, offering a decentralized alternative to centralized derivatives exchanges like Binance or Bybit.

Case Study: The Rise of GMX and "Real Yield"

GMX, a decentralized perpetuals exchange launched on the Arbitrum Layer 2, became a massive success by creating a novel model that benefited both traders and liquidity providers.

- Traders could connect their wallets and trade popular assets like BTC and ETH with up to 50x leverage, paying fees for their trades.
- Liquidity Providers could deposit actual assets like BTC, ETH, and stablecoins into a single, multi-asset pool (GLP). This pool acted as the counterparty to all trades on the platform.

The key innovation was that 100% of the trading fees generated by the leveraged traders were distributed back to the liquidity providers and those who staked the GMX governance token. Because these fees were paid in ETH and stablecoins (not an inflationary reward token), this was seen as a source of sustainable, "real yield." This model was incredibly popular and made GMX a cornerstone of the Arbitrum ecosystem.

Practical Application: Observing a Decentralized Trading

Terminal

You can get a feel for these powerful platforms without making a single trade.

- **Try This How-To:**

1. Go to the website of a decentralized perpetuals exchange like dYdX or GMX.
2. Navigate to their "Trade" or "Exchange" page.
3. You will see an interface that looks much like a professional trading terminal: a live price chart, a central order book (on dYdX) or price feed (on GMX), and options to go "Long" (betting the price will rise) or "Short" (betting it will fall).
4. Notice the "leverage slider," which allows traders to increase their position size.

This will give you a direct look at what a non-custodial, on-chain trading terminal for advanced financial instruments looks like.

Key Takeaways

- DeFi derivatives allow for advanced trading strategies like leverage and shorting.
- Perpetual swaps are futures contracts with no expiry date, making them the most popular derivative for crypto speculation.
- These platforms offer a non-custodial way to trade complex financial instruments, allowing users to maintain control of their funds.

Bridge to the Next Lesson

Trading with leverage is inherently risky, but the biggest and most unique risk in DeFi is often technical: the risk that a smart contract gets hacked. In our next lesson, we will look at the emerging field of DeFi insurance protocols, which aim to protect users from this very danger.

Lesson 09 - DeFi Insurance Protocols

An Introduction to Hedging Protocol Risk

You've deposited your funds into a DeFi protocol that has been audited and has billions of dollars in it. It feels safe. But in the world of crypto, there is no such thing as zero risk. Smart contracts can have unforeseen bugs, and protocols can get hacked, leading to the permanent loss of user funds. How can you protect yourself from this ever-present technical risk? The answer is an emerging and crucial sector of DeFi: decentralized insurance.

The Core Explanation: Coverage for On-Chain Events

DeFi insurance protocols offer a way for users to hedge against the risk of protocol failure. They function like a decentralized insurance company, allowing you to buy protection against specific, adverse on-chain events.

The general model works like this:

1. **Users Buy Coverage:** A user who has deposited funds into a specific DeFi protocol (e.g., Aave) can go to an insurance protocol and pay a premium to purchase 'coverage' on that protocol. The premium is priced based on the market's perceived risk of that protocol.

2. **Liquidity Providers Underwrite Risk:** The capital to pay out potential claims comes from other users who act as underwriters. They deposit their capital into the insurance protocol's pools and earn the premiums paid by the coverage buyers.
3. **Claims Process:** If the covered protocol suffers a loss from a defined event (like a confirmed smart contract exploit), the user who purchased coverage can file a claim. The insurance protocol's community (often its DAO) will then vote to approve or deny the claim based on the evidence. If approved, the user receives a payout from the underwriting pool.

This is a way of managing the inherent technical risks of interacting with a new and experimental financial system.

Case Study: Covering Your Aave Position

Let's consider a risk-averse user, Sarah, who has deposited $100,000 worth of stablecoins into the Aave lending protocol to earn a steady yield. While she trusts Aave, which is a very reputable protocol, she is aware that no smart contract is 100% safe from a potential hack.

To manage this risk, she goes to an insurance protocol like Nexus Mutual. She finds the option to buy "Aave v3 Coverage." The protocol quotes her a premium of, for example, 2.5% per year. She pays a $2,500 premium to get full coverage on her $100,000 deposit for one year.

A few months later, a sophisticated hacker finds a novel, unforeseen vulnerability in an Aave smart contract and manages to drain a portion of the protocol's funds. While uninsured users suffer a loss, Sarah is able to file a claim with Nexus Mutual. The DAO verifies the hack and approves her claim, and she is made whole. She paid a small premium to protect herself from a catastrophic technical failure.

Practical Application: Pricing Protocol Risk

The premiums charged by insurance protocols can be seen as the market's real-time assessment of a DeFi protocol's risk.

- **Try This How-To:**

1. Go to the website of a major DeFi insurance protocol like Nexus Mutual.
2. Navigate to their "Covers" or "Marketplace" section.
3. You will see a list of many different DeFi protocols that you can buy coverage for.
4. For each one, you will see the annual cost of the premium (the coverage cost).
5. Notice how this cost differs. A battle-tested, long-standing protocol like Uniswap will likely have a very low premium. A newer, less tested protocol will have a much higher premium. This difference is the market pricing in the perceived smart contract risk.

Key Takeaways

- DeFi insurance allows users to buy protection against protocol risks.
- Coverage typically protects against verifiable smart contract exploits.
- It is a growing sector aimed at making the DeFi space safer for users and institutions.

Bridge to the Next Lesson

Insurance protects you against the fallout from hacks. But how do these hacks actually work? It's not always as simple as a bug in the code. In our next lesson, we will differentiate between the two main types of DeFi exploits: smart contract hacks and economic hacks.

Lesson 10 - Smart Contract vs. Economic Hacks

An Introduction to How DeFi Breaks

"A hack is a hack," but in the world of DeFi, *how* a protocol is exploited can be very different. The outcome—lost funds—is the same, but the attack vectors are distinct. Understanding these differences is key to appreciating the complex security landscape of decentralized finance. Exploits generally fall into two broad categories: finding a flaw in the code versus cleverly manipulating the protocol's intended rules. This lesson will break down the two main ways that DeFi protocols get exploited.

The Core Explanation: Broken Code vs. Broken Logic

DeFi exploits can generally be classified into two types:

1. A 'Smart Contract Hack':

- **What it is:** This is the most straightforward type of exploit. It involves an attacker finding a bug or a flaw in the protocol's code itself and using it to drain funds.
- **Analogy:** This is like finding a spelling error or a loophole in a legal contract that allows you to do something the contract's writers never intended. The code itself is

broken. A classic example of a code bug is a "re-entrancy attack," which we will cover in the Expert level.

1. An 'Economic Exploit':

- **What it is:** This is a more subtle and often more complex type of attack. It involves using the protocol's intended mechanics in an unforeseen combination to manipulate the system for profit. The code works perfectly as written, but the *economic logic* of the system is broken.
- **Analogy:** This is like using the perfectly written rules of a legal contract in a clever sequence to produce a surprising and unintended outcome that benefits you. You aren't breaking the rules; you are using the rules against the system.

A very common tool for economic exploits is a 'flash loan attack.' A flash loan is a unique DeFi feature that allows a user to borrow a massive amount of capital (millions of dollars) with no collateral, on the condition that the loan is repaid within the same blockchain transaction. Attackers use this huge, temporary source of capital to manipulate asset prices on a DEX and trick a target protocol into thinking its collateral is worth more than it really is.

Case Study: The Mango Markets Exploit (Economic Exploit)

In October 2022, the Mango Markets lending protocol on the Solana blockchain was drained of over $100 million. This was a classic economic exploit.

- The attacker, Avraham Eisenberg, used a massive amount

of capital to intentionally and dramatically manipulate the price of the MNGO token upwards on a low-liquidity market.
- He then went to the Mango Markets lending protocol. The protocol's oracle correctly reported the new, artificially high price of MNGO.
- Eisenberg used his now massively overvalued MNGO tokens as collateral on the platform.
- The protocol's smart contracts, working exactly as intended, saw the value of his collateral and allowed him to borrow (and drain) essentially all of the protocol's other assets, like USDC and SOL.

He didn't find a bug in the code; he used a huge amount of capital to manipulate the protocol's inputs (the price of its collateral) and trick its perfectly functioning logic.

Practical Application: Analysing a Hack Post-Mortem

Reading about past DeFi exploits is one of the best ways to learn about security.

- **Try This How-To:**

1. Go to a website that documents and explains major DeFi hacks, like Rekt News.
2. Find the article about a hack that interests you.
3. As you read the "post-mortem" or explanation of how the hack worked, try to determine which category it falls into.
4. Ask yourself: Did the attacker find a specific line of code that was bugged (a smart contract hack), or did they use flash loans and price manipulation to trick the protocol

(an economic exploit)?

This analytical exercise helps you to better understand the different and complex threat vectors that exist in the DeFi space.

Key Takeaways

- Smart contract hacks exploit flaws and bugs in the protocol's code.
- Economic exploits manipulate the protocol's intended logic and economic incentives for profit.
- Flash loan attacks are a common tool used in economic exploits, allowing attackers to borrow massive capital with no collateral for a single transaction.

Bridge to the Next Lesson

Understanding these external risks is crucial. But there are also proactive steps you can take to protect your own wallet from being the weak link when you interact with these protocols. In our next lesson, we will cover some essential security best practices for using DeFi.

Lesson 11 - Security Best Practices for DeFi

An Introduction to Managing Your Digital Permissions

When you use a new app on your phone, it asks for permission to access your camera or contacts. In DeFi, when you use a new dApp, it asks for permission to access the tokens in your wallet. While this is a necessary step to interact with protocols, these permissions, if not managed properly, can create a permanent security vulnerability. This lesson will teach you about token approvals, the most overlooked aspect of wallet security, and how to practice good digital hygiene to keep your assets safe.

The Core Explanation: The Power of an "Approval"

When you want to trade a token on a DEX or deposit it into a lending protocol for the first time, you must first grant the protocol's smart contract permission to move that token from your wallet on your behalf. This is called a token 'approval'. You are signing a transaction that says, "I approve this smart contract to spend my USDC tokens."

The critical security issue arises from unlimited approvals. For user convenience, most dApps ask you to approve an *unlimited* amount of the token. This means you don't have to sign a new approval transaction for every single trade. While convenient, it creates a risk: an unlimited approval is a permission that lasts forever, unless you revoke it.

This means that if a dApp you used once and then forgot about is ever hacked or exploited, the attacker could potentially use that old, unlimited approval you granted to drain all of that specific token from your wallet—even if you haven't interacted with the protocol in months.

Case Study: The BadgerDAO Exploit

In December 2021, the DeFi protocol BadgerDAO was hacked, resulting in the loss of over $120 million of user funds. This was not a typical smart contract bug. Instead, the hackers managed to compromise the "front-end" of the protocol's website.

They injected malicious code that tricked users into signing transactions that granted a new, unlimited token approval to the hacker's own wallet. For weeks, users who interacted with the site were unknowingly giving the hacker permission to spend their tokens.

When the hacker decided to strike, they used these accumulated approvals to systematically drain the funds from the wallets of everyone who had been tricked. This was a powerful lesson that security is not just about the smart contract, but also about being extremely careful about which permissions you grant and to whom.

Practical Application: Revoking Your Approvals

Practicing good digital hygiene means periodically reviewing and revoking old permissions that are no longer needed.

- **Try This How-To**:

1. Go to a block explorer like Etherscan and log in with your wallet (or use a dedicated tool like revoke.cash).
2. In the main menu, find the "Token Approvals Checker" (on Etherscan it is under "More").
3. Connect your wallet. This is a safe, read-only action that allows the tool to scan the blockchain for your historical approvals.
4. The tool will show you a list of every smart contract that you have given spending permission to for every token in your wallet. You might be surprised at how long the list is.
5. You can then use the "Revoke" function to cancel any permissions for protocols that you no longer use or trust. This is the digital equivalent of changing the locks on your house.

Key Takeaways

- Be careful about which dApps you grant token approvals to.
- Approvals can be for a specific amount or, more dangerously, for an unlimited amount, which creates a lasting permission.
- Periodically review and revoke unnecessary approvals to protect your wallet from old or compromised protocols.

Bridge to the Next Lesson

Managing your wallet's security is crucial. Another key skill is learning how to analyse the health and safety of the protocols themselves before you decide to interact with them. In our next lesson, we will look at key metrics for analysing DeFi protocols.

Lesson 12 - Analysing DeFi Protocols

An Introduction to DeFi Due Diligence

With thousands of DeFi protocols competing for your capital, how do you tell the difference between a thriving, trusted blue-chip and a risky, deserted ghost town? Just as on-chain metrics can tell you about the health of a blockchain, a specific set of metrics can tell you about the health of a DeFi application. This lesson will teach you how to use key data points like Total Value Locked (TVL) and Protocol Revenue to perform due diligence and make more informed decisions about which protocols to use.

The Core Explanation: Measuring Health and Adoption
When evaluating a DeFi protocol, professional analysts focus on two key metrics that measure its market share and financial health:

1. Total Value Locked (TVL):

- **What it is:** TVL represents the total value of all assets that users have deposited into the protocol's smart contracts. It is the most common metric for gauging the overall scale and market share of a DeFi application.
- **What it means:** A high and, more importantly, a *growing* TVL is often a strong indicator of user trust, deep liquidity, and significant network effects. It shows that a large amount of capital is willing to trust the protocol's smart contracts and that the application has achieved a significant level of adoption.

1. Protocol Revenue:

- **What it is:** This is the total amount of fees that the protocol generates from its activity. For a DEX, this is trading fees. For a lending protocol, it's the interest paid by borrowers.
- **What it means:** Revenue is a direct measure of a protocol's usage and product-market fit. A protocol that generates significant and sustainable revenue is a healthy, long-term project that is providing a service people are willing to pay for. It is a sign of a real, functioning business, not just a speculative project.

Case Study: Uniswap vs. a Hypothetical DEX

Let's compare two protocols to see how these metrics tell a story.

- **Uniswap:** As the leading DEX, it consistently has one of the highest TVLs in all of DeFi, often in the billions of dollars. This indicates deep liquidity and widespread user trust. It also generates millions of dollars in trading fees (protocol revenue) *every single day*. This shows that it is a massively successful and heavily used financial utility.
- **Hypothetical DEX "NewSwap":** A new DEX launches and attracts some initial hype. However, after a few months, its TVL is only a few hundred thousand dollars. It generates only $50 in trading fees per day. This data tells you that, despite any marketing claims, "NewSwap" has failed to attract significant capital or user activity. It is a much riskier and less reliable place to trade than a market leader like Uniswap.

Practical Application: Using an Analytics Dashboard

The best part about DeFi is that this data is all public and easily accessible through analytics platforms.

- **Try This How-To:**

1. Go to the analytics website DeFiLlama. The homepage is a leaderboard of all DeFi protocols ranked by TVL.
2. This immediately gives you a sense of the market hierarchy.
3. Click on a major protocol from the top of the list, like Lido (a liquid staking protocol) or Aave (a lending pro-

tocol).

4. DeFiLlama will show you a detailed page with a chart of the protocol's historical TVL. You can also often find data on its daily fees and revenue.

Using this dashboard is the exact process that professional analysts use to assess a DeFi protocol's health, traction, and market share.

Key Takeaways

- Total Value Locked (TVL) measures the total assets deposited in a protocol, acting as a key indicator of market share and user trust.
- Protocol Revenue shows the fees generated by the protocol's activity, indicating its level of real-world usage.
- These metrics are essential for assessing a DeFi protocol's health and traction, allowing you to make data-driven decisions.

Bridge to the Next Lesson

These metrics are key to analysing protocols on a single chain, but DeFi is no longer confined to just Ethereum. To find the best opportunities, you often have to look across multiple blockchains. In our next lesson, we will explore the concept of multi-chain DeFi strategies.

Lesson 13 - Multi-chain DeFi Strategies

An Introduction to a Universe of Opportunity

For a long time, the world of DeFi was almost exclusively centered on the Ethereum blockchain. But that era is over. We now live in a vibrant multi-chain world, with dozens of Layer 1s and Layer 2s, each hosting its own unique and thriving DeFi ecosystem. A multi-chain strategy involves moving beyond a single network and leveraging the unique opportunities for yield, low fees, and innovation that exist across this expanding universe.

The Core Explanation: Expanding Your Horizons

A multi-chain DeFi strategy involves using DeFi protocols across various different blockchains (like Arbitrum, Solana, Polygon, and Avalanche) to find the best yields and lowest transaction fees. A single-chain user might be limited to the opportunities on Ethereum, while a multi-chain user can go where the action is.

A hypothetical multi-chain strategy could look like this:

1. **Borrow on the L1:** A user borrows stablecoins against their ETH on Aave on the Ethereum mainnet, where the protocol has the deepest liquidity and is the most secure.
2. **Bridge to an L2:** They then use a cross-chain bridge to move these stablecoins to a Layer 2 network like Arbitrum, where transaction fees are a fraction of the cost.
3. **Farm on the L2:** On Arbitrum, they use these stablecoins to provide liquidity to a new, high-yield DEX or yield farm, an opportunity that may not be available on the mainnet.

4. **Bridge Back:** After a period of farming, they can bridge their assets back to the Ethereum mainnet.

This kind of strategy requires a strong understanding of cross-chain bridges, managing wallets across different networks, and an awareness of the different security trade-offs of each chain. However, it also opens up a much wider landscape of potential opportunities.

Case Study: The Rise of the L2 Ecosystems

In 2022 and 2023, while the Ethereum mainnet remained expensive, a huge amount of innovation and user activity migrated to Layer 2s like Arbitrum and Optimism. Many of the most exciting and innovative new DeFi protocols chose to launch *exclusively* on these L2s to offer their users a better, cheaper experience.

- A user who was only active on the Ethereum mainnet would have completely missed out on being an early participant in these next-generation protocols.
- The multi-chain user, who was comfortable with bridging assets, was able to move capital to these L2s, become an early user of protocols like GMX or Velodrome, and often benefit from high initial yields and valuable retroactive airdrops.

This demonstrated that a multi-chain perspective was no longer just an option; it was a necessity for anyone wanting to stay at the cutting edge of DeFi.

Practical Application: Exploring the Multi-Chain Landscape

You can quantify the scale of these different blockchain

economies using analytics tools.

- **Try This How-To:**

1. Go to the analytics site DeFiLlama.
2. On the left-hand menu, click on "Chains."
3. The site will show you a leaderboard of all the major blockchains, ranked by their Total Value Locked (TVL).
4. You will see Ethereum at the top, but you will also see the massive, multi-billion dollar TVL on other chains like Tron, BNB Chain, Solana, and Arbitrum.

This data clearly illustrates that DeFi is a vast, multi-chain ecosystem, with significant economic activity happening across many different networks.

Key Takeaways

- A multi-chain strategy involves leveraging opportunities across multiple blockchains.
- The goal is often to find higher yields or lower transaction costs than are available on the Ethereum mainnet.
- This adds complexity and requires careful management of bridges and wallets, but it also opens up a much wider range of opportunities.

Bridge to the Next Lesson

Multi-chain strategies expand the universe of digital-native opportunities. But what if we could bring the value of traditional, real-world assets into this on-chain world? In our next lesson, we will look at one of the fastest-growing narratives in DeFi: Real-World Assets (RWAs).

Lesson 14 - Real-World Assets (RWA) in DeFi

An Introduction to Bridging Two Worlds

The DeFi ecosystem, for all its innovation, has largely been a self-contained world of crypto-native assets. The traditional financial world, with its trillions of dollars in real estate, stocks, and credit, has remained separate. Real-World Assets (RWAs) represent the crucial bridge being built to connect these two worlds. This narrative aims to bring the value of tangible, off-chain assets onto the blockchain, potentially unlocking trillions of dollars of new value for the DeFi ecosystem.

The Core Explanation: Tokenizing the Real World

RWAs involve "tokenizing" traditional, off-chain assets and bringing them into DeFi. The process involves creating a digital token on the blockchain that represents a legal claim on a real-world asset. This allows a physical or traditional financial asset to be represented and used within the digital world of DeFi.

Examples of assets that are being tokenized as RWAs include:

- **Private Credit:** Tokens that represent a share in a pool of loans made to real-world businesses.
- **U.S. Treasury Bonds:** Tokens that are fully backed by and redeemable for short-term U.S. government bonds.
- **Real Estate:** Tokens that represent fractional ownership

of a rental property, allowing the token holder to receive a share of the rental income.

Once these assets are tokenized, they can be used as building blocks in DeFi. For example, a stablecoin protocol could accept tokenized Treasury Bonds as collateral, or a user could borrow against their tokenized real estate. This narrative aims to bridge the gap between DeFi and traditional finance (TradFi).

Case Study: MakerDAO and U.S. Treasury Bonds

MakerDAO, the protocol behind the DAI stablecoin, has been a pioneer in integrating RWAs into its system. Historically, DAI was backed exclusively by volatile crypto assets like ETH and WBTC. While this was decentralized, it also exposed the protocol to high levels of crypto market volatility.

To increase stability and diversify its collateral, MakerDAO's governance voted to begin accepting RWAs. It has since created vaults that hold hundreds of millions of dollars' worth of tokenized U.S. Treasury Bonds. This means that the decentralized DAI stablecoin is now partially backed by one of the most stable and trusted assets in the entire traditional financial world. This move bridges the gap between the two systems, diversifies the collateral backing DAI, and provides a new, stable source of yield for the protocol.

Practical Application: Tracking the RWA Sector

You can track the growth of this emerging sector using specialized data platforms.

- **Try This How-To:**

1. Go to an RWA data analytics site like app.rwa.xyz.

2. On their dashboard, you will see a breakdown of the different types of real-world assets that have been tokenized and brought on-chain (e.g., private credit, treasuries, real estate).
3. You can see the total value of these tokenized assets and which protocols are the leaders in the space.

This gives you a live, data-driven look at the growth of this important new sector that aims to merge DeFi and TradFi.

Key Takeaways

- RWAs involve tokenizing traditional, off-chain assets and bringing them into DeFi.
- Examples include real estate, private credit, and government bonds.
- This narrative has the potential to bring trillions of dollars of value from traditional finance into the DeFi ecosystem, dramatically expanding its scale.

Bridge to the Next Lesson

RWAs bring physical and traditional financial assets into DeFi. But what about bringing another powerful class of *digital* assets—NFTs—into the financial system? In our final lesson of the Intermediate level, we will explore the innovative intersection of NFTs and DeFi, known as NFT-Fi.

Lesson 15 - NFTs in DeFi (NFT-Fi)

An Introduction to Financializing JPEGs

For a long time, NFTs have been seen primarily as digital art or collectibles—valuable, but highly illiquid. You could hold a CryptoPunk worth a million dollars, but you couldn't easily spend or borrow against it. NFT-Fi (or NFT Finance) is the exciting and emerging sector that aims to change this. It is the intersection of NFTs and Decentralized Finance, with the goal of unlocking the massive financial value of these unique digital assets and turning them into productive financial tools.

The Core Explanation: From Collectibles to Collateral

NFT-Fi aims to integrate NFTs into the DeFi ecosystem, making these illiquid digital collectibles into productive financial assets. This emerging sector is building a new suite of financial primitives for unique digital assets.

The key applications in NFT-Fi include:

1. **NFT Lending & Borrowing:** This is the most developed area. Protocols in this space allow users to use their valuable NFTs as collateral to borrow crypto. This allows NFT owners to unlock liquidity from their holdings without having to sell their prized assets.
2. **Fractionalization:** These are protocols that allow a user to lock up a single, very expensive NFT (like a Bored Ape) and issue many fungible tokens that each represent a small share of that NFT. This allows multiple people to own a piece of a "blue-chip" NFT, increasing its liquidity and making it accessible to a wider market.
3. **NFT Derivatives:** This allows traders to speculate on the

future floor price of a major NFT collection, similar to how they might trade perpetuals on Bitcoin or Ethereum.

These innovations bring more utility to NFTs, moving them beyond just being digital collectibles and integrating them into the broader DeFi economy.

Case Study: NFTfi - Peer-to-Peer Lending

NFTfi is a leading platform in the NFT lending space that operates on a peer-to-peer model.

- An NFT owner who needs liquidity can list their NFT (e.g., their CryptoPunk) on the NFTfi marketplace and request loan terms.
- Lenders on the platform can then browse the listed NFTs and make loan offers directly to the borrower (e.g., "I will lend you 50 ETH for 30 days at a 10% interest rate").
- If the borrower accepts an offer, a smart contract is created. The NFT is locked in the contract as collateral, and the lender's ETH is transferred to the borrower.
- If the borrower repays the loan plus interest on time, they get their NFT back. If they default, the smart contract automatically transfers ownership of the NFT to the lender.

This peer-to-peer model allows the market to organically price the risk and value of unique digital assets, creating a decentralized lending market for a new kind of collateral.

Practical Application: Browsing the NFT Loan Market

You can see this new financial market for digital collectibles in action.

- **Try This How-To:**

1. Go to the website for an NFT lending protocol like NFTfi or BendDAO.
2. Browse the marketplace or "loan book."
3. You will see a gallery of high-value NFTs from collections like Bored Ape Yacht Club and CryptoPunks that are currently being used as collateral for active loans.
4. You can often see the details of these loans: the loan amount (in ETH or a stablecoin), the interest rate, and the duration.

This provides a real-world look at the financialization of digital collectibles and the emerging world of NFT-Fi.

Key Takeaways

- NFT-Fi aims to integrate NFTs into the DeFi ecosystem, unlocking their financial value.
- Key applications include lending against NFTs and fractionalizing ownership of expensive assets.
- It makes illiquid digital collectibles into productive financial assets, allowing owners to access liquidity without selling.

10

Module 3 Recap

You have now completed your tour of the on-chain ecosystem and the final module of the Intermediate Level.

- You've learned about the key pillars of the Web3 economy, from the provable ownership of NFTs to the open financial system of DeFi and the community governance of DAOs.
- You have gained the practical skills to interact with this world, from making a swap on a DEX to understanding the basics of taxes and portfolio tracking.
- You've explored the cutting edge of DeFi, from the capital efficiency of liquid staking and yield aggregators to the promise of bringing Real-World Assets and NFTs into this new financial system.

You are no longer just an observer or a beginner; you are an experienced user who understands the mechanics, strategies, and risks of the DeFi world. You are now prepared to

move on to the Advanced Level, where you will develop true strategic expertise.

11

Level 3: Advanced

Goal: To develop strategic expertise. The user can analyse complex systems, manage significant risk, and identify emerging opportunities.

Module 1: Advanced On-Chain Analysis & Trading

Module Introduction: You have mastered the fundamentals and the core mechanics of the ecosystem. Welcome to the world of strategic expertise. This module is designed to elevate your skills from a knowledgeable user to a sophisticated analyst. You will learn how to leverage the blockchain's radical transparency to gain an edge, understand the invisible forces that impact your trades, and explore the advanced models that professionals use to evaluate a token's true economic substance.

Lesson 01 - Tracking 'Smart Money' Wallets

An Introduction to Following the Footprints

In traditional finance, "following the smart money" is a time-honoured strategy, but it's often based on rumours and delayed regulatory filings. In crypto, it's a science. The transparency of the blockchain allows you to watch the actions of the most influential and successful players—venture funds, project insiders, and legendary traders—in real-time. This lesson will teach you how to leverage this transparency to see what the "smart money" is doing before it becomes a mainstream headline.

The Core Explanation: Leveraging Radical Transparency

One of the most powerful uses of blockchain transparency is tracking the activity of 'smart money'—wallets belonging to VCs, project insiders, and highly profitable traders. While wallets on the blockchain are pseudonymous (just a string of characters), their activity is public.

Specialized on-chain analysis tools like Nansen, Arkham, or Dune Analytics are dedicated to de-anonymizing these wallets by analysing their connections and behaviour. Once a wallet is tagged as belonging to a major VC fund or a "whale" with a history of profitable trades, you can monitor their transactions in real-time.

This on-chain intelligence can provide powerful early signals:

1. **New Project Investments:** You can see when a wallet known for making smart, early-stage bets start accumulating a new, unknown token. This is often the earliest signal of a promising new project.

2. **Accumulation or Distribution:** You can observe when multiple smart money wallets are heavily buying a specific token (accumulation), signalling conviction, or when they are systematically selling (distribution), signalling a potential top.
3. **Emerging Narratives:** You can spot trends before they become mainstream by seeing which *sectors* smart money is rotating into. For example, seeing multiple funds start buying up tokens in the "Decentralized Science" (DeSci) category could signal an emerging narrative.

Case Study: The GCR Story

GCR is a legendary pseudonymous trader who famously turned a small portfolio into hundreds of millions of dollars by correctly predicting market movements, including shorting the top of the 2021 bull market. Because his Ethereum wallet address is publicly known, he became one of the most-watched "smart money" accounts in the entire ecosystem.

On-chain analysts and regular users alike would monitor his wallet's every move. When he started heavily accumulating a new token, the market took notice. When he sold a position, it was seen as a major signal. In one famous instance, his large purchases of a particular token were a key catalyst that brought widespread attention to the asset. This is a real-world example of how the actions of a single, highly respected on-chain entity can be used as a powerful data point by the rest of the market.

Practical Application: Your First Sleuthing Steps

While advanced tools require subscriptions, you can perform basic "smart money" tracking yourself using a block explorer.

- **Try This How-To:**

1. Find an article or social media post that discusses a recent "seed round" investment by a major VC fund (like Andreessen Horowitz or Paradigm) into a new crypto project.
2. The article will often mention the total amount invested.
3. Go to the block explorer for that project's chain (e.g., Etherscan) and look up the project's main token contract.
4. Look at the "Top Holders" list. Can you identify any large, recent transfers from the project's treasury to a new wallet that might correspond with the investment round?

Click on that potential VC wallet. What else is in it? What other moves has it made?

This is the foundational work of an on-chain analyst: following the money to uncover insights.

Key Takeaways

- On-chain analysis tools allow for the identification and tracking of influential wallets.
- Monitoring 'smart money' can reveal investment trends and token accumulations.
- This strategy leverages the inherent transparency of public blockchains to generate insights that are impossible in traditional markets.

Bridge to the Next Lesson

Tracking smart money is about observing the visible actions of others. But there is an even deeper, more invisible force at play on the blockchain that affects every single trade you make, often without you even knowing it. In our next lesson, we will explore the "invisible tax" of Maximal Extractable Value, or MEV.

Lesson 02 - MEV (Maximal Extractable Value) Explained

An Introduction to the "Invisible Tax"

When you submit a trade on a decentralized exchange, you expect to get the price you see on the screen. But often, you get a slightly worse price. Why? The answer is a complex and fascinating phenomenon known as Maximal Extractable Value (MEV). It is a hidden, "invisible tax" that sophisticated actors can extract from the blockchain by strategically reordering, inserting, or censoring transactions. Understanding MEV is crucial for any serious DeFi user, as it is a fundamental force that shapes the on-chain trading landscape.

The Core Explanation: The Value of Transaction Ordering

Maximal Extractable Value (MEV) is the maximum value that can be extracted from block production in excess of the standard block reward and gas fees. It exists because the participants who build the blocks (miners in PoW, validators in PoS) have the ultimate power to decide the order of transactions within that block. This ability to control transaction ordering is valuable, and that value can be extracted.

This creates a hidden economy of "searchers" (sophisticated bots) who scan the mempool for profitable opportunities and "builders" who construct the most profitable blocks for the validators.

Common forms of MEV include:

1. **Arbitrage:** A searcher spots a price difference for the same token on two different DEXs. They can create a transaction that buys on the cheaper DEX and sells on the more expensive one, and pay a high fee to a validator to ensure their transaction is included for a risk-free profit.
2. **Liquidations:** In lending protocols, when a user's collateral drops below a certain threshold, they can be liquidated. Searchers constantly monitor for these opportunities and race to be the first to execute the liquidation to claim the reward.
3. **Sandwich Attacks:** This is a malicious form of MEV that directly harms users. A searcher sees a large user trade in the mempool. They front-run the user by placing a buy order just before theirs, then let the user's trade push the price up, and immediately back-run the user by placing a sell order right after. This "sandwiches" the user's trade, extracting value and causing the user to get a worse price (higher slippage).

Case Study: The Sandwich Attack

Imagine a user, Sarah, wants to make a large swap on Uniswap, buying $100,000 worth of a token called XYZ. She submits her transaction to the mempool.

1. An MEV bot ("searcher") sees this large buy order before

it is confirmed.

2. **Front-run:** The bot instantly submits its own buy order for XYZ, paying a very high gas fee to ensure its transaction is placed *before* Sarah's in the block. This pushes the price of XYZ up slightly.
3. **Victim's Trade:** Sarah's $100,000 buy order now executes at a slightly worse average price because of the bot's front-run. Her large purchase pushes the price up even more.
4. **Back-run:** The MEV bot immediately submits a sell order for the XYZ tokens it just bought. It sells them at the now higher price, capturing a small, nearly risk-free profit.

Sarah's trade was "sandwiched." The MEV bot profited directly from her trade, and as a result, she received fewer XYZ tokens for her $100,000. This happens thousands of times a day in DeFi.

Practical Application: Seeing MEV in the Wild

The world of MEV is no longer a dark forest; it is now transparent and observable.

- **Try This How-To:**

1. Go to a website that visualizes the MEV supply chain, like explore.flashbots.net.
2. This platform shows a live feed of "MEV bundles"—sequences of transactions crafted by searchers and submitted to block builders to extract value.
3. You can often see specific arbitrage and sandwich attacks as they are happening, labelled for you.

Exploring this data makes the abstract concept of MEV a tangible, real-time phenomenon and reveals the scale of this complex and invisible on-chain economy.

Key Takeaways

- MEV is the value extracted by reordering or censoring transactions in a block.
- Common examples are arbitrage, liquidations, and front-running.
- MEV can negatively impact regular users by increasing their trading costs through phenomena like sandwich attacks.

Bridge to the Next Lesson

MEV is a highly technical aspect of blockchain mechanics that affects a token's price in the short term. A more fundamental but equally advanced area of analysis is looking deeper into a token's long-term economic design. In our next lesson, we will go beyond basic tokenomics and into advanced tokenomic analysis and modelling.

Lesson 03 - Advanced Tokenomic Analysis and Modelling

An Introduction to a Token's "Business Model"

In the beginner level, we learned about basic tokenomics. Now, we go deeper. Advanced tokenomic analysis treats a token not just as an asset, but as the centerpiece of a complex digital economy. It involves modelling how value flows through a protocol's ecosystem and, most importantly, how (or if) that value accrues back to the token itself. This is how professional analysts determine if a token has a sustainable "business model" or if it's just a tool for speculation.

The Core Explanation: Value Accrual and Token Sinks

Advanced tokenomic analysis goes beyond simple supply caps. It involves modelling a token's value accrual and its flow within its ecosystem. The central question is: "As the protocol becomes more successful, is there a clear and direct mechanism that makes the token more valuable?"

Key areas to analyse are:

1. **Vesting Schedules:** You must analyse not just the existence of insider tokens, but the specific timeline on which they unlock. A "vesting cliff," where a large amount of team and investor tokens unlock on a single day, can create a predictable and massive sell-pressure event that you need to be aware of.
2. **Token Sinks:** These are mechanisms that are designed to remove tokens from the liquid, circulating supply, which can be very bullish. Common examples include:

- **Burning:** The protocol uses a portion of its revenue to buy back tokens from the open market and permanently destroy them, reducing the total supply.

- **Long-Term Staking:** Mechanisms that incentivize users to lock up their tokens for long periods, often in exchange for a greater share of rewards or governance power.

1. **Value Accrual:** This is the most critical component. How does the protocol's revenue flow back to the token holder? Is it through...

- Buybacks and Burns? (As described above).
- Fee Sharing ("Real Yield")? Does a portion of the protocol's revenue, paid in a stable asset like ETH or USDC, get distributed directly to token stakers?
- Governance Rights? Do the tokens give control over a valuable treasury or the protocol's future fee streams?

Case Study: The "Fee Switch" Debate

Uniswap, the leading DEX, generates hundreds of millions of dollars in trading fees per year. For a long time, 100% of these fees went to the Liquidity Providers. The UNI governance token had control over the protocol, but no direct claim on its massive revenue. This was considered a weak value accrual mechanism.

A long-standing governance debate has been about activating the "fee switch." This proposal would redirect a small portion of the trading fees (e.g., 1/10th) away from LPs and distribute it to UNI token holders who have staked their tokens.

This is a perfect case study of value accrual. If the fee switch is turned on, there will be a direct, programmatic link between the protocol's success (trading volume) and the value returned to the token holders. This would significantly strengthen the UNI token's "business model," transforming it from a pure governance token into a productive, yield-bearing asset.

Practical Application: Analyzing Value Accrual

You can analyze the value accrual model of any major DeFi protocol by doing some research.

- **Try This How-To:**

1. Choose a major, revenue-generating DeFi protocol that you are interested in (e.g., Aave, GMX, MakerDAO).
2. Go to its official documentation or analytics pages (sites like Token Terminal are excellent for this).
3. Try to answer these three questions:

- Does this protocol generate significant, sustainable revenue?
- How does that revenue flow? (Does it go to LPs, the treasury, or token holders?)
- Does the native token have a clear mechanism (like fee sharing or burning) to capture a portion of that revenue?

Answering these questions is the core of performing an advanced value accrual analysis.

Key Takeaways

- Vesting schedules are a critical indicator of future token supply inflation and potential sell pressure.
- Effective 'token sinks' (like burn mechanisms) reduce

the circulating supply and can be a bullish driver of value.

- A strong tokenomic model clearly links the protocol's success to the token's value through a direct value accrual mechanism.

Bridge to the Next Lesson

Understanding a token's value accrual is key to deciding if it's a good long-term hold. Another advanced strategy involves not just holding the token, but actively using it within DeFi to generate a return. In our next lesson, we will explore the advanced and active strategy of liquidity provisioning.

Lesson 04 - Liquidity Provisioning as a Strategy

An Introduction to Active Market Making

In the Intermediate level, you learned the basics of providing liquidity and the risks of impermanent loss. That is a passive strategy. At the advanced level, liquidity provisioning (LPing) transforms into an active and complex strategy, particularly with the advent of "concentrated liquidity" AMMs. This lesson will introduce you to this more sophisticated form of market making, where efficiency and active management can dramatically increase your returns, but also your risks.

The Core Explanation: The Power of Concentrated Liquidity

While basic liquidity provisioning is straightforward, advanced strategies involve actively managing your position. The key innovation that enables this is 'concentrated liquidity,' pioneered by Uniswap v3.

- **Traditional AMM (e.g., Uniswap v2):** When you provide liquidity, your capital is spread out evenly along the entire price curve, from zero to infinity. This means a huge portion of your capital is sitting unused unless the price of the asset is trading at extreme highs or lows. It is very capital inefficient.
- **Concentrated Liquidity AMM (e.g., Uniswap v3):** This model allows you to act as a more sophisticated market maker. Instead of providing liquidity across the entire price range, you can concentrate your capital within a specific, narrow price range where you expect the most trading to occur.

For example, for an ETH/USDC pool where ETH is trading at $3,000, you might concentrate your liquidity between $2,900 and $3,100. Because all your capital is being put to work in this tight range, you will earn a much larger share of the trading fees for the same amount of capital. This can dramatically increase your capital efficiency and fee earnings. However, it also exposes you to much higher impermanent loss and requires active management, as you must reposition your range if the price moves outside of it.

Case Study: The Stablecoin LP

Let's consider an LP providing liquidity to a USDC/DAI pool. Both tokens are stablecoins pegged to $1.

- **On a Traditional AMM:** The LP provides liquidity across the full range from $0 to infinity. Since virtually all trading happens between $0.99 and $1.01, most of their capital is never used, and they earn very low fees.

- **On a Concentrated Liquidity AMM:** A sophisticated LP provides the same amount of capital but concentrates it in a very tight range, for example, from $0.999 to $1.001. Because their capital is thousands of times more efficient (all of it is working where the trades are happening), they can earn significantly higher fee revenue than the first LP. However, they must actively monitor the pool. If one of the stablecoins were to lose its peg and trade at $0.98, their position would be entirely converted to the de-pegged asset, and they would need to decide whether to reposition their liquidity at a loss.

Practical Application: Simulating a Position

You can get a tangible sense of the trade-offs of concentrated liquidity using online simulators.

- **Try This How-To:**

1. Do a web search for a "Uniswap v3 Simulator" or "Concentrated Liquidity Calculator."
2. These tools allow you to create a hypothetical LP position for a pair like ETH/USDC.
3. First, set a very wide price range for your liquidity. Note the projected fee revenue.
4. Now, keep the same amount of capital but narrow the price range significantly around the current market price.
5. Observe how the projected fee revenue increases dramatically. This visually demonstrates the concept of capital efficiency. Now, move the projected price of ETH

outside your narrow range and see the effect on your position's value to understand the risk.

Key Takeaways

- Concentrated liquidity allows LPs to provide capital in specific price ranges, rather than across the entire price curve.
- This can result in significantly higher fee revenue and capital efficiency compared to traditional LPs.
- The trade-off is an increased risk of impermanent loss and the need for active management if the price moves outside your chosen range.

Bridge to the Next Lesson

Active liquidity provisioning is a way to profit from market activity. But what if you could design a strategy to profit regardless of which direction the market moves? In our next lesson, we will explore the complex world of delta-neutral and market-neutral strategies.

Lesson 05 - Delta-Neutral and Market-Neutral Strategies

An Introduction to Directionless Profit

Most investing is directional—you are making a bet that the price of an asset will go either up or down. But what if you could structure a trade to be profitable regardless of which way the market moves? Delta-neutral strategies are an advanced technique designed to do just that. The goal is to isolate and profit from market inefficiencies, like funding rates or volatility, rather than from the price direction itself. This lesson will introduce you to this sophisticated style of trading.

The Core Explanation: Hedging for Yield

Delta-neutral strategies are designed to have a "delta" of zero, meaning your portfolio's value is not significantly affected by small changes in the underlying asset's price. You are effectively hedged against market movements.

The most common example in crypto is 'funding rate farming':

1. **The Setup:** A trader goes long on a spot asset (e.g., they buy 1 ETH on a spot exchange like Coinbase) while simultaneously going short on that same asset on a perpetuals market (e.g., they short 1 ETH on a derivatives exchange like dYdX).
2. **The Hedge:** Their exposure to the price of ETH is now "neutral." If the price of ETH goes up, their spot position gains value while their short position loses value by a similar amount. If the price goes down, the reverse is true. Their net position value remains relatively stable.

3. **The Profit Mechanism:** So how do they profit? They aim to collect the funding payments from the perpetuals market. Funding is a mechanism that keeps the price of a perpetual contract close to the spot price. In a bull market, when many traders are going long with leverage, the funding rate is often positive, meaning longs must pay shorts a small fee every few hours. The delta-neutral farmer's goal is to collect these positive funding payments from their short position, while their exposure to price movements is hedged.

Case Study: The Bull Market Funding Farmer

During the peak of the 2021 bull market, sentiment was extremely bullish. The funding rates on major exchanges for assets like Bitcoin and Ethereum were consistently and highly positive, sometimes exceeding 50-100% APR.

Delta-neutral traders executed the funding rate farming strategy at scale. They would buy spot ETH and short ETH perpetuals. They were immune to the volatile price of ETH moving up or down, but every 8 hours, they would collect a significant funding rate payment from the mass of leveraged long traders.

While this strategy seems risk-free, it is not. The primary risk is liquidation. A sudden, violent price spike (a "scam wick") could liquidate the trader's short position, destroy their hedge and leave them with only the long spot position, which could then crash in value. These strategies are complex and carry their own unique risks.

Practical Application: Observing Funding Rates

You can see the raw material for these strategies on data websites.

- **Try This How-To:**

1. Go to a data site that tracks derivatives data, like coinglass.com or velfina.com.
2. Find the section for "Funding Rates."
3. You will see a table showing the current funding rates for BTC or ETH perpetuals across all the major centralized and decentralized exchanges.
4. Notice how the rates are sometimes positive (longs pay shorts) and sometimes negative (shorts pay longs). Also, notice how the rates become much more extreme during periods of high market volatility. These are the exact rates that delta-neutral farmers are analysing and trying to capture.

Key Takeaways

- Delta-neutral strategies aim to isolate and profit from market inefficiencies, not from the direction of price movements.
- Funding rate arbitrage is a popular market-neutral strategy where traders hedge their price exposure to collect payments from leveraged traders.
- These strategies are complex and carry their own unique risks, such as the liquidation of the hedge during extreme volatility.

Bridge to the Next Lesson

Delta-neutral strategies often involve using derivatives like perpetuals. Another powerful class of derivatives is options, which allow for even more complex strategies. In our next lesson, we will explore how crypto options work and how they are being made accessible through structured products.

Lesson 06 - Crypto Options and Structured Products

An Introduction to Advanced Risk Management Tools

Beyond simple spot trading and futures, the world of advanced finance is dominated by options. These versatile derivative contracts are the essential tools that sophisticated investors use to hedge risk, speculate on volatility, and generate income from their existing holdings. While options can be complex, a new wave of DeFi "structured products" is making these powerful strategies accessible to the average user for the first time.

The Core Explanation: The Right, Not the Obligation

Options are derivative contracts that give the buyer the right, but not the obligation, to buy or sell an asset at a predetermined price (the 'strike price') on or before a specific date (the 'expiration date').

There are two basic types of options:

1. **A 'Call' Option:** Gives the owner the right to buy an asset at the strike price. You would buy a call option if you are bullish and believe the price of the asset will rise significantly.
2. **A 'Put' Option:** Gives the owner the right to sell an asset at the strike price. You would buy a put option if you are bearish and believe the price will fall, as it acts as a form

of insurance.

While options can be used for speculation, one of their most popular uses is for income generation through options selling. This is where DeFi Options Vaults (DOVs) come in.

- DOVs are protocols that have simplified this process. Users can deposit assets (like ETH or WBTC) into a vault, and the vault's smart contract then automatically runs a specific, recurring options-selling strategy to generate yield for the depositors.

Case Study: The Covered Call Strategy

The most common strategy used by DOVs is the "covered call." Let's say a user, Sarah, holds 1 ETH and is a long-term believer, but she doesn't think the price will rise dramatically in the next month.

- **The Strategy:** She deposits her 1 ETH into a "covered call" DOV. The vault's smart contract automatically sells a call option against her ETH with a strike price that is well above the current market price (e.g., if ETH is $3,000, the vault might sell a call option with a $3,500 strike price that expires in one week).
- **The Income:** The vault collects the premium (the price paid by the option buyer) from selling this option and distributes it to Sarah and the other depositors as yield.
- **The Trade-off:** Sarah earns income on her ETH. However, she has capped her potential upside. If the price of ETH were to unexpectedly skyrocket to $4,000, her ETH would be "called away" and sold at the lower strike price of

$3,500.

DOVs automate this weekly process, allowing users to consistently generate yield in sideways or moderately bullish markets.

Practical Application: Exploring DOV Platforms

You can see the various automated options strategies available in DeFi.

- **Try This How-To:**

1. Go to the website of a major DOV protocol like Ribbon Finance, Thetanuts Finance, or Friktion (on Solana).
2. Browse their "Vaults" or "Products."
3. You will see different vaults for different assets (BTC, ETH, etc.) and different strategies (like "Covered Call" or "Put Selling").
4. Look at the historical APY (Annual Percentage Yield) for these vaults. This shows you the real-world yield that can be generated by automating these complex options-selling strategies.

Key Takeaways

- Call options give the right to buy; put options give the right to sell.
- Options are versatile tools for hedging risk, speculating on volatility, and generating income.
- DeFi Options Vaults (DOVs) automate complex options strategies, like covered call selling, to generate a consis-

tent yield for depositors.

Bridge to the Next Lesson

Options vaults are a legitimate way to use derivatives to generate yield. However, derivatives, and particularly another unique DeFi primitive, can also be used for more nefarious purposes, like powering the economic exploits we've discussed. In our next lesson, we will explore the uses and abuses of flash loans.

Lesson 07 - Flash Loans: Uses and Abuses

An Introduction to Instant, Uncollateralized Capital

What if you could borrow a million dollars, or even a billion, with zero collateral? In traditional finance, this is impossible. In DeFi, it happens thousands of times a day. Flash loans are a uniquely DeFi primitive that allows a user to borrow a massive amount of capital for the duration of a single, atomic transaction. They are a powerful tool for legitimate arbitrage and a devastating weapon for malicious exploits. This lesson explores this mind-bending concept and its dual-edged nature.

The Core Explanation: Borrowing at the Speed of a Block

A flash loan is a unique DeFi primitive that allows a user to borrow an essentially unlimited amount of capital without any collateral, on the absolute condition that the loan is repaid within the same blockchain transaction.

The key mechanic that makes this possible is atomicity. An Ethereum transaction is "atomic," meaning it either executes completely, or it fails completely and is reverted, as if it never happened.

1. **Borrow:** At the start of a transaction, a user can call a flash loan provider (like Aave) and borrow a huge sum (e.g., 100,000 ETH).
2. **Execute:** The user can then use that 100,000 ETH to perform a series of other actions within the *same transaction* (e.g., complex arbitrage trades across multiple DEXs).
3. **Repay:** By the end of the transaction, the user's code must repay the full 100,000 ETH, plus a small fee.
4. **Succeed or Fail:** If the loan is successfully repaid, the entire transaction is confirmed. If, for any reason, the loan cannot be repaid, the entire transaction is reverted. The initial borrowing never happened, and the protocol loses nothing.

This allows for incredibly capital-efficient arbitrage and collateral swaps. However, it is most famous for its abuse in economic exploits, where attackers use the massive, uncollateralized capital to manipulate markets and drain protocols.

Case Study: The Beanstalk Farms Exploit

In April 2022, the Beanstalk Farms protocol was drained of $182 million in one of the most audacious flash loan attacks in history.

1. **Borrow:** The attacker took out a massive flash loan of nearly $1 billion worth of various crypto assets.
2. **Acquire Votes:** They used this capital to buy a huge quantity of Beanstalk's governance token, giving them over two-thirds of the total voting power.

3. **Pass Malicious Proposal:** In the same transaction, they used this voting power to instantly pass a malicious governance proposal that transferred all of the protocol's $182 million in treasury funds to their own wallet.
4. **Repay:** They then repaid the initial $1 billion flash loan.

The entire attack—borrowing, voting, and stealing—happened in the span of a single Ethereum transaction that lasted less than 13 seconds. This was a devastating demonstration of how flash loans can be weaponized to attack a protocol's governance system.

Practical Application: Observing a Flash Loan

You can see these complex, atomic transactions on a block explorer.

- **Try This How-To:**

1. Go to an analytics platform for a lending protocol like AaveScan or look at the Aave protocol's contract on Etherscan.
2. Find the section that lists "Flash Loans."
3. Click on the transaction ID for one of the loans.
4. The block explorer will show you a single, complex transaction. If you trace the flow of funds, you will see a huge amount of capital being borrowed from the Aave pool at the beginning and then being paid back at the very end, with a series of other actions (like DEX swaps) happening in between. This makes the concept of an "atomic" transaction visible.

Key Takeaways

- Flash loans are uncollateralized loans that must be repaid in the same transaction.
- They are a powerful tool for arbitrage and increasing capital efficiency.
- They are also the primary tool used in many high-profile DeFi economic exploits, particularly for price manipulation and governance attacks.

Bridge to the Next Lesson

Flash loans are often used to exploit a protocol's economic logic. But what about attacks that are designed to exploit the social or community layer, such as governance and airdrop distributions? In our next lesson, we will explore Sybil attacks and the broader concept of economic security.

Lesson 08 - Sybil Attacks and Economic Security

An Introduction to the Problem of Fake Identities

On the internet, a famous cartoon proclaimed, "nobody knows you're a dog." In Web3, this is doubly true: nobody knows if you are one person with one wallet, or one person with one thousand wallets. A Sybil attack is the age-old internet problem of a single entity creating numerous fake identities to gain an unfair advantage. This lesson will explore why this is a major challenge for decentralized systems and how it relates to the broader concept of a protocol's economic security.

The Core Explanation: One User, Many Wallets

A Sybil attack is when an attacker creates a large number of pseudonymous identities (in crypto, this means wallets) to overwhelm a network or influence a system. This is a major concern in two key areas:

1. **Airdrops:** When a project announces it will airdrop a valuable token to its early users, it creates an incentive for "Sybil farmers." A single person might create thousands of wallets and perform minimal actions with each one to try and qualify for the airdrop thousands of times, taking a disproportionately large share of the distribution.
2. **DAO Governance:** In a simple "one token, one vote" system, a Sybil attack is less of a concern. However, in systems that try to be more democratic (e.g., "one person, one vote" via identity solutions), an attacker could create thousands of fake identities to gain outsized voting power.

This leads to the broader concept of Economic Security. This refers to a protocol's resilience against manipulation, even if its code is bug-free. The key question to ask is: "How much would it cost an attacker to break or exploit this protocol?" A protocol is considered economically secure if the cost of performing an attack is significantly greater than any potential profit the attacker could gain.

Case Study: A Hypothetical Governance Attack

Imagine a small DeFi protocol with a DAO that governs its treasury, which holds $5 million in stablecoins. The DAO's governance token, GOV, has a total market cap of only $2 million.

- The governance system is simple: one token equals one vote, and a 51% majority is needed to pass a proposal.
- An attacker sees this discrepancy. The cost to attack the protocol is the cost to acquire 51% of the GOV tokens, which is just over $1 million.
- The potential profit from the attack is the entire $5 million treasury.

The attacker spends $1.1 million on the open market to buy 51% of the GOV tokens. They then create and instantly pass a governance proposal to transfer the full $5 million treasury to their own wallet. The smart contracts worked perfectly as written, but the protocol was not economically secure because the cost of the attack ($1.1M) was far less than the potential profit ($5M).

Practical Application: Spotting Anti-Sybil Measures

Projects are constantly developing more sophisticated ways to defend against Sybil attacks, especially for airdrops.

- **Try This How-To:**

1. Find the official blog post or documentation that announced the eligibility criteria for a recent, major airdrop (e.g., Arbitrum, Optimism, or zkSync).
2. Read through the criteria. You will notice that it's never just one simple action. It's usually a complex, weighted list of requirements, such as:

- Bridging a certain amount of assets.

- Performing transactions in multiple different months.
- Interacting with a minimum number of different smart contracts.
- A minimum transaction volume.

1. These complex criteria are not arbitrary; they are specifically designed as an anti-Sybil measure. By requiring a history of genuine, diverse, and non-trivial activity, they make it much more difficult and expensive for a single person to "farm" the airdrop with thousands of fake, low-effort wallets.

Key Takeaways

- A Sybil attack involves using numerous fake identities (wallets) to gain an unfair advantage.
- This is a major challenge for fair airdrop distribution and decentralized governance.
- Economic security is as important as smart contract security; a protocol is only secure if the cost of an attack is greater than the potential profit.

Bridge to the Next Lesson

Economic security is a key measure of a DAO's health. Another critical indicator is the health and management of its finances. In our next lesson, we will learn how to analyse DAO treasuries as a proxy for their long-term viability.

Lesson 09 - Analysing DAO Treasuries

An Introduction to an Organization's War Chest

"Show me the money." In the corporate world, you analyse a company's health by looking at its balance sheet and cash flow statements. In the world of DAOs, the equivalent is the treasury. The DAO's treasury is its lifeblood—the pool of capital it uses to fund development, pay contributors, and grow its ecosystem. Analysing the composition and management of this treasury is one of the most effective ways to gauge a DAO's long-term health and sustainability.

The Core Explanation: A Window into a DAO's Health

The health of a Decentralized Autonomous Organization (DAO) can often be determined by analysing its treasury. Because these treasuries are held in public wallets, they offer a transparent view into the DAO's financial position.

Key analysis points include:

1. **Diversification:** This is the most important factor. Is the treasury held mostly in its own native, volatile governance token, or has the DAO been disciplined and diversified into more stable assets like stablecoins (USDC, DAI) and established blue-chips like ETH? A treasury that is 90%+ its own token is a massive red flag, as a crash in the token's price could bankrupt the organization.
2. **Runway:** This is a measure of sustainability. Based on the DAO's current expenses (e.g., payments to core contributors), how many months or years can the DAO continue to operate before its treasury runs out? A long runway (measured in years) is a sign of a healthy, well-

managed organization.

3. **Revenue Sources:** Where is the treasury's capital coming from? Is it funded solely by the continuous emission (inflation) of its own token, or does the underlying protocol generate real, sustainable revenue from fees that flow into the treasury? A DAO backed by real revenue is far more sustainable than one that simply prints its own money to pay its bills.

Case Study: The Bear Market Litmus Test

The 2022 crypto bear market was a brutal but effective test of DAO treasury management.

- **The Weak DAOs:** Many DAOs that had launched during the bull market held almost their entire treasury in their own native governance token. When the bear market hit, the price of their token crashed by 90-95%. Consequently, the value of their treasury—and thus their ability to fund operations—also crashed by 90-95%. They were forced to dramatically cut costs, contributors left, and many of these DAOs effectively died.
- **The Strong DAOs:** In contrast, DAOs that had been disciplined during the bull market had a different experience. They had used their high token price to strategically diversify a significant portion of their treasury into stablecoins. When the bear market hit, the value of their native token still crashed, but their large stablecoin reserves meant they had a long financial runway. They were able to continue building, paying their contributors, and even expanding throughout the downturn.

This was a clear, real-world lesson: prudent treasury diversification is a key differentiator between a DAO that can survive a full market cycle and one that cannot.

Practical Application: Performing a Treasury Analysis

You can analyse the treasury of any major DAO using public tools.

- **Try This How-To:**

1. Go to a DAO analytics platform like DeepDAO or a portfolio viewer like Zapper.
2. Search for a major DAO that you are interested in (e.g., Arbitrum, Optimism, Uniswap, Aave).
3. These platforms will often have a "Treasury" or "Finances" tab that shows you a pie chart of the DAO's treasury holdings.
4. Ask yourself the key questions: What percentage is held in its native token versus stablecoins or ETH? Does it look well-diversified and prepared for a market downturn?

This is the first and most important step in evaluating a DAO's long-term financial viability.

Key Takeaways

- A well-managed DAO treasury is diversified beyond its own native token.
- "Runway" is a critical metric for a DAO's long-term sustainability, indicating how long it can fund its operations.
- Analysing treasury management is a key part of evaluat-

ing a DAO's viability and resilience to market cycles.

Bridge to the Next Lesson

Analysing treasuries is a form of fundamental analysis that combines financial and on-chain data. But there are even more advanced, purely quantitative on-chain indicators that can give us a macro-level view of market sentiment and valuation. In our final lesson of this module, we will explore some of these powerful tools.

Lesson 10 - Quantitative On-Chain Indicators

An Introduction to the Market's Vital Signs

What if you could measure the entire market's profitability in real-time? Or determine if a blockchain's valuation is justified by its economic activity? Quantitative on-chain indicators are advanced metrics that provide a "macro" view of the market's health and sentiment. They move beyond analysing individual wallets or protocols to take the vital signs of the entire network, helping analysts to identify potential market tops and bottoms.

The Core Explanation: From Micro to Macro

Beyond simple metrics like active addresses, quantitative on-chain indicators provide deeper market insights by creating ratios and models based on the blockchain's data.

Here are three of the most well-known indicators:

1. Spent Output Profit Ratio (SOPR):

- **What it is:** SOPR is a ratio that indicates whether, on average, the coins being sold on a given day are being sold at a profit or a loss.
- **How to read it:** A SOPR value greater than 1 suggests that holders are, on average, selling at a profit (taking profits). A value less than 1 suggests holders are selling at a loss (panic selling). A SOPR value of exactly 1 often acts as support or resistance, as it's the market's break-even point.

1. Market Value to Realized Value (MVRV) Ratio:

- **What it is:** MVRV is a ratio that compares the asset's current total market cap (Market Value) to the aggregated cost basis at which all coins were last moved (Realized Value). In simple terms, it measures the total unrealized profit held by all investors.
- **How to read it:** A high MVRV ratio (e.g., above 3.0 for Bitcoin) signals that there are large unrealized profits in the system, which can indicate a market top is near. A low MVRV ratio (e.g., below 1.0) signals that the market, on average, is holding at a loss, which can indicate a market bottom.

1. Network Value to Transactions (NVT) Ratio:

- **What it is:** The NVT ratio is often described as the crypto equivalent of the Price-to-Earnings (P/E) ratio for a stock. It compares the network's value (market cap) to the value of the transactions it is processing.
- **How to read it:** A high NVT ratio can suggest that the

network's valuation is becoming "frothy" and is outpacing its actual transactional use. A low NVT ratio suggests the valuation is well-supported by on-chain economic activity.

Case Study: MVRV and Bitcoin's Market Tops

The MVRV ratio has been an uncannily accurate indicator of Bitcoin's major market cycle tops and bottoms.

- At the peak of the 2013, 2017, and 2021 bull markets, the MVRV ratio reached extreme high levels. This indicated that the average holder had massive, unrealized profits, creating a huge potential overhang of sell-side pressure. These MVRV peaks coincided almost perfectly with the final price peaks of the market cycle.
- Conversely, during the darkest days of the 2015, 2018, and 2022 bear markets, the MVRV ratio dropped below 1.0. This signalled that the average holder was now "underwater" (holding their coins at an unrealized loss). Historically, this has marked the periods of maximum financial opportunity and the best times for long-term accumulation.

This shows how a macro on-chain indicator can provide powerful, data-driven context for understanding market cycles.

Practical Application: Exploring Live On-Chain Charts

Many of these advanced indicators are available to view for free on specialized charting websites.

- **Try This How-To:**

1. Go to a free on-chain charting site like lookintobitcoin.com.
2. Find the chart for the "MVRV Z-Score." This is a popular and easy-to-read version of the MVRV ratio that uses standard deviations to identify the extremes.
3. Look at the historical chart. You can visually see how the indicator has moved into the red "overvalued" zone near major market tops and the green "undervalued" zone near major market bottoms.

Exploring this chart is one of the best ways to get a feel for the cyclical nature of the crypto markets through a quantitative lens.

Key Takeaways

- SOPR provides insight into holder profitability and sentiment, showing whether the market is taking profits or panic-selling at a loss.
- MVRV helps identify potential market tops and bottoms by measuring the total unrealized profit in the system.
- NVT Signal can be used to assess whether a blockchain's valuation is justified by its usage, acting like a P/E ratio for the network.

12

Module 1 Recap

You have now completed the first module of the Advanced Level, graduating from standard analysis to sophisticated, crypto-native techniques.

- You've learned how to leverage the blockchain's transparency to track "smart money" and understand the "invisible tax" of MEV.
- You can now perform advanced tokenomic analysis, focusing on crucial concepts like value accrual, vesting schedules, and token sinks.
- You understand advanced trading and income-generating strategies, from active liquidity provisioning and delta-neutral farming to the use of crypto options and structured products.
- Finally, you have been introduced to the world of quantitative on-chain indicators, the tools used to take the vital signs of the market itself.

You are now equipped with the analytical framework of a professional, ready to dive even deeper into the technology and protocols that define Web3.

Module 2: Web3 & Protocol Deep Dives

Module Introduction: You've learned how to analyse protocols from the outside. Now, we dive into the core architectural debates and technologies that are shaping the future of Web3. This module will take you deeper into the cryptographic magic of Zero-Knowledge Proofs, the competing philosophies of blockchain design, and the emerging technologies that are enabling a more decentralized, private, and user-owned internet. This is where you learn to think like a protocol designer.

Lesson 01 - SNARKs vs. STARKs

An Introduction to Cryptographic Magic

Imagine being able to prove that you know a secret, without revealing the secret itself. This is the essence of Zero-Knowledge Proofs (ZKPs), a form of cryptographic magic that is revolutionizing blockchain technology. ZKPs are the key to unlocking both scalability and privacy in Web3. This lesson will introduce you to this powerful concept and the two leading technologies that make it a reality: zk-SNARKs and zk-STARKs.

The Core Explanation: Proving Without Revealing

A Zero-Knowledge Proof is a cryptographic method where one party (the 'prover') can prove to another party (the 'verifier') that a given statement is true, without conveying any information apart from the fact that the statement is true. In crypto, this has two primary applications:

1. **Scalability:** A ZK-Rollup can execute thousands of transactions off-chain and then generate a single, small proof that says, "I have correctly processed 10,000 transactions, and the final state is X." The Ethereum mainnet only needs to verify this single proof, rather than re-executing all 10,000 transactions.
2. **Privacy:** A user can prove they have sufficient funds to make a payment without revealing their total balance or transaction history.

There are two main types of ZKPs, each with its own trade-offs:

- zk-SNARKs (Succinct Non-Interactive Argument of Knowledge):
- **Pros:** They produce very small proof sizes ("succinct") and have very fast verification times, making them highly efficient on-chain.
- **Cons:** They require a "trusted setup." This is a cryptographic ceremony that must be performed when the protocol is created to generate a secret key. If the data used in this ceremony is not destroyed, it could be used to create fake, valid-looking proofs.
- zk-STARKs (Scalable Transparent Argument of Knowledge):

- **Pros:** They are "transparent," meaning they require no trusted setup. They also have the advantage of being quantum-resistant, making them more future-proof.
- **Cons:** Their proof sizes are significantly larger than SNARKs, which makes them more expensive to verify on-chain.

Case Study: The Privacy Coin Zcash

Zcash (ZEC) was one of the first and most prominent projects to implement zk-SNARKs for on-chain privacy. It allows users to choose between two types of transactions: transparent and "shielded."

- A transparent transaction works just like Bitcoin, with the sender, receiver, and amount visible on the public blockchain.
- A shielded transaction uses a zk-SNARK. The transaction is still recorded on the blockchain, but the sender, receiver, and amount are all encrypted. The attached zk-SNARK proves to the network that the transaction is valid (the sender owned the funds, no new coins were created out of thin air) without revealing any of the confidential details.

Zcash is a real-world, long-running application of Zero-Knowledge Proofs being used to provide powerful privacy guarantees.

Practical Application: The "Where's Wally?" Analogy

This analogy helps to grasp the core concept of a ZKP.

- **Try This How-To:**

1. Imagine a giant "Where's Wally?" picture. You want to prove to your friend that you have found Wally, but you don't want to show them where Wally is.
2. You could take a huge piece of cardboard, cut a small Wally-sized hole in it, and place it over the picture so that only Wally is visible through the hole.

You can then show this to your friend. They can see Wally with their own eyes and are convinced that you know where he is. However, you have given them zero knowledge about his location relative to the rest of the picture.

The cardboard with the hole is the "proof." It proves the statement is true ("I have found Wally") without revealing the secret information (his location).

Key Takeaways

- ZK-proofs allow for verification of information without revealing the information itself.
- zk-SNARKs are small and fast but rely on a trusted setup ceremony.
- zk-STARKs are larger and slower but are transparent and quantum-resistant.

Bridge to the Next Lesson

SNARKs and STARKs are the underlying cryptographic proofs that power ZK-Rollups. But as we learned, ZK-Rollups are just one of the two major scaling paradigms. In our next lesson, we will compare them directly with their main competitor: Optimistic Rollups.

Lesson 02 - Optimistic Rollups vs. ZK-Rollups

An Introduction to the Great Scaling Debate

In the Intermediate level, you learned that "rollups" are the primary Layer 2 solution for scaling Ethereum. However, the rollup ecosystem is divided into two competing camps with fundamentally different security models. On one side are Optimistic Rollups, which assume transactions are honest unless proven otherwise. On the other are ZK-Rollups, which demand mathematical proof of honesty upfront. This lesson will dive into this great scaling debate, exploring the trade-offs between these two dominant paradigms.

The Core Explanation: Fraud Proofs vs. Validity Proofs

These are the two dominant Layer 2 scaling paradigms, and their core difference lies in how they prove the validity of their off-chain transactions to the Ethereum mainnet.

1. Optimistic Rollups (e.g., Arbitrum, Optimism):

- **Security Model:** "Innocent Until Proven Guilty"
- **How they work:** They 'optimistically' post batches of transactions to the L1, assuming they are valid without providing any upfront proof. This makes them relatively simple and EVM-compatible.
- **The Catch:** To ensure security, there is a 7-day 'challenge period'. During this window, anyone can submit a 'fraud proof' to the L1 if they spot an invalid transaction. If the proof is successful, the fraudulent transaction is reverted, and the block producer is penalized. Their security is based on economic incentives and game theory.

1. ZK-Rollups (e.g., zkSync, StarkNet):

- **Security Model:** "Guilty Until Proven Innocent with Mathematical Proof"
- **How they work:** Instead of assuming validity, they generate a cryptographic 'validity proof' (a SNARK or STARK) for each batch of transactions.
- **The Advantage:** This proof mathematically guarantees the validity of every transaction in the batch. The L1 smart contract only needs to verify this single proof. This means there is no long challenge period, and withdrawals can be processed much faster. Their security is based on cryptographic certainty.

The key tradeoff is between the economic security of Optimistic Rollups and the cryptographic security of ZK-Rollups. ZK-Rollups are generally considered the long-term scaling solution, but the technology is more complex and computationally intensive.

Case Study: The 7-Day Withdrawal Period

The most tangible difference for a user between these two systems is the time it takes to withdraw funds back to the Ethereum mainnet.

- A user on an Optimistic Rollup like Arbitrum who wants to move their ETH back to the L1 using the native bridge must wait for the 7-day challenge period to expire. This is a necessary security measure, but it is a significant user experience drawback, as their capital is locked and illiquid for a full week.
- A user on a ZK-Rollup like zkSync can bridge their assets

back to the L1 as soon as their transaction is included in a batch and its validity proof is posted and verified on-chain, which typically takes only minutes to an hour.

This stark difference in withdrawal times highlights the practical trade-offs between the two systems. (Note: Third-party bridges often provide faster withdrawals for Optimistic Rollups, but they do so by introducing their own liquidity and trust assumptions).

Practical Application: Identifying Rollup Types

You can easily see the current state of market adoption for these two competing technologies.

- **Try This How-To:**

1. Go to the analytics website L2BEAT.com.
2. The homepage lists the top Layer 2 networks. Each one is clearly categorized under the "Type" column as either an "Optimistic Rollup" or a "ZK Rollup."
3. Compare the Total Value Locked (TVL) and the recent transaction volume for the top protocol from each category (e.g., Arbitrum vs. zkSync).

This shows you the current state of market adoption and dominance for these two competing scaling technologies.

Key Takeaways

- Optimistic Rollups use a fraud-proof system with a long withdrawal period, assuming transactions are valid unless challenged.

- ZK-Rollups use a validity-proof system, allowing for near-instant withdrawals by providing mathematical proof of correctness.
- The key tradeoff is between the economic security of Optimistic Rollups and the cryptographic security of ZK-Rollups.

Bridge to the Next Lesson

This debate between rollup types is part of a larger and even more fundamental architectural debate in the blockchain space. Should a blockchain try to do everything in one highly integrated package, or should it be broken down into specialized, interchangeable parts? In our next lesson, we will explore the competing design philosophies of Modular vs. Monolithic blockchains.

Lesson 03 - Modular vs. Monolithic Blockchains

An Introduction to a New Architectural Paradigm

"Should a blockchain try to do everything itself, or should it be a specialist?" This is the core question behind the modular vs. monolithic debate, one of the most important architectural trends shaping the future of the blockchain industry. Just as the industrial revolution moved from all-in-one artisans to specialized assembly lines, some believe blockchains must also specialize to achieve global scale. This lesson will break down these two competing design philosophies.

The Core Explanation: All-in-One vs. a la Carte

A blockchain has to perform three core functions:

- **Execution:** Running smart contracts and processing transactions.
- **Settlement:** Finalizing transactions and resolving disputes (like fraud proofs).
- **Data Availability:** Ensuring that the data for all transactions is published and available for anyone to verify.

The two design philosophies differ on how these functions should be handled:

1. The 'Monolithic' Design Philosophy:

- **What it is:** A monolithic blockchain, like Solana, aims to have a single, highly-optimized Layer 1 that handles all three core functions: Execution, Settlement, and Data Availability.
- **The Goal:** To achieve extremely high performance and a simple developer experience within a single, tightly integrated package. The entire system is optimized to work together as one unit.

1. The 'Modular' Thesis:

- **What it is:** The modular thesis, which is best exemplified by Ethereum's rollup-centric roadmap, argues that these functions should be separated into specialized, interchangeable layers for better scalability and flexibility.
- **The Goal:** To create a "modular stack" where each component is the best in its class. For example:

- A rollup like Arbitrum can act as the specialized Execution Layer.
- Ethereum can act as the decentralized and secure Settlement Layer.
- And a new, specialized chain like Celestia can be used as a cheap and efficient Data Availability Layer.

Case Study: The Ethereum Rollup-Centric Roadmap

Ethereum has made a conscious and strategic bet on a modular future. Instead of trying to make the base Layer 1 itself incredibly fast for transaction execution (which could compromise decentralization), Ethereum is optimizing its base layer to be the most secure and decentralized Settlement and Data Availability layer in the world.

Upgrades like "The Merge" (moving to PoS) and the upcoming "Danksharding" are all designed to make the main chain cheaper and more efficient at storing the data from Layer 2 rollups. The vision is for a universe of thousands of specialized rollups (for gaming, DeFi, social media, etc.) to handle execution, all while inheriting the ultimate security and finality of the Ethereum base layer. This is a strategic bet that a modular, specialized assembly line will ultimately produce more scalability than a single, all-in-one monolithic design.

Practical Application: The Computer Building Analogy

You can think about this debate in terms of building a computer.

- **Try This How-To:**

1. The monolithic approach is like buying an all-in-one

iMac from Apple. It is a beautiful, highly optimized, and tightly integrated system that works perfectly out of the box. However, it is a closed system, and it is very difficult to upgrade or customize individual components.

2. The modular approach is like building your own custom PC. You choose the best specialized components from different manufacturers—the best CPU from Intel, the best graphics card from Nvidia, the best storage from Samsung. By combining these best-in-class components, you can create a system that is potentially more powerful, flexible, and customizable than the all-in-one.

This analogy helps to clarify the fundamental trade-offs between the two design philosophies.

Key Takeaways

- Monolithic chains like Solana integrate all core functions on one layer for high performance.
- Modular chains separate Execution, Settlement, and Data Availability into specialized layers.
- The modular thesis suggests that specialization will lead to more scalable and customizable blockchains, with Ethereum's rollup-centric roadmap being the prime example.

Bridge to the Next Lesson

The modular thesis allows for a universe of specialized execution layers built on a shared settlement layer. But what if a single, large application needs its own, completely sovereign blockchain, with full control over its own rules and security? In our next lesson, we will explore the "App-Chain Thesis."

Lesson 04 - The App-Chain Thesis

An Introduction to Sovereign Applications

Why should a blockbuster application, with millions of users and transactions, must share its resources and compete for space on a congested, general-purpose blockchain? The App-Chain Thesis is a powerful idea that argues it shouldn't. It is the belief that for Web3 to reach a global scale, the largest and most successful decentralized applications will eventually need to become their own sovereign blockchains, fully customized for their specific purpose.

The Core Explanation: From dApp to App-Chain

The App-Chain (or App-Specific Blockchain) Thesis posits that large-scale dApps will eventually need their own sovereign blockchains rather than competing for blockspace on a shared L1 or L2. Frameworks like the Cosmos SDK and Avalanche Subnets are specifically designed to make it easier for developers to build these custom chains.

The primary benefits of an app-chain are:

1. **Customization and Performance:** An app-chain allows a dApp to customize its entire technology stack. The developers can choose their own consensus mechanism, their own virtual machine, and even design their own

fee structure, optimizing every component for their specific use case (e.g., a high-frequency trading app could optimize for speed, while a social media app could optimize for storage).

2. **No More "Noisy Neighbours":** On a shared blockchain, a popular NFT mint or a new game can cause gas fees to skyrocket for every other application on the network. An app-chain avoids this problem entirely, as the application has its own dedicated blockspace.
3. **Value Capture:** The dApp can capture all the economic value it generates. This includes transaction fees and any MEV, which can be redirected back to the app's own token holders and community treasury, rather than being paid out to the validators of the underlying Layer 1.

Case Study: The dYdX Chain

dYdX, one of the largest decentralized perpetuals exchanges in the world, provides a perfect case study for the app-chain thesis.

- dYdX originally launched as a Layer 2 application on Ethereum. It was successful, but the team found that to achieve the ultra-high performance and throughput needed to truly compete with centralized exchanges, they were limited by the constraints of the shared Ethereum environment.
- In 2022, they made the bold decision to migrate away from Ethereum and build their own sovereign blockchain, the dYdX Chain, using the Cosmos SDK.
- This move allowed them to build a fully customized, in-

memory order book that could handle a much higher volume of transactions than was possible on Ethereum. It was a major validation of the app-chain thesis, demonstrating that for certain high-performance applications, becoming a sovereign chain is the optimal long-term strategy.

Practical Application: Exploring the Cosmos

The Cosmos ecosystem is the living embodiment of the app-chain thesis.

- **Try This How-To:**

1. Go to a Cosmos ecosystem explorer website, like mapofzones.com.
2. You will see a stunning visual representation of dozens of interconnected but independent blockchains.
3. Many of these are app-chains—blockchains dedicated to a single purpose. For example, Osmosis is an app-chain DEX, Akash is an app-chain for decentralized cloud computing, and Celestia is an app-chain for data availability.

This visual exploration shows the app-chain thesis in action: a universe of sovereign, specialized blockchains all interconnected.

Key Takeaways

- An app-chain is a blockchain dedicated to a single application.
- This allows for deep customization and avoids competi-

tion for blockspace with "noisy neighbors."

- The Cosmos ecosystem is a prime example of the app-chain thesis in action, enabled by its software development kit (SDK).

Bridge to the Next Lesson

App-chains give applications sovereignty over their digital world. But what about giving individuals sovereignty over their digital *identity*? In our next lesson, we will explore the critically important and emerging concept of Decentralized Identity.

Lesson 05 - Decentralized Identity and Verifiable Credentials

An Introduction to Owning Your "You"

Who are you online? Right now, your digital identity is a fragmented collection of profiles and accounts controlled by giant corporations (Google, Apple, Facebook) and governments. You don't own your identity; you are merely renting it from these centralized providers. Decentralized Identity (DID) is a powerful new framework that aims to flip this model on its head, creating a self-sovereign identity for the internet that you, and only you, truly own and control.

The Core Explanation: Your Universal, Self-Owned ID

The Decentralized Identity framework is designed to give you control over your personal data. It consists of two core components:

1. **Decentralized Identifiers (DIDs):**

- A DID is a globally unique ID that you create, own, and control, not one that is issued to you by a company or government.
- It is stored on a blockchain or other distributed ledger, and it acts as your root of trust, like your own self-generated passport number for the internet. You can use it to sign in to services and prove that you are you, without relying on a third party like Google.

1. **Verifiable Credentials (VCs):**

- A VC is a digital, tamper-proof attestation or claim about you, which has been cryptographically signed by an issuer.
- The Flow: An issuer (like a university) can give you a VC that represents your diploma. You store this VC in your personal "identity wallet." You can then present this VC to a verifier (like a potential employer) to prove you have a degree. The verifier can cryptographically check the signature and know the credential is valid, without ever needing to contact the university directly.

This model gives you granular control over who you share your personal information with and prevents a single company from controlling your digital life.

Case Study: Applying for a Loan in a Web3 World
Imagine you want to apply for a loan in a DeFi protocol.

- **The Old Way (Web2):** You would have to manually

provide your bank statements, credit score report, employment letters, and other sensitive personal documents directly to the lender, giving them full access to all your private data.

- **The New Way (Web3 with DIDs/VCs):** You would have Verifiable Credentials in your identity wallet for each of these claims:
- A VC from your bank attesting to your account balance.
- A VC from a credit agency attesting to your credit score.
- A VC from your employer attesting to your income. You could then use Zero-Knowledge Proofs to present only the specific proofs the lender's smart contract needs (e.g., "Proof that credit score is > 700," "Proof that income is > $50k/year") without revealing the actual underlying data. You prove you are qualified without exposing all your personal information.

Practical Application: Seeing the Standards Emerge

While the DID ecosystem is still in its early stages, it is being built on serious, open standards.

- **Try This How-To:**

1. Do a web search for the "W3C DID Specification."
2. The World Wide Web Consortium (W3C) is the main international standards organization for the Internet, responsible for standards like HTML and CSS.
3. You will find that they have a dedicated working group that is formalizing the technical standards for DIDs and VCs.

This shows that Decentralized Identity is not just a niche crypto concept, but a serious, globally-coordinated effort to build a new, more private and user-centric identity layer for the entire internet.

Key Takeaways

- DIDs are user-owned identifiers that are not reliant on a central authority.
- Verifiable Credentials are tamper-proof, digital attestations of claims (like a degree or license).
- This model gives users control over who they share their personal information with, enhancing privacy and security.

Bridge to the Next Lesson

Decentralized Identity gives you control over your personal *data*. But where should that data, and all the data for the entire Web3 ecosystem, be *stored*? In our next lesson, we will explore the crucial infrastructure of decentralized storage.

Lesson 06 - Decentralized Storage

An Introduction to Uncensorable Data

You own an NFT, but where is the actual image for that NFT stored? You use a dApp, but where is the website's front-end code hosted? In many cases today, the answer is a centralized server owned by a company like Amazon or Google. This creates a critical vulnerability: if that server goes down, your NFT becomes a dead link and your dApp is unusable. Decentralized storage is the solution—a new paradigm for storing data that is censorship-resistant, resilient, and not reliant on any single company.

The Core Explanation: Content vs. Location

Decentralized storage networks provide a censorship-resistant and resilient alternative to centralized cloud providers like Amazon Web Services (AWS). They achieve this by distributing data across a global network of independent node operators.

There are two main models to understand:

1. InterPlanetary File System (IPFS):

- **What it is:** IPFS is a peer-to-peer network for storing and sharing data in a distributed file system.
- **Key Innovation:** Data on IPFS is content-addressed, not location-addressed. When you want to access a file on the traditional web, you type in its location (e.g., http://website.com/image.jpg). On IPFS, you request a file by its unique hash, known as a Content Identifier (CID). The network then finds that content from whichever nodes are holding it. This makes the data resilient, as it can be stored on many computers at once.

1. Arweave:

- **What it is:** Arweave offers a different and more ambitious model: permanent, immutable storage.
- **Key Innovation:** Users pay a one-time, upfront fee to store data forever. This is made possible by a crypto-

economic model where the fees are placed into an endowment. The interest from this endowment is used to pay a network of miners to perpetually store the data. It is designed for data that needs to be preserved immutably for generations.

Case Study: Securing NFT Metadata

The metadata for a "blue-chip" NFT project like the Bored Ape Yacht Club or CryptoPunks is incredibly valuable. This metadata includes the image itself and the list of traits that determine its rarity.

- If that metadata is stored on a link to a company's private server (http://...), it has a single point of failure. If that company goes out of business or the server goes down, the NFT effectively becomes a broken link, and its value could be destroyed.
- To solve this, major NFT projects have moved to secure their metadata on permanent, decentralized storage networks. Many projects now explicitly state that their art is "Stored on Arweave" or "Stored on IPFS." This ensures that the art and traits for the NFT will remain online, accessible, and verifiable forever, completely independent of the company that originally created the project. It is a promise of true permanence for digital assets.

Practical Application: Checking an NFT's Storage

You can often check for yourself where an NFT's data is stored.

- **Try This How-To:**

1. Go to an NFT marketplace like OpenSea.
2. Navigate to the page for a major NFT collection (e.g., Bored Ape Yacht Club).
3. Click on a specific NFT and scroll down to the "Details" section.
4. You will often see a link for the "Metadata." Click on it.

Look at the URL that opens in your browser. Does it start with ipfs:// or link to a domain like arweave.net? If so, you are looking at an NFT whose data is being secured on a decentralized storage network. If it links to a normal website, its data is centrally stored.

Key Takeaways

- Decentralized storage is critical for ensuring the metadata of NFTs and the front-ends of dApps remain permanently online.
- IPFS is a distributed file system for content-addressed data storage.
- Arweave is designed for permanent data storage, paid with a single upfront fee.

Bridge to the Next Lesson

Decentralized storage is a crucial part of the Web3 technology stack. But just as important as the technology are the human systems that govern these new protocols. In our next lesson, we will look at advanced DAO structures and the key debates shaping the future of decentralized governance.

Lesson 07 - Advanced DAO Structures and Governance Debates

An Introduction to the Challenges of Digital Democracy

The simple "one token, one vote" model that launched the DAO revolution was powerful, but it's not perfect. As DAOs have grown into complex organizations managing billions of dollars, they've encountered real-world governance challenges like voter apathy (most token holders don't vote) and plutocracy (whales with the most tokens have all the power). This lesson explores the advanced and experimental structures that DAOs are now implementing to become more efficient, resilient, and truly decentralized.

The Core Explanation: Evolving Beyond Simple Voting

Simple token voting often fails at scale. To solve this, advanced DAOs are experimenting with new governance structures to improve efficiency and broaden participation.

The key innovations include:

1. **Pods and Sub-DAOs:** A large, monolithic DAO can be slow and bureaucratic. To combat this, many are adopting a model of 'Sub-DAOs' or 'Pods.' These are specialized working groups within the larger DAO that are given their own autonomous budgets and mandates. For example, a "Marketing Sub-DAO" or a "Grants Pod" can make its own decisions and spend its own budget without requiring a full vote from the entire organization for every small decision. This dramatically increases the DAO's efficiency.
2. **Delegation:** To combat voter apathy, many of the largest DAOs have implemented delegation systems. In this

model, token holders who don't have the time or expertise to vote on every proposal can delegate their voting power to an active, informed representative they trust. These delegates effectively become "protocol politicians" who are expected to stay informed and vote on behalf of their constituents. This creates a form of liquid democracy.

3. **Reputation-Based Governance:** There is a major ongoing debate about moving beyond pure token-based voting. Some DAOs are experimenting with non-transferable, reputation-based tokens or NFTs that are granted based on contributions and expertise, not just wealth. The goal is to give more power to the most dedicated community members.

Case Study: The Optimism Collective's Two Houses

Optimism, a major Ethereum Layer 2, has one of the most innovative governance models in the space. Recognizing the limitations of pure token voting, they created a bicameral (two-house) governance system called The Optimism Collective.

- **The Token House:** This is made up of OP token holders. They vote on day-to-day governance matters, protocol upgrades, and the allocation of ecosystem incentives. This represents the "plutocratic" side of governance, where capital has a say.
- **The Citizens' House:** This is made up of individuals who have been granted a non-transferable, identity-based "Citizenship" NFT based on their contributions to the community. This house is responsible for voting on the

allocation of public goods funding from the protocol's revenue. This represents the "democratic" side of governance, based on one person, one vote.

This two-house system is a real-world experiment in balancing the interests of capital (token holders) with the interests of the community (active contributors), creating a more robust and equitable governance structure.

Practical Application: Observing Protocol Politicians

You can see the system of delegation in action on governance websites.

- **Try This How-To:**

1. Go to a governance portal for a major DAO that uses delegation, such as the Optimism or Aave governance websites.
2. Find the section for "Delegates."
3. You will see a leaderboard of the top delegates, showing how much voting power has been entrusted to them by other token holders.
4. Many delegates will have a profile where they introduce themselves, outline their voting philosophy, and provide a history of their past votes.

This is like observing the candidates and representatives in a new digital political system, where transparency is paramount.

Key Takeaways

- Simple token voting can lead to low participation (voter apathy) and control by wealthy holders (plutocracy).
- Sub-DAOs and delegate systems are being implemented to improve governance efficiency and combat voter apathy.
- The field of DAO governance is highly experimental and constantly evolving as organizations try to find the right balance between decentralization and effectiveness.

Bridge to the Next Lesson

DAO governance is evolving to better manage digital organizations. A key area that many of these DAOs are focused on is the multi-billion-dollar world of on-chain gaming. In our next lesson, we will explore the evolution of GameFi and its economic models.

Lesson 08 - GameFi and Play-to-Earn Economic Models

An Introduction to the Player-Owned Economy

What if the time you spent playing a video game, and the rare items you earned, had real, tangible value that you truly owned? This is the revolutionary promise of GameFi (Game Finance). The initial "Play-to-Earn" (P2E) model took the world by storm, but its flawed economics revealed important lessons. This lesson explores the evolution of GameFi, from the unsustainable hype of P2E to the more mature and promising "Play-and-Own" models of the future.

The Core Explanation: From P2E to Play-and-Own

GameFi is the combination of gaming with decentralized

finance. It uses blockchain technology and NFTs to create games where players have true ownership of their in-game assets and can participate in a real, open economy.

The evolution of GameFi economic models can be broken down into two stages:

1. Play-to-Earn (P2E):

- **The Model:** This was the first popular model, pioneered by games like Axie Infinity. The core loop was that players could earn fungible tokens with real-world value simply by playing the game.
- **The Flaw:** These early economies were often highly inflationary and functioned like a leaky bucket. They relied on a constant influx of new players (and their capital) to pay for the earnings of the existing players. When new player growth stalled, there was more selling pressure on the reward token than buying pressure, and the value of the token would inevitably crash. They were often more "earn" than "play."

1. Play-and-Earn / Play-to-Own:

- **The Model:** The industry is now evolving towards more sustainable models. The focus is on creating genuinely fun and engaging games first, with blockchain elements serving to *enhance* the experience.
- **The Difference:** The core of these new models is true ownership of in-game assets (as NFTs). The goal is not just to earn a daily wage, but to own your unique items, characters, and cosmetics, which you can then freely

trade on an open market. The economic design focuses on creating sustainable, player-driven economies that rely on in-game spending and trade, rather than just inflationary rewards.

Case Study: The Rise and Fall of Axie Infinity's Economy

During its peak in 2021, Axie Infinity was a global phenomenon. It was a digital pet battling game where players could earn a token called Smooth Love Potion (SLP). For a time, players in developing nations like the Philippines were able to earn significantly more money playing the game than from their traditional jobs, creating a powerful "scholarship" economy.

However, the game's P2E economy was highly inflationary. Millions of new SLP were being created every day by players, but there were not enough "sinks" (ways to spend SLP within the game) to absorb this supply. The economy became completely reliant on new players buying the "Axie" NFTs needed to start playing. When the bear market hit and new player growth stopped, the price of SLP collapsed by over 99%, demonstrating the inherent unsustainability of the early P2E model.

Practical Application: The Traditional Gaming Economy

The "Play-to-Own" model is an evolution of a multi-billion-dollar economy that already exists in traditional gaming.

- Try This How-To:

1. Look at the Steam Community Market for a major traditional game like *Counter-Strike* or *Dota 2*.

2. You will see a vibrant, player-driven economy for in-game cosmetic items ("skins"), with some rare items selling for thousands of dollars.
3. However, players do not truly own these items. They exist within a closed ecosystem, and players can never "cash out" their items for real money through official channels.

The "Play-to-Own" model of Web3 gaming aims to take this existing player behavior and give them true, open-market property rights for their in-game assets.

Key Takeaways

- Early Play-to-Earn (P2E) models often suffered from unsustainable, inflationary token designs that relied on new player growth.
- The industry is shifting focus to gameplay quality and true asset ownership (Play-and-Own).
- Sustainable GameFi economies need "token sinks" and value generated from player enjoyment and trade, not just inflationary rewards.

Bridge to the Next Lesson

GameFi is about building economies and communities within games. But what if you could take the same principles of user ownership and apply them to the social layer of the entire internet? In our next lesson, we will explore the ambitious world of Decentralized Social platforms.

Lesson 09 - Decentralized Social Platforms

An Introduction to Owning Your Social Graph

Your social media profile—your content, your connections, your followers—is one of your most valuable digital assets, yet you don't own it. It is locked inside the walled gardens of companies like Meta and X. Decentralized Social (DeSo) is a movement to solve the core problems of Web2 social media, such as data monopolization and censorship, by building a new social layer for the internet where you are in complete control of your online identity.

The Core Explanation: A Portable, User-Owned Identity

Decentralized Social (DeSo) aims to give users true ownership of their "social graph" (their identity, content, and connections). Instead of each social media app being its own closed silo, DeSo protocols create a shared, open, and permissionless social layer that any application can plug into.

Leading protocols like Farcaster and Lens Protocol are building this new paradigm. Here's how it works:

1. **You Own Your Identity:** Your core profile and identity are tied to your crypto wallet, not to an application. You control it.
2. **You Own Your Content:** Every post you make is a piece of data that you own and can, in some cases, even be an NFT.
3. **You Own Your Connections:** Your list of followers and friends (your social graph) is portable.

This creates an open ecosystem. Developers can build new social media apps (clients) without having to bootstrap a user base from scratch; they can simply plug into the existing social graph. Users, in turn, can move freely between these different apps without losing their audience or their identity. If you get banned from one app, your identity and followers remain intact, and you can simply start using another one.

Case Study: The Farcaster Ecosystem

Farcaster is a leading decentralized social protocol. It clearly demonstrates the separation between the protocol and the applications built on top of it.

- **The Protocol:** Farcaster itself is the underlying, decentralized network that stores user identities and the links between them.
- **The Clients:** There are dozens of different applications, or "clients," that you can use to interact with the Farcaster protocol. Warpcast is the most popular, and it looks and feels much like Twitter. However, there are other clients that look like Reddit, or are designed for specific communities.

A user can create an identity on Farcaster and then use Warpcast one day and a different client the next. Their posts, followers, and profile will be consistent across all of them because all these apps are reading from the same, user-owned, open social layer. This is a powerful demonstration of a portable identity that is free from the control of a single application.

Practical Application: Exploring a DeSo Ecosystem

You can see the variety of applications being built on these open social graphs.

- **Try This How-To:**

1. Go to the website for Lens Protocol or Farcaster.
2. Find their "Ecosystem" or "Apps" page.
3. You will see a gallery of dozens of different applications—social feeds, video apps, publishing platforms, link-in-bio tools—all built on top of the same, shared social graph.

This visually demonstrates the concept of a portable identity layer, where one core profile can be used across many different front-end experiences, fostering a more open, competitive, and censorship-resistant social media landscape.

Key Takeaways

- DeSo aims to give users ownership of their social graph (identity, content, connections).
- Protocols like Farcaster and Lens create a shared social layer that different applications can plug into.
- This creates a more open, competitive, and censorship-resistant social media landscape, where users can move freely without being locked into a single platform.

Bridge to the Next Lesson

DeSo aims to bring transparency and user ownership to our social lives. But what if you want the opposite—true privacy for your financial life? While most blockchains are public, some are designed specifically for confidentiality. In our final lesson of this module, we will explore the world of privacy coins and technologies.

Lesson 10 - Privacy Coins and Technologies

An Introduction to Financial Confidentiality

Blockchains like Bitcoin and Ethereum are radically transparent. Every transaction is a public record for the world to see. While this is great for auditing, it is not ideal for financial privacy. Imagine if your every purchase, your salary, and your total net worth were visible to your neighbors, your employer, and your competitors. Privacy coins are a specialized category of cryptocurrencies designed to solve this problem, using advanced cryptography to provide transaction confidentiality on a public blockchain.

The Core Explanation: Obfuscation vs. Zero-Knowledge

While most blockchains are pseudonymous (your identity is a string of characters, not your real name), they are not anonymous. On-chain analysis can often link your real-world identity to your wallet. Privacy coins are designed to be truly anonymous by obscuring the transaction details.

There are two main technological approaches to achieving on-chain privacy:

1. Obfuscation (used by Monero - XMR):

- Monero's privacy is mandatory for all transactions. It achieves this by mixing user transactions together using a combination of clever cryptographic techniques:
- **Ring Signatures:** These group a sender's transaction with many other "decoy" transactions, making it im-

possible for an outside observer to know who the true sender was.

- **Stealth Addresses:** These are unique, one-time public addresses that are created for every single transaction, so you cannot link multiple payments to the same recipient.
- **RingCT (Confidential Transactions):** This technique encrypts the amount of the transaction.

1. Zero-Knowledge Proofs (used by Zcash - ZEC):

- Zcash offers optional privacy through "shielded" transactions. It uses the zk-SNARKs we learned about in a previous lesson.
- When a user makes a shielded transaction, the zk-SNARK proves to the network that the transaction is valid (the sender had the funds, the numbers add up correctly) without revealing any of the confidential details—the sender's address, the receiver's address, or the transaction amount are all encrypted.

Case Study: The Need for Commercial Privacy

Imagine a large company that wants to start using a blockchain to pay its suppliers.

- If they use Ethereum, all of their financial activity would be public. Their competitors could see exactly who their suppliers are, how much they are paying them, and how often. This is highly sensitive commercial information that they would never want to make public.
- By using a privacy-preserving blockchain or technology, the company could pay its suppliers on-chain while

keeping all of the transaction details confidential. This is a crucial requirement for any serious enterprise adoption of blockchain technology. The need for financial privacy is not just for individuals; it is a fundamental requirement of business.

Practical Application: Comparing Block Explorers

You can visually see the difference between a transparent and a private blockchain by looking at their block explorers.

- **Try This How-To:**

1. First, go to Etherscan, the block explorer for the transparent Ethereum blockchain. Look at the latest transactions. You can see the "From" address, the "To" address, and the "Value" for every single one.
2. Now, go to the block explorer for Monero (like xmrchain.net). Look at its list of latest transactions. You will see that the sender, receiver, and amount for *every* transaction are completely obscured.

This stark visual contrast is the best way to understand the difference between a transparent public ledger and a privacy-preserving one.

Key Takeaways

- Privacy coins aim to provide transaction confidentiality on a public blockchain.
- Monero uses obfuscation techniques like Ring Signatures to mix user transactions, making its privacy mandatory.

- Zcash uses zero-knowledge proofs (zk-SNARKs) to provide cryptographic, optional privacy for its "shielded" transactions.

13

Module 2 Recap

You have now completed a deep dive into the core architectural debates and technologies that define Web3.

- You understand the cryptographic magic of Zero-Knowledge Proofs and the trade-offs between SNARKs and STARKs.
- You can explain the great scaling debate between Optimistic and ZK-Rollups, and the even broader architectural debate between Modular and Monolithic blockchains.
- You grasp the strategic importance of the App-Chain Thesis and the emerging technologies that are enabling a more user-owned internet, such as Decentralized Identity, Decentralized Storage, advanced DAO governance models, and Privacy Technologies.

You are now equipped with the advanced technical knowledge to understand not just what protocols do, but how they

are built and why they are designed in a particular way.

Module 3: The Regulatory & Macro Landscape

Module Introduction: A protocol's success is not just determined by its technology or community; it is also profoundly shaped by the outside world. This final module of the Advanced Level will zoom out, exploring the critical external forces that impact the crypto industry. You will learn about the different regulatory approaches being taken around the globe, the powerful influence of macroeconomic trends like interest rates, and the tools used by law enforcement to navigate the transparent world of the blockchain.

Lesson 01 - MiCA in Europe

An Introduction to a Comprehensive Rulebook

For years, the crypto industry has operated in a state of regulatory uncertainty, often described as a "wild west." While some jurisdictions have taken a piecemeal or enforcement-first approach, the European Union has done something revolutionary: it has created a single, comprehensive, and clear rulebook for the entire continent. This landmark regulation is called MiCA (Markets in Crypto-Assets), and it is setting a potential global standard for how to regulate the digital asset industry.

The Core Explanation: Creating a Unified Market

MiCA is the European Union's comprehensive regulatory

framework for crypto. It is a single piece of legislation that creates harmonized rules for crypto-assets across all 27 EU member states.

The primary goals of MiCA are:

- **Consumer Protection:** To ensure that investors are protected from scams and that their assets are held safely.
- **Market Integrity:** To prevent market abuse, insider trading, and manipulation.
- **Legal Certainty:** To provide clear rules of the road for businesses, so they know what is required to operate legally.

MiCA provides a clear legal framework for crypto-asset service providers (CASPs) and issuers, covering everything from the operation of exchanges and wallet providers to the stringent requirements for issuing stablecoins. This holistic approach contrasts sharply with the more fragmented, enforcement-led approach seen in jurisdictions like the United States.

Case Study: The "Passporting" Advantage

Imagine a new crypto exchange, "EuroCoin," wants to offer its services to customers across the entire European Union.

- **Before MiCA:** To operate legally, EuroCoin would have had to navigate the complex and differing licensing requirements of 27 different member states. This would have been an incredibly expensive and time-consuming process.
- **After MiCA:** EuroCoin can now apply for a single MiCA license in any one EU country (e.g., France or Germany).

Once that license is granted, they can "passport" it across the entire EU bloc, giving them legal access to a massive, unified market of over 450 million people.

This creation of a single, unified market is one of the most significant impacts of the MiCA regulation, making the EU an attractive region for crypto businesses to establish themselves.

Practical Application: Observing Corporate Compliance

You can see how seriously established crypto companies are taking this landmark regulation.

- **Try This How-To:**

1. Go to the official blog or news section of a major global crypto exchange like Coinbase, Kraken, or Circle (the issuer of the USDC stablecoin).
2. Use their search function to look for "MiCA."
3. You will likely find detailed articles and press releases explaining how they are preparing for MiCA compliance, applying for licenses in various EU countries, and what the new rules will mean for their European customers.

This shows how MiCA is not just a theoretical document; it is a real-world regulation that is actively shaping the business strategies of the largest players in the industry.

Key Takeaways

- MiCA is the European Union's comprehensive regulatory framework for crypto.

- It provides clear rules for exchanges, wallet providers, and stablecoin issuers, creating legal certainty.
- This approach contrasts with the more fragmented, enforcement-led approach seen in other jurisdictions like the US.

Bridge to the Next Lesson

The EU's comprehensive approach is one model. In the United States, however, the situation is far more complex, with two major agencies battling for control over the crypto industry. In our next lesson, we will explore the critical jurisdictional conflict between the SEC and the CFTC.

Lesson 02 - SEC vs. CFTC

An Introduction to the Battle for Crypto's Crown

Who regulates crypto in the world's largest economy? The answer is complicated and highly contested. The central conflict in U.S. crypto regulation is a battle for jurisdiction between two powerful agencies: the SEC and the CFTC. Their fundamentally different views on what crypto *is* have created a landscape of legal uncertainty that has profoundly shaped the industry in the United States and across the world. This lesson will break down this crucial conflict.

The Core Explanation: Securities vs. Commodities

In the United States, regulatory authority over crypto is contested between two key agencies:

1. The Securities and Exchange Commission (SEC):

- **Mandate:** The SEC's primary mission is to protect investors and regulate the securities markets (e.g., stocks and bonds).
- **View on Crypto:** The SEC, particularly under its current leadership, has taken the broad view that most cryptocurrencies (besides Bitcoin) are securities. They argue that most altcoins are sold as investment contracts where buyers expect to profit from the efforts of a central development team. Therefore, they should be regulated under the same strict disclosure laws as stocks.

1. The Commodity Futures Trading Commission (CFTC):

- **Mandate:** The CFTC's primary mission is to regulate the commodities derivatives markets (e.g., futures and options on assets like oil, wheat, or gold).
- **View on Crypto:** The CFTC has taken the view that major cryptocurrencies like Bitcoin and Ether are commodities. As such, they believe they should have oversight over the spot markets for these assets and exclusive jurisdiction over their derivatives markets.

This jurisdictional conflict creates significant uncertainty. Is an asset a security, a commodity, or something else entirely? The answer determines which agency has power over it and which set of decades-old laws applies to this new technology.

Case Study: The Ripple (XRP) Lawsuit

The SEC's enforcement-led approach was put on full display in December 2020 when it filed a major lawsuit against Ripple Labs. The SEC alleged that Ripple's token, XRP, was an unregistered security and that the company had been illegally selling it to the public for years.

The multi-year legal battle that followed became one of the most closely watched cases in crypto history. The outcome was complex: in July 2023, a federal judge issued a summary judgment with a split decision:

- Sales of XRP directly from Ripple to institutional investors were deemed to be securities offerings.
- Sales of XRP to the public on exchanges were *not* deemed to be securities offerings.

This created a complicated and still-debated legal precedent, but it was a landmark case that directly challenged the SEC's broad assertion that all tokens are securities. It is the prime example of the high-stakes consequences of the security vs. commodity debate in the US.

Practical Application: Observing the Public Stances

You can often see this jurisdictional tension play out in the public statements of the agency leaders.

- Try This How-To:

1. Find the official X (Twitter) accounts for the current chairs of the SEC and the CFTC.
2. Browse their recent posts or transcripts of their public speeches that relate to "crypto" or "digital assets."
3. You will often see them framing the asset class through the lens of their respective agencies. The SEC Chair will typically focus on investor protection and securities law compliance. The CFTC Chair will often talk about market risk and the need for regulation of crypto commodities.

This provides a direct look at their differing public stances and the ongoing battle for regulatory control.

Key Takeaways

- The SEC typically classifies crypto assets as securities, seeking to regulate them under investor protection laws.
- The CFTC typically classifies major crypto assets as commodities, seeking to regulate their markets.
- This lack of clear jurisdiction between the two agencies is a major source of regulatory uncertainty in the U.S.

Bridge to the Next Lesson

While government agencies debate how to regulate decentralized assets, they are also actively exploring how to create their own forms of digital money. In our next lesson, we will explore the global rise of Central Bank Digital Currencies, or CBDCs.

Lesson 03 - CBDCs (Central Bank Digital Currencies)

An Introduction to the State's Response

What if your national currency, like the Australian Dollar, was a purely digital token issued directly by the central bank? This is the concept behind a Central Bank Digital Currency (CBDC). As cryptocurrencies have grown, governments and central banks around the world have accelerated their own research into issuing digital money. A CBDC represents the digitization of the traditional financial system, and its rise could have major implications for the future of both crypto and personal financial privacy.

The Core Explanation: Digitized, Not Decentralized

A Central Bank Digital Currency (CBDC) is a digital form of a country's fiat currency that is a direct liability of the central bank. It is crucial to understand how a CBDC is fundamentally different from a cryptocurrency like Bitcoin:

- **Centralized vs. Decentralized:** A CBDC is 100% centralized and controlled by the government's central bank. Bitcoin is run by a decentralized, global network of participants.
- **Permissioned vs. Permissionless:** A CBDC would be a permissioned system. The central bank would control who can use the network and could potentially reverse transactions or freeze funds. Cryptocurrencies are permissionless; anyone can use them without asking for approval.
- **Trust-Based vs. Trustless:** A CBDC relies on trust in the government. Cryptocurrencies are designed to be trustless, relying on cryptography and consensus.

A CBDC represents the digitization of traditional money, not the creation of a new decentralized asset. The potential implications for the crypto industry are twofold: a CBDC could act as a major competitor to privately issued stablecoins, but it could also introduce the general public to the concept of digital wallets, potentially acting as a gateway to the broader digital asset world.

Case Study: China's Digital Yuan (e-CNY)

China is one of the furthest ahead in the world in developing and piloting a CBDC. The Digital Yuan (e-CNY) has been trialled in dozens of cities and used by hundreds of millions of citizens, allowing them to use a digital wallet on their phone to make payments for everything from public transport to groceries.

While the e-CNY offers efficiency and convenience, it also provides the Chinese government with an unprecedented level of surveillance and control over its citizens' financial activity. Because the ledger is controlled by the central bank, the government can theoretically track every single transaction in real-time. Furthermore, there are concerns that a CBDC could be programmed with rules, such as expiry dates on funds to force spending, or restrictions on what the money can be used to buy. The e-CNY is a powerful case study of both the potential benefits and the significant privacy and control concerns of a state-run digital currency.

Practical Application: Tracking Global CBDC Progress

The development of CBDCs is a global phenomenon, with nearly every major country exploring the concept.

- **Try This How-To:**

1. Go to the website of the Atlantic Council, a non-partisan think tank.
2. Search for their "CBDC Tracker."
3. They maintain an interactive map of the world showing the status of CBDC development in every country. You can see which countries are in the research phase, which are in pilot programs (like China), and which, if any, have fully launched.

This provides a clear and authoritative global overview of this major financial and geopolitical trend.

Key Takeaways

- A CBDC is a centralized, digital version of a country's fiat money, controlled by the central bank.
- They are fundamentally different from decentralized cryptocurrencies like Bitcoin.
- The global development of CBDCs could act as both a competitor and a catalyst for the crypto industry, while also raising significant privacy concerns.

Bridge to the Next Lesson

CBDCs are a top-down, government-driven force that will shape the future of finance. But the crypto markets are also deeply affected by broader, bottom-up economic forces that impact all risk assets. In our next lesson, we will explore the powerful impact of macroeconomics on the crypto world.

Lesson 04 - Impact of Macroeconomics on Crypto

An Introduction to "No Market is an Island"

For a long time, many believed the crypto market was an isolated ecosystem, a separate financial world that moved to its own rhythm, immune to the forces of the "real world." That belief has been shattered. It is now clear that the crypto market is deeply intertwined with and sensitive to global macroeconomic trends. Understanding these broad economic forces—like interest rates and inflation—is no longer optional; it is essential for analyzing and navigating modern crypto market cycles.

The Core Explanation: Risk-On vs. Risk-Off

'Macro' refers to the broad economic trends related to interest rates, inflation, and economic growth that are driven by the actions of central banks and governments. The state of the macro environment determines the market's overall appetite for risk.

There are two key environments to understand:

1. 'Risk-On' Environment:

- **Characterized by:** Low interest rates, high liquidity (central banks are "printing money"), and positive economic growth.
- **Investor Behaviour:** When money is cheap and the economy is strong, investors are more willing to take risks. They move their capital into speculative, high-growth assets in search of high returns.
- Impact on Crypto: A risk-on environment is generally bullish for crypto, as capital flows freely into speculative assets.

1. 'Risk-Off' Environment:

- **Characterized by:** Rising interest rates, tight liquidity (central banks are trying to slow the economy), and economic uncertainty.
- **Investor Behaviour:** When money becomes expensive and the future is uncertain, investors become risk-averse.

They pull their capital out of speculative assets and move it into "safer" assets like government bonds or the US Dollar.

- **Impact on Crypto:** A risk-off environment is generally bearish for crypto, as capital flows out of the ecosystem.

In recent years, cryptocurrencies, particularly Bitcoin, have shown a high correlation with the traditional stock market, especially the tech-heavy Nasdaq index, often trading like a high-beta technology stock.

Case Study: The 2022 Bear Market

The crypto bear market of 2022 was a perfect, and brutal, case study in the power of macroeconomics. In response to skyrocketing global inflation, central banks around the world, led by the U.S. Federal Reserve, began one of the most aggressive interest rate hiking cycles in history.

- This created a powerful "risk-off" environment. The cost of borrowing money soared, and liquidity was drained from the financial system.
- Investors, who had been piling into speculative assets in 2021, now fled to safety.
- The crypto market experienced a massive crash, losing nearly two-thirds of its value. Crucially, this crash moved in very high correlation with the Nasdaq stock index, which was also hit hard by the rising rates.

This period definitively proved that crypto is no longer an insulated market; it is a globally traded risk asset that is highly sensitive to the decisions made by central banks.

Practical Application: Observing Market Correlations

You can see the relationship between crypto and traditional markets for yourself on a chart.

- **Try This How-To:**

1. Go to a charting website like TradingView.
2. Pull up a weekly chart of Bitcoin (BTCUSD).
3. Use the "Compare" or "Add Symbol" feature to overlay the chart of the Nasdaq 100 index (NDX) onto the same chart.
4. Look at the period from 2020 to the present. You will be able to visually see the high correlation between the two assets, especially during major market moves up and down.

This is a clear, visual representation of crypto's connection to the broader macro environment.

Key Takeaways

- Crypto assets are sensitive to global macroeconomic conditions.
- Low interest rates and high liquidity ('risk-on') are generally bullish for crypto.
- High interest rates and tight liquidity ('risk-off') are generally bearish for crypto.

Bridge to the Next Lesson

Macro forces affect the market from the outside. But how do regulators and law enforcement see what's happening on the *inside* of the blockchain? In our next lesson, we will explore the powerful and growing world of on-chain forensic analysis.

Lesson 05 - On-Chain Forensic Analysis

An Introduction to "Following the Money"

"Every transaction leaves a trace." This old saying has never been more true than on a public blockchain. This creates a fascinating paradox: the blockchain offers pseudonymity, but it also offers a level of radical transparency that makes it a powerful tool for financial investigation. This has given rise to a new industry of on-chain "crypto detectives"—forensic analysis firms that can "follow the money" with unprecedented precision.

The Core Explanation: De-anonymizing the Blockchain

While blockchain addresses are pseudonymous, they are not anonymous. The public and permanent nature of the ledger allows for powerful on-chain forensic analysis.

Companies like Chainalysis and Elliptic are the leaders in this field. They specialize in:

1. **De-anonymizing Transactions:** They use advanced heuristics and massive data sets to link real-world identities (e.g., individuals, exchanges, illicit actors) to specific blockchain addresses. They do this by clustering wallets, analysing transaction patterns, and integrating data from public and private sources.
2. **Tracking the Flow of Funds:** Their software can trace the path of illicit funds from a hack or a darknet market,

through complex mixing services, all the way to a cash-out point like a centralized exchange.
3. **Providing Compliance Software:** They provide tools to exchanges, banks, and government agencies to help them with anti-money laundering (AML) compliance, allowing them to screen for transactions coming from sanctioned addresses or known illicit sources.

These firms play a crucial role in making the crypto ecosystem safer and are essential partners for law enforcement agencies investigating crypto-related crime.

Case Study: The 2016 Bitfinex Hack Recovery

In 2016, the Bitfinex crypto exchange was hacked, and nearly 120,000 Bitcoins were stolen. At the time, this was a devastating blow to the industry. For years, the stolen coins lay dormant, but the hackers eventually began trying to launder the money through a complex web of thousands of transactions across multiple chains.

However, because the Bitcoin blockchain is a permanent and public ledger, law enforcement, with the help of on-chain forensic firms, was able to meticulously trace the flow of every single coin. After years of painstaking investigation, in 2022, the U.S. Department of Justice was able to identify the hackers and gain access to the private keys associated with the stolen funds.

They successfully seized and recovered over 94,000 of the stolen Bitcoin, worth over $3.6 billion at the time of the seizure. This was a landmark case that demonstrated that even with sophisticated laundering techniques, the transparency of the blockchain can be a powerful tool for justice.

Practical Application: Reading a Forensic Report

You can get a direct look into the world of a crypto detective by reading their public reports.

- **Try This How-To:**

1. Go to the official blog or "Press Room" section of the Chainalysis or Elliptic website.
2. Browse their case studies or annual reports. You will find fascinating, detailed breakdowns (often with charts) of how they traced funds from major North Korean hacks, ransomware attacks, or darknet markets.
3. Reading one of these reports will give you a direct insight into the tools and techniques of on-chain forensic analysis and show how the public nature of the blockchain can be a powerful tool for law enforcement.

Key Takeaways

- On-chain forensic firms analyse public blockchains to track funds and identify illicit activity.
- These tools are used by governments and exchanges for compliance and investigations.
- This demonstrates that most blockchains are transparent, not anonymous, and that illicit funds can often be traced.

Bridge to the Next Lesson

On-chain forensics helps law enforcement apply existing laws to the world of crypto. But the most fundamental legal question in the U.S. is which laws apply in the first place. Is a token a commodity, or is it a security? In our next lesson, we will explore the crucial legal framework used to answer this question: The Howey Test.

Lesson 06 - The Howey Test

An Introduction to the Orange Grove Standard

What does a 1940s legal case about Floridian orange groves have to do with the cutting edge of Web3 technology? Everything, it turns out. The Howey Test is a decades-old legal framework from that very case, and it has become the central battleground for determining whether a crypto asset is a security in the United States. Understanding this simple, four-part test is essential for grasping the core of the regulatory conflict in the world's largest capital market.

The Core Explanation: Defining an "Investment Contract"

In the United States, the primary legal framework for determining if an asset is a security is the 'Howey Test,' which is derived from the 1946 Supreme Court case *SEC v. W. J. Howey Co.*

The test defines an "investment contract" (which is a type of security) as a transaction that has four distinct prongs:

1. An investment of money...
2. ...in a common enterprise...
3. ...with a reasonable expectation of profits...
4. ...to be derived from the efforts of others.

The U.S. Securities and Exchange Commission (SEC) applies this old test to modern crypto assets. The SEC's argument is that most Initial Coin Offerings (ICOs) and altcoins qualify as securities because they meet these four prongs: people invest money (1) into a common project (2) expecting the token to go up in value (3) based on the work of a central development team or foundation (4).

If a token is deemed to be a security, it falls under the strict jurisdiction of the SEC and is subject to extensive registration and disclosure laws.

Case Study: The SEC vs. LBRY, Inc.

LBRY was a decentralized, blockchain-based content-sharing platform with a native token called LBC. In 2021, the SEC sued LBRY, Inc., arguing that their sales of LBC tokens were illegal, unregistered securities offerings.

- The SEC's argument was a straightforward application of the Howey Test. They claimed that people who bought LBC were investing in a common enterprise (the LBRY network) with the expectation of profit, and that this profit was dependent on the managerial and entrepreneurial efforts of the LBRY company, which developed and promoted the network.
- In a key ruling in 2022, a federal judge sided with the SEC, agreeing that the token sales met the criteria of the Howey Test. The case was seen as a major victory for the SEC's broad application of the Howey Test to a functioning crypto protocol. It highlighted that even tokens with clear utility could be classified as securities if their initial sale and subsequent promotion led buyers to expect a profit based on the efforts of a central entity.

Practical Application: The Original Orange Grove

To truly understand the Howey Test, it helps to understand the simple facts of the original case.

- **Try This How-To:**

1. Do a web search for a summary of the 1946 Supreme Court case, *SEC v. W. J. Howey Co.*
2. You will learn that the case was about a company in Florida that owned a large orange grove. To finance their operations, they sold sections of this grove to guests at their hotel.
3. Crucially, the hotel guests didn't want to actually farm the oranges themselves. The contract included a deal where the hotel's staff would manage the groves, harvest the oranges, and then share the profits with the guests.
4. The Supreme Court ruled that these land sale contracts were, in fact, "investment contracts" (securities) because the guests were investing money, expecting a profit, based on the efforts of the Howey Company.

Understanding this simple origin story makes it much clearer how the SEC is now applying this same four-part logic to ICOs and token sales.

Key Takeaways

- The Howey Test is a legal framework used in the U.S. to define what constitutes a security.
- The test has four prongs: an investment of money, in a

common enterprise, with an expectation of profit, from the efforts of others.

- Whether a token is a security or a commodity is one of the most important unresolved legal questions in crypto, and the SEC's application of this decades-old test is highly contentious.

Bridge to the Next Lesson

The Howey Test is a U.S.-specific legal framework. But the push for crypto regulation is a global phenomenon. In our next lesson, we will look at an important international standard that is impacting every crypto exchange in the world: the FATF Travel Rule.

Lesson 07 - The FATF Travel Rule

An Introduction to Global Compliance

Your crypto transactions, especially when they move between exchanges, are not as private as you might think. A global anti-money laundering rule, born in the world of traditional banking, is now being applied to the crypto industry. The FATF "Travel Rule" is an international standard that requires crypto exchanges to collect and share customer information, fundamentally changing the nature of inter-exchange transfers and bringing crypto compliance in line with the global banking system.

The Core Explanation: Attaching Data to Transactions

The Financial Action Task Force (FATF) is an international, inter-governmental body that sets the global standards to combat money laundering and terrorist financing. While its recommendations are not legally binding, its member countries (including Australia, the US, and most of Europe) are expected to implement them into their national laws.

The 'Travel Rule' is one of its most important recommendations. It requires financial institutions (which now include crypto exchanges, or "Virtual Asset Service Providers") to:

1. Obtain and hold required and accurate originator (sender) and beneficiary (recipient) information for virtual asset transfers.
2. Pass this information to the next financial institution in the chain.

In practice, this means that for transactions above a certain threshold (typically around $1,000 USD), when you withdraw crypto from Exchange A to your account on Exchange B, Exchange A must electronically send your personal information (like your name and address) along with the transaction data to Exchange B. This increases compliance burdens and challenges the purely pseudonymous, peer-to-peer nature of early crypto transactions.

Case Study: An Inter-Exchange Transfer

Let's look at how the Travel Rule changes a simple transaction.

- Before the Travel Rule: A user wants to withdraw 1 Bitcoin from their account on Exchange A to their deposit address on Exchange B. They would simply initiate a standard Bitcoin transaction on the blockchain. The only information that "travels" is the on-chain transaction data.

- After the Travel Rule: The user initiates the same withdrawal. Now, behind the scenes, a new process happens. Exchange A's compliance system is required to send a separate, secure message to Exchange B containing the sender's name, physical address, and other identifying information, as well as the recipient's name. Exchange B must receive and store this information before it can credit the user's account with the 1 Bitcoin.

This brings crypto exchange transfers under the same regulatory umbrella as traditional bank wire transfers.

Practical Application: National Implementation

You can see how these global standards are implemented at a national level by government bodies.

- **Try This How-To:**

1. Go to the official website for AUSTRAC (Australian Transaction Reports and Analysis Centre), which is Australia's primary financial intelligence agency.
2. Use their search function to look for their official guidance on the "Travel Rule" for "digital currency exchange providers" (the legal term for crypto exchanges).
3. You will find official government documentation explaining how Australian businesses are expected to comply with these international FATF standards.

This shows how global recommendations from an organization like the FATF are translated into binding national laws that crypto companies must follow.

Key Takeaways

- The FATF sets global anti-money laundering (AML) standards.
- The Travel Rule requires crypto service providers to share customer data during transactions between exchanges.
- This rule is designed to bring the crypto industry in line with traditional banking regulations.

Bridge to the Next Lesson

The Travel Rule is a major compliance challenge for centralized exchanges. But the biggest challenge for regulators is how to apply rules to financial systems that have no central company at all. In our next lesson, we will explore the complex challenges of DeFi regulation.

Lesson 08 - DeFi Regulation Challenges

An Introduction to Regulating Code

How do you regulate a piece of software? How do you apply laws designed for corporations to autonomous smart contracts that run on a global, decentralized network? This is the fundamental and fascinating challenge of DeFi regulation. Traditional financial laws are designed to target identifiable, centralized intermediaries. DeFi, by its very nature, has none. This lesson will explore the unique challenges that regulators face and the novel approaches they are considering.

The Core Explanation: Who is Responsible?

Regulating Decentralized Finance presents a massive challenge for authorities because it breaks the traditional regulatory model. The laws we have are designed to hold a specific, legally identifiable intermediary (like a bank, a broker, or an exchange) responsible.

DeFi protocols, however, are autonomous smart contracts with no central operator. This creates the key question for regulators: "Who do we regulate?". If a DeFi protocol is exploited or used for illicit activity, who is legally responsible?

Regulators are grappling with this and exploring several potential approaches:

1. **Regulating the Developers:** One approach is to hold the software developers who originally wrote the smart contract code liable for its use. This is highly contentious, as it could have a chilling effect on open-source software development.
2. **Regulating the DAOs:** Another approach is to treat the DAO that governs a protocol as a legally recognizable entity and hold it responsible. This is also complex, as many DAOs are loosely structured, global organizations.
3. **Regulating the On-Ramps and Off-Ramps:** This is currently the most common approach. It involves focusing regulation on the centralized "choke points" that connect the DeFi ecosystem to the traditional financial system. This means applying strict AML/KYC rules to centralized exchanges and stablecoin issuers.

Case Study: The U.S. Treasury's Sanctioning of Tornado Cash

Tornado Cash is a fully decentralized, non-custodial privacy protocol on Ethereum. It is a set of smart contracts that allows users to deposit and withdraw ETH in a way that breaks the on-chain link between the source and destination, enhancing privacy.

In August 2022, the U.S. Department of the Treasury's Office of Foreign Assets Control (OFAC) took the unprecedented step of adding the Tornado Cash protocol's smart contract addresses to the U.S. sanctions list. The government alleged it had been used by North Korea to launder hundreds of millions of dollars.

This was a landmark and highly controversial event. It was one of the first times a government had sanctioned a piece of open-source, autonomous code rather than a person or a company. The action raised complex legal and philosophical questions about whether code itself can be sanctioned and the implications for financial privacy and freedom of speech, a debate that is still ongoing in the courts.

Practical Application: The Self-Driving Car Analogy

The liability questions in DeFi are similar to those in other emerging technologies.

- **Try This How-To:**

1. Consider a self-driving car that is involved in an accident.
2. Think about the question: Who is legally at fault?
3. Is it the person in the driver's seat who wasn't actively driving? Is it the owner of the car? Is it the company that wrote the autonomous driving software? Or is it the manufacturer that built the car?

There is no easy answer. This is a real-world analogy for

the complex liability questions that regulators face with DeFi. The question of "who to regulate" in a decentralized, autonomous system is one of the biggest challenges they face.

Key Takeaways

- DeFi's decentralized nature makes it difficult to apply traditional, entity-based regulations.
- Regulators are exploring novel approaches, such as targeting developers, DAOs, or the centralized on-ramps.
- The question of "who to regulate" in a decentralized system is a core challenge for authorities worldwide.

Bridge to the Next Lesson

While general DeFi regulation remains a complex and slow-moving challenge, authorities are moving much faster on one specific and systemically important area of the ecosystem. In our next lesson, we will focus on the intense regulatory scrutiny being applied to stablecoins.

Lesson 09 - Stablecoin Regulation

An Introduction to "What's Backing Your Digital Dollar?"

Stablecoins are the bedrock of the crypto economy, acting as the primary bridge to the traditional financial system. Their massive scale and importance have placed them directly in the crosshairs of global regulators. The central question they are asking is: "What is truly backing your digital dollar, and is it safe?" This lesson will explore why stablecoins are a primary focus for regulators and the types of rules we can expect to see in the future.

The Core Explanation: The Focus on Reserves

Due to their crucial role in the crypto ecosystem and their direct link to the traditional financial system, stablecoins are a primary focus for regulators. A crisis in a major stablecoin could have cascading effects on the broader financial world.

The main concerns for regulators are:

1. **Ensuring Adequate Reserves:** Regulators want to ensure that fiat-backed stablecoins (like USDC and USDT) have legitimate, high-quality, and audited reserves to back their tokens 1-to-1. They want to prevent a situation where a stablecoin issuer does not have enough liquid assets to meet a wave of redemptions.
2. **Preventing Systemic Risk:** The largest stablecoins have tens of billions of dollars in circulation. If a major one were to fail, it could cause massive disruption not just in the crypto markets, but also in the traditional commercial paper markets where they hold some of their reserves.

To address these concerns, regulators around the world are looking to implement rules that would require major stablecoin issuers to meet standards similar to those for banks or money market funds. This would likely include strict requirements for the quality and liquidity of their reserves, regular public audits, and robust risk management procedures.

Case Study: The Collapse of Terra/UST

The dramatic failure of the multi-billion dollar "algorithmic" stablecoin, TerraUSD (UST), in May 2022 was a watershed moment that massively accelerated the global push for stablecoin regulation.

UST was not backed by real-world reserves. Instead, it relied on a complex and ultimately fragile algorithm linked to a sister token, LUNA. When the system entered a "death spiral," the value of both tokens collapsed to near zero, wiping out over $40 billion of investor value in a matter of days.

Regulators and central bankers around the world immediately pointed to the UST collapse as the prime example of the systemic risks that unbacked or poorly backed stablecoins could pose to the broader financial system. This event moved stablecoin regulation from a theoretical discussion to an urgent, top-tier priority for policymakers globally.

Practical Application: Verifying Reserves

In response to regulatory pressure and user demand for transparency, major stablecoin issuers are now providing regular public disclosures about their reserves.

- **Try This How-To:**

1. Go to the official website of Circle, the regulated U.S. company that issues the USDC stablecoin.
2. Find their "Transparency," "Trust," or "Reserves" section.
3. You will see that they provide monthly attestation reports from major, independent accounting firms (like Deloitte). These reports detail the exact composition and value of the cash and U.S. Treasury bond reserves that fully back all the USDC in circulation.

This level of voluntary transparency is a direct response to regulatory pressure and is becoming the expected industry standard for major stablecoin issuers.

Key Takeaways

- Regulators are highly focused on the systemic risks posed by stablecoins.
- The main goal is to ensure that stablecoin reserves are fully backed, liquid, and transparent.
- Future regulations will likely impose bank-like requirements on major stablecoin issuers.

Bridge to the Next Lesson

We've looked at specific regulations from around the world, from MiCA in Europe to the agency battles in the U.S. But what does it all mean for the bigger picture? In our final lesson of the Advanced Level, we will look at the future of crypto policy.

Lesson 10 - The Future of Crypto Policy

An Introduction to a Maturing Industry

The era of crypto being an unregulated "wild west" is coming to an end. Around the world, policymakers are moving from a state of observation to one of action. The future of crypto policy will not be a single, global standard, but rather a patchwork of different approaches. However, clear trends are emerging. This final lesson will look at the key themes that will shape the future of crypto policy and what it means for the industry's transition into a mature and integrated part of the global financial system.

The Core Explanation: Key Themes in Global Regulation

The future of crypto policy is likely to be a journey towards greater regulatory clarity, but also increased compliance burdens. The industry is moving from the fringes to the mainstream, and with that comes a new set of rules and responsibilities.

We can expect to see several key themes dominate the regulatory landscape in the coming years:

1. **A Move Towards Clarity:** There will be a continued push away from "regulation by enforcement" towards clear, legislated rulebooks, following the comprehensive model set by Europe's MiCA.
2. **Increased Compliance:** Stricter Anti-Money Laundering (AML) and Counter-Financing of Terrorism (CFT) requirements for all crypto businesses will become the global norm, harmonizing the industry with traditional banking standards.
3. **Asset Differentiation:** Regulators will likely create different and more nuanced rules for different types of crypto assets. They will probably not treat Bitcoin (a commodity), a pre-mined altcoin (potentially a security), and a stablecoin (a payment instrument) all under the same framework.
4. Managing Systemic Risk: There will be a heavy and continued focus on the largest and most systemically important parts of the ecosystem, particularly major stablecoin issuers and the points where the DeFi and traditional financial systems intersect.

The industry's ability to engage constructively with policymakers will be crucial in shaping a balanced and innovation-friendly regulatory future.

Case Study: The Approval of Spot Bitcoin ETFs

For a decade, the U.S. SEC repeatedly rejected applications for a Spot Bitcoin ETF (Exchange-Traded Fund), a financial product that would allow mainstream investors to easily gain exposure to Bitcoin through their traditional brokerage accounts.

However, after a major crypto asset manager, Grayscale, successfully sued the SEC and won in court—with a judge ruling that the SEC's rejection was "arbitrary and capricious"—the agency was finally forced to approve the ETFs in January 2024.

This was a landmark moment for the industry in several ways:

- It was a major victory where the industry used the legal system to force regulatory clarity.
- It created a fully regulated product that bridged the gap between crypto and traditional finance.
- The subsequent success of the ETFs, which saw billions of dollars of inflows, demonstrated the immense pent-up demand for crypto from mainstream investors. It was a major step in the maturation and integration of crypto into the global financial system.

Practical Application: Following the Advocates

You can get a direct insight into the high-level conversations that are shaping the future of regulation by following the work of industry advocacy groups.

- **Try This How-To:**

1. Find the official website or X (Twitter) account of a major crypto advocacy group in your region. In the US, this would be organizations like the 'Blockchain Association' or 'Coin Center.' In Australia, it would be 'Blockchain Australia.'
2. Look for their "Policy" or "Research" section. You can often find detailed policy papers, blog posts, and responses to government consultations.
3. Reading these documents will give you a direct look into the sophisticated, high-level conversations that are happening between the industry's top minds and government policymakers to shape the future of regulation.

Key Takeaways

- The future of crypto regulation will involve a balance between fostering innovation and managing risk.
- Expect clearer rules but also stricter compliance for crypto businesses worldwide.
- Ongoing dialogue between the industry and regulators is essential for shaping effective and sensible policy.

14

Module 3 Recap

You have now completed your deep dive into the external forces that shape the crypto landscape.

- You've analysed the different regulatory approaches being taken around the world, from the comprehensive MiCA framework in Europe to the jurisdictional conflict between the SEC and CFTC in the United States.
- You understand the rise of state-controlled CBDCs, the powerful impact of macroeconomic trends on crypto's market cycles, and the tools of on-chain forensics.
- You can explain the key legal frameworks like the Howey Test and global compliance standards like the FATF Travel Rule, and you have a clear view of the key themes that will shape the future of crypto policy.

You have now completed the Advanced Level. You possess not only the technical and analytical skills to navigate the ecosystem but also the strategic understanding of the external forces that shape its destiny. You are now prepared

to enter the final level of our curriculum: the Expert Level.

15

Level 4: Expert

Goal: To push the boundaries of knowledge and transition from an expert user to an innovator and leader in the space. This level is for those who want to build, design, and fundamentally shape the future of Web3.

Module 1: Protocol Development & Security

Module Introduction: You have learned to analyze and use protocols from the outside. Now, we look from the inside out. This module provides a foundational understanding of what it takes to build on the blockchain. You'll learn the basics of the primary smart contract language, the tools professional developers use, and the adversarial mindset required to identify critical security vulnerabilities. This is your introduction to thinking like a Web3 developer and a security researcher.

Lesson 01 - Solidity Fundamentals

An Introduction to the Language of Immutable Money

Imagine writing a legal contract that, once signed, could never be altered, amended, or stopped. It would execute its terms with perfect, robotic precision forever. That is the power and the peril of writing a smart contract.

Solidity is the language used to write these immutable agreements on the world's most active blockchain, Ethereum. Understanding its fundamentals isn't just for developers; it's for anyone who wants to grasp the true nature of programmable money and the challenges of building in Web3.

The Core Explanation: Building with Digital Bricks

Solidity is a high-level, contract-oriented programming language for implementing smart contracts on EVM-compatible blockchains. It was heavily influenced by languages like C++ and JavaScript, but it is specifically designed to operate within the unique and constrained environment of the Ethereum Virtual Machine (EVM).

An expert must understand its core components and the paradigm shifts from traditional development:

- **The Paradigm Shift:** The fundamental difference from traditional software is twofold: immutability and cost. Once a smart contract is deployed to the blockchain, its code can never be changed. A bug cannot be "patched" in the traditional sense. Furthermore, every single operation that writes data to the blockchain costs the user a transaction fee (gas), making security and optimization paramount.
- Core Components:

- **Pragmas:** Directives at the top of a file that declare the compiler versions to be used.
- **State variables:** Variables whose values are permanently stored on the blockchain, representing the contract's "memory".
- **Functions:** The executable units of code that define how the contract can be interacted with, using visibility specifiers (public, private, internal, external).
- **Modifiers:** Reusable pieces of code for checking conditions before a function is executed.
- **Events:** Used for logging contract activities, which allows off-chain applications to listen for things happening inside the contract.

Case Study: The ERC-20 Token Standard

Perhaps the most famous example of Solidity's power is the ERC-20 token standard. Before this standard, every new token on Ethereum was a completely custom smart contract. This made it very difficult for wallets and exchanges to support them, as they would have to write new custom code for every single token.

The ERC-20 standard, written in Solidity, defined a common interface that all fungible tokens should follow. It specified a standard set of functions that every ERC-20 token must have, such as balanceOf(address), transfer (address, uint), and approve (address, uint).

This simple act of standardization caused an explosion of innovation. It allowed any wallet, exchange, or dApp to instantly and automatically support any new token that followed the standard. This laid the groundwork for the ICO (Initial Coin Offering) boom of 2017 and the entire DeFi ecosystem that followed. It is a perfect case study of how a well-designed smart contract standard can create powerful network effects.

Practical Application: Reading a Live Contract

You can see the structure of a real-world Solidity contract on a block explorer.

- **Try This How-To:**

1. Go to Etherscan and find the contract address for a well-known token like USDC or SHIB.
2. Navigate to the "Contract" tab. You will see the verified Solidity source code.
3. You don't need to understand everything. Just scroll through the code and try to identify the key components we discussed: the pragma at the top, the state variables (like balances), and the function definitions for transfer and balanceOf.

This makes the abstract structure of a smart contract tangible and real.

Key Takeaways

- Solidity is the primary language for EVM smart contract development.
- Immutability and gas costs are core constraints that dictate development patterns, forcing a focus on security and optimization.
- Mastering concepts like state, functions, modifiers, and events is non-negotiable for any aspiring developer.

Bridge to the Next Lesson

Writing code in Solidity is only one part of the equation. Professional developers rely on sophisticated toolkits to test, debug, and deploy their contracts safely. In our next lesson, we will explore the industry-standard development environments, Hardhat and Foundry.

Lesson 02 - Hardhat & Foundry

An Introduction to Mission Control

You wouldn't build a skyscraper with a hammer and a handsaw, and you don't build a multi-million-dollar DeFi protocol by writing code in a simple text editor. Professional smart contract development requires a sophisticated mission control center—a development environment that manages the entire lifecycle of a contract, from writing the first line of code to deploying it securely onto the mainnet. This lesson introduces the two industry titans, Hardhat and Foundry, that make professional Web3 development possible.

The Core Explanation: The Developer's Toolkit

Professional smart contract development relies on sophisticated development environments that provide a comprehensive suite of tools for compiling, deploying, testing, and debugging contracts. These frameworks handle all the complex boilerplate, allowing developers to focus on the core logic of their application. The two undisputed leaders are Hardhat and Foundry.

1. Hardhat:

- **What it is:** A JavaScript-based development environment that has been the industry standard for several years.
- It provides a flexible and highly extensible platform with a rich plugin ecosystem. Its core features include a local blockchain simulation for rapid testing, integration with JavaScript testing libraries, and powerful deployment scripting.

1. Foundry:

- **What it is:** A newer, Rust-based toolkit that has rapidly gained popularity for its high speed and developer-friendly approach.
- **Key Features:** Because it is written in Rust, Foundry is significantly faster at compiling and testing contracts. Its killer feature is

Solidity-native testing, which allows developers to write their tests directly in Solidity instead of switching to JavaScript. It also has built-in support for "fuzz testing," a powerful technique for finding bugs.

An expert developer should be proficient in at least one of these frameworks to manage a professional workflow.

Case Study: The Importance of Comprehensive Testing

In August 2021, a cross-chain bridge protocol was exploited, allowing an attacker to drain the protocol of its funds. The post-mortem analysis revealed that the bug was subtle but could have been caught with more rigorous testing.

Specifically, a "fuzz test"—a technique popularized by Foundry where the testing framework automatically bombards functions with a huge number of random inputs—

would have likely discovered the edge case that the attacker exploited. The protocol had standard unit tests for the "happy paths" but lacked tests for unexpected or malicious inputs. This incident became a powerful case study for the entire industry on the absolute necessity of comprehensive testing suites, a core feature that frameworks like Hardhat and Foundry are designed to facilitate.

Proficiency in writing comprehensive test suites is a critical skill for any developer.

Practical Application: A Developer's Workflow

You can get a feel for a developer's workflow by watching a short tutorial.

- **Try This How-To:**

1. Go to YouTube and search for a "Hardhat tutorial" or "Foundry tutorial" for beginners.
2. Watch the first 15-20 minutes. You don't need to understand the code itself.
3. Pay attention to the developer's process: they will write code in one window and use commands in a separate "terminal" window to compile the contract, run a local test network, and run a test script that checks their code for errors.

This will give you a direct visual understanding of a developer's day-to-day workflow using these powerful tools.

Key Takeaways

- Hardhat and Foundry are the industry standards for

Ethereum development.

- These tools manage the entire lifecycle of a smart contract, from compilation to deployment.
- Proficiency in writing comprehensive test suites is a critical skill for any smart contract developer.

Bridge to the Next Lesson

Even with the best tools and the most rigorous testing, vulnerabilities can still exist. The history of crypto is littered with hacks caused by a single, infamous type of bug. In our next lesson, we will dissect the most notorious smart contract vulnerability of all time: the re-entrancy attack.

Lesson 03 - Re-entrancy Attacks

An Introduction to the Ghost in the Machine

Imagine a bank's ATM that has a fatal flaw: when you ask to withdraw cash, it gives you the money *before* it updates your account balance. What would you do? You would ask for the money again, and again, and again, before the machine can register the first withdrawal. This is the logic behind a re-entrancy attack, the most infamous smart contract vulnerability in history, responsible for the legendary hack of "The DAO". Understanding this attack is a rite of passage for any student of smart contract security.

The Core Explanation: The Dangers of External Calls

A re-entrancy attack occurs when a function makes an external call to another, untrusted contract before it resolves its own state changes (like updating a user's balance).

Here's how the attack unfolds:

1. An attacker creates a malicious smart contract.
2. The attacker deposits funds into a vulnerable target contract (let's call it "VictimBank").
3. The attacker then calls the withdraw function on VictimBank.
4. The vulnerable withdraw function first checks the attacker's balance, then sends the ETH to the attacker's contract, and *only then* does it update the attacker's balance to zero.
5. This is the fatal flaw. When the attacker's contract receives the ETH, its code is programmed to immediately "re-enter" the VictimBank, calling the withdraw function again before the first call has finished.
6. Because the attacker's balance has not yet been set to zero, the VictimBank sees a valid balance and sends the funds again. This loop continues, draining the contract's funds, until the attacker stops or the contract is empty.

The primary defence is the 'Checks-Effects-Interactions' pattern. This is a strict programming pattern where you perform all internal checks first, then make all changes to state variables (the Effects), and only as the very last step do you make any external calls to other contracts (the Interactions).

Case Study: The 2016 DAO Hack

This is the canonical example. The DAO was a decentralized investment fund that raised over $150 million worth of ETH in 2016. It's withdraw function contained a classic re-entrancy vulnerability: it sent ETH to the user *before* updating their internal balance ledger.

An attacker exploited this flaw precisely as described above. They used a malicious smart contract to repeatedly call the withdraw function, draining 3.6 million ETH (worth ~$50 million at the time) from the fund. The event was so catastrophic that it led to the contentious hard fork that split the blockchain into Ethereum (which reversed the hack) and Ethereum Classic (which did not). It remains the most important lesson in smart contract security history.

Practical Application: Spotting the Vulnerability

You don't need to be a developer to understand the flawed logic.

- **Try This How-To:**

1. Do a web search for a simplified code example of a "re-entrancy attack."
2. You will find two small code blocks to compare.
3. Vulnerable Code: Look at the withdraw function. You will see that the line of code that sends the Ether (often msg.sender.call.value(...)) comes *before* the line of code that updates the user's balance (e.g., balances[msg.sender] = 0).
4. Secure Code: In the corrected version, you will see the order is flipped. The balance is updated to zero *first* (the "Effect"), and the Ether is sent *last* (the "Interaction").

Visually comparing these two small code blocks is the best way to understand the vulnerability and the simple elegance of its solution.

Key Takeaways

- Re-entrancy is a critical vulnerability where an external call is used to re-enter a function before it completes.
- The Checks-Effects-Interactions pattern is the standard defence against this attack.
- Understanding this and other vulnerabilities is essential for smart contract security.

Bridge to the Next Lesson

Understanding specific bugs like re-entrancy is a key part of the adversarial mindset required for security. In our next lesson, we will explore the broader mindset of a smart contract auditor, whose job is not to build, but to break.

Lesson 04 - Smart Contract Auditing: The Mindset

An Introduction to Adversarial Thinking

A developer builds a house, brick by brick, ensuring everything works as planned. An auditor's job is to try and find a way to burn that house down. A smart contract audit is a crucial, adversarial process that serves as the final security checkpoint before a protocol handling significant value goes live. It is not about checking for best practices; it is a systematic hunt for every possible vulnerability. This lesson will explore the unique, adversarial mindset required to be a smart contract auditor.

The Core Explanation: The "Unhappy Path"

A smart contract audit is a systematic, adversarial review

of the codebase to discover vulnerabilities, logical errors, and economic exploits. The mindset of an auditor is fundamentally different from that of a developer.

- A developer's mindset is focused on the 'happy path'. Their primary goal is to make the system function correctly as intended. They ask, "Does my code work?".
- An auditor's mindset is focused on every possible 'unhappy path' and edge case. Their job is not to confirm that the code works, but to discover how it can be broken. They ask not just 'does the code work?', but 'how can I break this code?' and 'how can I abuse the system's logic for profit?'.

Audits cover both low-level, code-specific bugs (like re-entrancy or integer overflows) and higher-level, complex economic logic flaws that might only emerge when different parts of the protocol interact in unexpected ways. A rigorous audit from a reputable firm is a critical signal of a project's commitment to security.

Case Study: The Wormhole Bridge Hack ($320M)

In February 2022, the Wormhole bridge, a complex protocol connecting Ethereum and Solana, was exploited for over $320 million. The post-mortem analyses revealed the cause was an incredibly subtle cryptographic bug in one of the Solana-side smart contracts.

The attacker found a flaw that allowed them to fake a verification signature, tricking the Solana program into believing that a valid deposit had been made on the Ethereum side. This allowed them to mint 120,000 "wrapped" ETH on Solana without any corresponding collateral being locked on

Ethereum.

This case highlights the immense complexity and high stakes of auditing. A pre-deployment audit with a sufficiently adversarial mindset and deep, specialized expertise in that specific cryptographic library might have been able to identify this vulnerability. It serves as a powerful reminder of the value of deep, specialized security reviews before deploying protocols that secure hundreds of millions of dollars.

Practical Application: Reading an Audit Report

You can get a direct look into the adversarial process of a professional security audit.

- **Try This How-To:**

1. Go to the website of a major smart contract auditing firm like Trail of Bits, OpenZeppelin, or CertiK.
2. Find their blog or "Publications" section, where they often post public audit reports for major DeFi protocols.
3. You don't need to understand the code. Just read the "Summary" and the list of "Findings."
4. Notice how the findings are categorized by severity: Critical, High, Medium, Low. This gives you a direct look into the output of an audit and the adversarial process of identifying and prioritizing vulnerabilities.

Key Takeaways

- Auditing is an adversarial process focused on finding vulnerabilities.
- It requires a mindset geared towards breaking the system,

not just making it work.
- Audits cover both code-level bugs and higher-level economic logic flaws.

Bridge to the Next Lesson

Auditing focuses on preventing the code from being broken. But what if the code works perfectly, yet the system is still exploitable because the *incentives* are wrong? In our final lesson of this module, we will explore the crucial and overarching field of mechanism design.

Lesson 05 - Mechanism Design: An Introduction

An Introduction to Building Systems for Selfish People

"How do you build a system that works, even when everyone using it is trying to cheat for their own personal gain?" This is the central question of mechanism design. It is a fascinating field of economics and game theory that is absolutely essential for building sustainable decentralized protocols. It's about designing the rules of a game in such a way that the rational, self-interested actions of individual players lead to a desirable and secure outcome for the whole system.

The Core Explanation: Aligning Incentives

Mechanism design is a field of economics and game theory that focuses on designing protocols or 'mechanisms' where the rational actions of individual participants lead to a desired system-wide outcome. In Web3, this is crucial for creating sustainable tokenomics, effective governance systems, and secure DeFi protocols.

The core of mechanism design is to assume that all users are rational, self-interested actors who will exploit the system for personal gain if possible. Given this assumption, the key questions are:

- 'How will rational, self-interested users behave within this system?'.
- 'How can we design the incentives to prevent them from breaking it?'.

An expert understands that a protocol's long-term security depends as much on the strength of its

economic incentives as it does on the quality of its code. Good mechanism design aligns individual incentives with the overall health of the protocol.

Case Study: Ethereum's EIP-1559

The upgrade to Ethereum's fee market, known as EIP-1559, was a masterclass in mechanism design.

- **The Old Mechanism:** The fee market was a simple "first-price auction." Users would blindly bid to get their transactions included, leading to wild price swings and a terrible user experience.
- **The Problem:** The incentives were misaligned. There was no predictable fee, and all fees went to the miners, creating misaligned incentives.
- **The New Mechanism (EIP-1559):** The upgrade introduced a new system with a "base fee" that is algorithmically adjusted based on network demand. The crucial part is that this base fee is burned, not paid to validators.

Users can then add an optional "priority fee" (a tip) to the validator to get their transaction included faster.

- **The Result:** This new mechanism achieved several desired outcomes. It made gas fees more predictable for users, and the burning of the base fee created a powerful deflationary "token sink" for ETH, directly linking network usage to the scarcity of the asset. It was a change in the protocol's *mechanism* designed to align incentives for a better system-wide outcome.

Practical Application: The Congestion Charge Analogy

You can see the logic of mechanism design in the real world.

- **Try This How-To:**

1. Consider a traffic congestion charge in a major city centre like London.
2. Desired System-Wide Outcome: Less traffic congestion.
3. Mechanism: Charge drivers a fee to enter the city centre during peak hours.
4. Assumed Rational Behaviour: Rational, self-interested drivers will change their behaviour (drive at off-peak times, use public transport, or carpool) to avoid the fee.
5. Result: The rational actions of individuals (avoiding a personal cost) lead to the desired system-wide outcome (less traffic for everyone).

This is the core logic of mechanism design: using incentives to shape behaviour to achieve a collective goal.

Key Takeaways

- Mechanism design applies game theory to build robust decentralized systems.
- It assumes users are rational actors who will exploit the system for personal gain if possible.
- Good mechanism design aligns individual incentives with the overall health of the protocol.

16

Module 1 Recap

You have now completed the first module of the Expert Level, moving from analysis to the core principles of building and securing Web3 protocols.

- You've learned the fundamentals of Solidity, the language of smart contracts, and the professional development environments like Hardhat and Foundry used to build with it.
- You understand the most infamous smart contract vulnerability, the re-entrancy attack, and the crucial "Checks-Effects-Interactions" pattern used to prevent it.
- You have explored the adversarial mindset of a smart contract auditor, whose job is not to build, but to break.
- Finally, you've been introduced to the overarching field of mechanism design, the art of building systems that are secure not just in their code, but in their economic incentives.

You are now equipped with the foundational knowledge to understand how Web3 protocols are designed, built, and secured from the inside out.

Module 2: Quantitative Finance & Research

Module Introduction: You've learned how to build and secure a protocol. Now, you will learn to model and measure it with the rigor of a quantitative analyst, or "quant." This module moves beyond descriptive metrics into the world of predictive modelling and advanced financial theory. You will learn how professionals' model complex DeFi protocols, analyse the sophisticated mechanics of AMMs and options markets, and understand the architecture of the bots that operate in the blockchain's hidden economy.

Lesson 01 - Introduction to DeFi Quantitative Modeling

An Introduction to Modelling a Digital Economy

Beyond the individual metrics, there are the models. A quantitative model is a mathematical representation of a complex system, designed to understand its behaviour and predict its future outcomes under various conditions. In DeFi, where every protocol is a miniature, self-contained economy, quantitative modelling is the essential tool that analysts, risk managers, and protocol designers use to stress-test their systems and forecast their financial futures. This is where data analysis evolves into economic science.

The Core Explanation: From Data to Simulation

Quantitative modelling in DeFi involves creating mathematical representations of protocols to understand their behaviour. This goes far beyond simply tracking historical TVL or revenue. It involves building a dynamic model, often in a spreadsheet or a programming language, that simulates the interplay of key variables.

The goals of such a model include:

1. **Assessing Economic Security:** Simulating extreme market conditions to see if a protocol remains solvent. For a lending protocol, this means modelling a "liquidation cascade" to see if it would result in bad debt.
2. **Predicting Revenue:** Forecasting a protocol's future fee generation based on a set of assumptions about market growth, trading volume, and market share.
3. **Understanding Complex Systems:** DeFi protocols are path-dependent, meaning the outcome of one event influences the next. Models are used to understand these complex feedback loops, such as how token emissions affect token price, which in turn affects the attractiveness of yield farming, which affects the protocol's TVL.

Case Study: Modelling a Lending Protocol's Risk

A lending protocol like Aave needs to set its risk parameters (like the Loan-to-Value ratio and liquidation thresholds) for a new collateral asset. A quantitative analyst ("quant") on their risk team will not just guess these numbers.

- They will build a sophisticated model that ingests historical price data for the new asset, its volatility, and its liquidity on major DEXs.

- They will then run thousands of Monte Carlo simulations—a modelling technique that simulates a range of possible future outcomes. These simulations will model thousands of different market scenarios, including a 50% crash in the asset's price, extreme network congestion that could delay liquidations, and high slippage on DEXs.
- By running these simulations, the quant can determine the optimal LTV and liquidation threshold that will keep the protocol solvent even under the most extreme, black-swan stress conditions. This is a core function of quantitative modelling in DeFi risk management.

Practical Application: Exploring a Public Model

Many research firms and individual quants on social media publish their models, offering a transparent look into their analytical process.

- **Try This How-To:**

1. Do a web search for a "DeFi protocol revenue model" or "tokenomics simulation spreadsheet."
2. You will often find articles from crypto research firms (like Blockworks Research or Messari) or individuals where they share their detailed models.
3. Download or view one of these spreadsheets. You don't need to be a financial expert to understand the basics. Look at the "Assumptions" tab, where the analyst sets their inputs (e.g., future user growth, market share). Then look at the "Forecast" tab to see how the model uses these assumptions to project future revenues.

Exploring one of these models gives you a direct look into the world of DeFi quantitative analysis.

Key Takeaways

- Quantitative modelling uses mathematics and simulation to understand protocol dynamics.
- It is used to forecast revenue, stress-test economic security, and analyse tokenomics.
- This field treats DeFi protocols as complex, interconnected economic systems.

Bridge to the Next Lesson

One of the most complex and heavily modelled systems in all of DeFi is the Automated Market Maker. In our next lesson, we will look at the advanced mechanics of AMMs and a more accurate way to measure the risk to those who provide them with capital.

Lesson 02 - Advanced AMM Mechanics & LVR

An Introduction Beyond Impermanent Loss

In the Intermediate level, you learned about Impermanent Loss (IL) as the basic measure of risk for liquidity providers (LPs). For quantitative analysts, however, IL is a flawed and overly simplistic metric. To truly understand the economics of being an LP, we must introduce a more precise and powerful measure: Loss-versus-Rebalancing (LVR). This lesson will take you deeper into AMM mechanics and explain why

LVR is the professional standard for quantifying the true cost of providing liquidity.

The Core Explanation: The Cost of Being the Counterparty

Beyond the basic x*y=k model, experts analyse AMMs through more sophisticated lenses. A key insight is that LPs are, by definition, always taking the "other side" of every trade against informed arbitrageurs.

- When the price of an asset moves on an external market (like Binance), the price in an AMM pool becomes stale.
- An arbitrageur will immediately trade against the pool to bring its price back in line with the market, making a small, risk-free profit.
- This profit for the arbitrageur is a direct loss for the liquidity providers.

Loss-versus-Rebalancing (LVR) (pronounced "Clever") is the metric that quantifies this exact loss.

- **Definition:** LVR measures the loss an LP incurs due to adverse price movements compared to a constantly rebalancing portfolio. A rebalancing portfolio (like one a sophisticated market maker would run) constantly adjusts its prices. An AMM is passive and must be "rebalanced" by arbitrageurs.
- **What it means:** LVR provides a truer measure of the cost of providing liquidity against informed traders. It mathematically formalizes the value that is extracted from passive LPs by active arbitrageurs over time. For an LP position to be truly profitable, the fees earned must be greater than the LVR incurred.

Case Study: The Arbitrageur's Profit is the LP's Loss

Let's consider a major price movement in the ETH/USD pair.

- The price of ETH is stable at $3,000. An ETH/USDC liquidity pool is balanced.
- News breaks, and the price of ETH instantly jumps to $3,030 on all major centralized exchanges.
- For a moment, the AMM pool is still offering ETH at the stale price of $3,000.
- An arbitrageur's bot instantly detects this. It buys the "cheap" ETH from the AMM pool and sells it on Binance for a profit. This action pushes the AMM's price up to match the market.

The profit that the arbitrageur just made was extracted directly from the liquidity providers. LVR is the precise mathematical formalization of this loss. It is a constant, unavoidable "cost of business" for passive LPs, driven by the volatility of the underlying assets.

Practical Application: Reading the Research

The concept of LVR comes from a landmark academic paper that has shaped how all sophisticated market participants now view AMM risk.

- **Try This How-To:**

1. Do a web search for the academic paper: "Loss-versus-Rebalancing for Automated Market Makers" or a detailed summary of it.
2. While the mathematics in the paper are highly advanced,

reading the "Introduction" and "Conclusion" sections will provide a deep appreciation for the advanced financial theory being developed to accurately model and understand the risks and returns of being a liquidity provider.

3. You will see how the authors frame LVR as a more accurate and descriptive term than the often-misleading "Impermanent Loss."

Key Takeaways

- Advanced AMM analysis involves modelling the value extracted from LPs by arbitrageurs.
- Loss-versus-Rebalancing (LVR) is a more precise measure of LP risk than Impermanent Loss.
- LVR quantifies the cost imposed on LPs by informed traders who are constantly rebalancing the pool, and it must be overcome by trading fees for the position to be profitable.

Bridge to the Next Lesson

Modeling AMMs is about understanding the risks and returns of spot markets. But an even more complex and forward-looking area for quantitative analysis is the options market. In our next lesson, we will explore Implied Volatility and the insights that can be gained from volatility surfaces.

Lesson 03 - On-Chain Options & Volatility Surfaces

An Introduction to the Market's Crystal Ball

What does the market *think* will happen next? While most indicators look at past price action, Implied Volatility (IV) is a powerful, forward-looking metric derived from options prices that acts as the market's collective forecast of future price movement. By analysing the "volatility surface," quantitative analysts can gain deep insights into market sentiment and expectations, essentially reading the market's crystal ball.

The Core Explanation: Pricing Future Volatility

Implied Volatility (IV) is the market's forecast of a likely movement in an asset's price. It is a key variable used in options pricing models. A high IV means the market expects large price swings in the future, while a low IV means the market expects a period of calm.

By plotting the Implied Volatility of options with different strike prices and different expiration dates, one can construct a 'volatility surface.' This is a 3D plot that provides a rich, nuanced view of market sentiment.

A key feature of this surface is its 'skew'.

- In a "normal" market, the skew is often to the downside. This means that out-of-the-money put options (bets on a price crash) have a higher IV than out-of-the-money call options.
- This happens because investors are often more afraid of a sudden crash than they are hopeful of a sudden rally. As a result, they are willing to pay a higher premium for "downside protection" (put options), which pushes up

the implied volatility for those options. The shape of this skew can reveal the market's perception of risk.

Case Study: The Pre-Halving Volatility Skew

Let's consider the period leading up to a major, scheduled event like a Bitcoin halving.

- In the months before the event, quantitative analysts will closely watch the Bitcoin volatility surface.
- They might observe that the implied volatility for call options (bets on a price increase) with an expiration date just *after* the halving begins to rise significantly. At the same time, the IV for put options might remain flat.
- This would create a "call skew" or "smile," indicating that the market is actively and aggressively betting on a price surge following the halving. Traders are willing to pay a high premium for the right to buy Bitcoin at a higher price in the future, and this demand is reflected directly in the implied volatility.

This provides a data-driven insight into the market's forward-looking expectations, which is far more powerful than just looking at the current spot price.

Practical Application: Viewing a Volatility Surface

You can view these complex data sets on the websites of major crypto derivatives exchanges.

- **Try This How-To:**

1. Go to a major crypto derivatives exchange website that has a public data or analytics section (like Deribit).

2. Find their "Volatility Surface" or "Options Skew" chart for Bitcoin or Ethereum.
3. You will see a 3D graph (or a 2D representation of it) plotting Implied Volatility, Strike Price, and Time to Expiration.
4. Even without understanding all the mathematical details, you can visually see the shape of the surface and how market expectations are not uniform, with different levels of volatility being priced in for different future scenarios.

Key Takeaways

- Implied Volatility (IV) is a key metric derived from options prices that indicates expected future price movement.
- A volatility surface is a 3D plot of IV, strike price, and time to expiration, providing a rich view of market expectations.
- The shape of the surface, particularly its 'skew,' reveals market sentiment and the market's perception of risk for upside vs. downside moves.

Bridge to the Next Lesson

Analysing options markets is one way to understand market expectations. But some quants are not just analyzing the market; they are actively participating in its micro-structure by building automated bots to capture inefficiencies. In our next lesson, we will look at the conceptual architecture of an

MEV searcher bot.

Lesson 04 - Building an MEV Searcher Bot (Conceptual)

An Introduction to the On-Chain Hunters

In the hidden, real-time economy of MEV, the hunters are not humans, but highly optimized, automated bots. These "searchers" are constantly scanning the mempool, the blockchain's waiting room, for any profitable opportunity they can find, from simple arbitrage to complex liquidations. Understanding the conceptual architecture of a searcher bot is key to understanding the micro-structure of on-chain markets and the sophisticated actors who operate within it.

The Core Explanation: The Anatomy of a Searcher

An MEV 'searcher' is an automated bot that scans the mempool for profitable opportunities like DEX arbitrage or liquidations. Building one is a highly competitive and specialized field, but the conceptual architecture involves several key components:

1. **A Node Connection:** The bot needs a direct, high-speed connection to a blockchain node to see the pending transactions in the mempool as they are broadcast. The faster it sees the transactions, the bigger its advantage.
2. **A Simulator:** It is too slow and expensive to test potential trades on the live network. Instead, searchers use a simulator, which is often a private fork of the mainnet. This allows the bot to test thousands of potential transaction orderings and strategies against the current state of the mempool without executing

them.

3. **A Profitability Calculator:** For every potential opportunity, the bot must calculate its profitability. This involves factoring in the potential revenue against the very high gas costs (priority fees or "bribes") needed to ensure the block builder includes their transaction exactly where they want it.
4. **A Transaction Bundler:** Once a profitable opportunity is found, the bot packages its transaction(s) into a "bundle" and submits it directly to block builders through a private communication channel like Flashbots. This prevents other searchers from seeing and front-running their own strategy in the public mempool.

Case Study: A Simple Arbitrage Searcher in Action

Let's trace the actions of a simple arbitrage searcher bot:

1. **Monitor:** The bot is connected to an Ethereum node and is constantly monitoring the mempool for new transactions.
2. **Identify:** It sees two large, unrelated trades involving the ETH/USDC pair on two different DEXs (Uniswap and Sushiswap).
3. **Simulate:** Its simulator instantly calculates that after these two trades execute, the price of ETH will be slightly different on each DEX for a brief moment.
4. **Calculate:** The profitability calculator confirms that a trade buying on the cheaper DEX and selling on the more expensive one will net a profit of 0.1 ETH, even after paying a high priority fee to the block builder.
5. **Bundle & Submit:** The bot creates a bundle of three

transactions (the two user trades plus its own arbitrage trade in the middle) and submits this bundle via Flashbots to be included in the block. If successful, the bot captures a small, risk-free profit.

Practical Application: Exploring the Tools

You can explore the infrastructure that these sophisticated searcher bots use.

- **Try This How-To:**

1. Go to the official documentation for Flashbots.
2. Find the section for "MEV-geth" or their general documentation for searchers.
3. You don't need to be a developer to understand the high-level concepts. Reading the introductory paragraphs will give you a direct insight into the tools and infrastructure that searchers use. You will see discussions about "bundles," "private transactions," and the "block builder auction," which are the core primitives of this hidden economy.

Key Takeaways

- MEV searching involves monitoring the mempool for profitable opportunities.
- Key components include a node, a transaction simulator, and a profitability calculator.
- Searchers often use services like Flashbots to privately submit transaction bundles to block builders.

Bridge to the Next Lesson

MEV bots are a major source of risk for traders, but an even bigger systemic risk in DeFi is the potential for a lending protocol to become insolvent during a market crash. In our final lesson of this module, we will explore how quantitative analysts model this critical risk.

Lesson 05 - Risk Modeling for Lending Protocols

An Introduction to Stress-Testing a Digital Bank

What happens to a DeFi lending protocol during a market apocalypse? When asset prices are crashing and the network is congested, can the protocol's liquidation engine keep up, or will it fail and accumulate massive amounts of bad debt? Risk modelling is the crucial, quantitative discipline of stress-testing these decentralized banks to ensure they can survive even the most extreme and volatile market shocks.

The Core Explanation: Preparing for the Cascade

Experts assess the risk of lending protocols by modelling their resilience to market shocks. This involves stress-testing the protocol's liquidation engine and analysing the quality of its collateral assets. It's about finding the breaking point of the system before it happens in the real world.

The key parameters to model include:

- **'Loan-to-Value' (LTV) Ratios:** The percentage of collateral value that a user can borrow against.
- **'Liquidation Thresholds':** The collateralization ratio at which a loan becomes eligible for liquidation.
- **'Liquidation Penalties':** The bonus or fee paid to liquida-

tors, which incentivizes them to repay risky debt.

A robust risk model will use historical data and statistical methods to simulate a severe market crash. The goal is to determine if the protocol could handle the resulting cascade of liquidations—where liquidations push the price of the collateral down further, causing even more liquidations—without accumulating bad debt and becoming insolvent. The results of these models are used to set safe LTV and liquidation parameters for each collateral asset.

Case Study: The "CRV Crisis" of 2023

In mid-2023, the founder of Curve Finance, a major DeFi protocol, had taken out massive loans (hundreds of millions of dollars) from various lending protocols, using his own CRV token as collateral. When the price of the CRV token began to fall sharply, it threatened to trigger the liquidation of this massive position.

The risk was systemic. If all of his positions were liquidated at once on the open market, the sell pressure would have crashed the price of CRV to near zero. This would have left the lending protocols holding worthless collateral, causing them to accumulate tens of millions of dollars in bad debt.

In response, quantitative risk modelling firms and the DAOs of the lending protocols worked around the clock. They published detailed models simulating the potential impact of the cascade and proposed real-time risk parameter adjustments (like temporarily halting new CRV borrowing) to protect the protocols from insolvency. It was a live, high-stakes demonstration of the critical importance of risk modelling in DeFi.

Practical Application: Reading a Risk Assessment

The risk analysis for major DeFi protocols is often done transparently in public governance forums.

- **Try This How-To:**

1. Go to the official governance forum for a major lending protocol like Aave or Compound.
2. Find their risk management section or search for a proposal related to "onboarding a new asset" or "adjusting risk parameters."
3. You will often find detailed analyses from professional risk modeling firms like Gauntlet, Chaos Labs, or Gauntlet.
4. Read through one of these reports. You will see their simulation results and their specific recommendations for the appropriate LTV and liquidation threshold for the asset in question. This is a direct look into the world of professional DeFi risk management.

Key Takeaways

- Risk modeling for lending protocols focuses on their ability to withstand liquidation cascades.
- Setting appropriate LTVs and liquidation parameters for each collateral asset is critical.
- Stress-testing involves simulating extreme market downturns to check for insolvency risk.

17

Module 2 Recap

You have now completed a deep dive into the world of quantitative finance and research in Web3.

- You've moved beyond simple metrics to understand how professionals use quantitative models to simulate and stress-test the complex economic systems of DeFi protocols.
- You can explain the advanced mechanics of AMMs, including the more precise risk metric of Loss-versus-Rebalancing (LVR).
- You understand how on-chain options markets and volatility surfaces can be used to gauge the market's forward-looking expectations.
- You grasp the conceptual architecture of MEV searcher bots and the crucial process of risk modelling that keeps DeFi lending protocols safe.

You are now equipped with the quantitative frameworks

used by the most sophisticated analysts and researchers in the space.

Module 3: Governance & Protocol Politics

Module Introduction: You've learned how protocols are built, secured, and modelled. We now arrive at the final, most human layer: politics. In a decentralized world, power is not absolute; it is negotiated. Protocol Politics is the "meta-game" of influencing these decentralized systems. This module will take you into the world of governance, diplomacy, and strategy, where the players are not just users, but VCs, whales, and delegates, and where the art of persuasion can be as powerful as a line of code.

Lesson 01 - Introduction to Protocol Politics

An Introduction to the Human Layer

It's not just about the code; it's about the people. A decentralized protocol can be technically perfect, but its success or failure often comes down to the complex, messy, and fascinating world of human coordination. Protocol Politics is the meta-game of influencing the direction of a decentralized protocol. It's a strategic arena where social coordination, lobbying, coalition-building, and public perception are just as important as technical merit. Understanding this human layer is the final step to becoming an expert.

The Core Explanation: The Game of Influence

Protocol Politics is the interplay between a protocol's various stakeholders, each with their own competing interests. Decisions are not made in a vacuum; they are the result of a political process.

The key players in this game are:

- **Core Developers:** The team that builds and maintains the protocol. They often have deep technical knowledge and a long-term vision.
- **Large Token Holders ("Whales"):** Individuals or entities that hold a significant percentage of the governance tokens, giving them substantial voting power.
- **Venture Capital (VC) Firms:** Early investors who often hold large token allocations and have a strong financial incentive to see the protocol succeed.
- **Delegates:** The "protocol politicians" in DAOs with delegation systems, who are responsible for representing the interests of the token holders who have delegated to them.
- **The Community:** The broad base of regular users and small token holders.

An expert in this domain understands how to navigate these human and political layers—building consensus, forming coalitions, and persuading different stakeholder groups—to achieve strategic objectives for the protocol.

Case Study: The Uniswap Fee Switch Debate

The long-running debate over Uniswap's "fee switch" is a perfect case study in protocol politics. The proposal is simple: divert a small portion of the protocol's trading fees to UNI token holders. However, its political implications are immense.

- **Stakeholders' Interests:** VCs and large token holders (like a16z, a major investor) have a strong financial incentive to turn the switch on, as it would create a revenue stream for the token. Some Liquidity Providers, however, are against it, as it would reduce their share of the fees. The core development team has historically been cautious, worried it could introduce regulatory risks.
- **The Politics:** The debate has played out for years on public forums and social media. Major VCs have published detailed blog posts outlining their position. Delegates have been lobbied by different factions. The final decision is not just a technical one; it is a political negotiation between powerful, competing interests.

Practical Application: Observing the Parliamentary Floor

You can watch these political debates unfold in real-time.

- **Try This How-To:**

1. Go to the governance forum of a major, contentious protocol (like Uniswap).
2. Find a major proposal that has a long discussion thread (the fee switch is a great example).
3. Read through the comments. You will see different stakeholder groups arguing their positions. You might see a delegate from a university blockchain club explaining why they are voting a certain way, or a VC firm publishing a long, detailed post with their rationale.

This is the "parliamentary floor" of protocol politics, and it is happening completely in public.

Key Takeaways

- Protocol Politics is the human layer of decision-making in DAOs.
- It involves navigating the competing interests of various powerful stakeholders, including developers, VCs, and the community.
- Success in governance requires social and political acumen, not just technical skill.

Bridge to the Next Lesson

Navigating protocol politics requires more than just a good idea; it requires the ability to communicate that idea in a formal, persuasive, and comprehensive way. In our next lesson, we will cover the essential skill of crafting an effective governance proposal.

Lesson 02 - Crafting Effective Governance Proposals

An Introduction to the Art of Persuasion

An idea is not a plan. In the formal world of DAO governance, a simple suggestion in a Discord channel has zero chance of becoming a reality. To enact change, you must craft an effective governance proposal. This is a masterclass in communication, research, and persuasion. It is a comprehensive document that must not only present an idea, but also justify it with data, anticipate objections, and build social consensus before a single vote is cast.

The Core Explanation: The Anatomy of a Winning Proposal

An effective governance proposal must go far beyond a simple idea. It is a formal document that provides the community with all the information they need to make a reasoned decision.

A strong proposal includes several key components:

1. **A Clear Problem Statement:** It must begin by clearly and concisely defining the problem it aims to solve, ideally with supporting data.
2. **A Detailed Proposed Solution:** This section must lay out the specific, actionable solution, including any required code changes, smart contract interactions, or new parameter settings.
3. **A Robust Rationale:** It must provide a compelling argument for *why* this solution is the right one, explaining its benefits to the protocol and its users.
4. **An Analysis of Risks and Trade-offs:** A credible proposal honestly addresses the potential downsides, risks, and trade-offs of the proposed change.
5. **A Pre-Vote "Temperature Check":** Before moving to a formal, binding on-chain vote, most successful proposals start with an informal "temperature check" poll on the governance forum to gauge community sentiment and gather feedback.

Proposals that fail often do so because they lack one or more of these crucial components, appearing ill-prepared and failing to build the necessary social consensus.

Case Study: A Hypothetical Aave Proposal

Let's compare a weak proposal to a strong one for the Aave lending protocol.

- Weak Proposal: A user posts on the forum, "Title: Add XYZ Token as Collateral. Body: I think we should add XYZ token, it's a good project." This proposal has no data, no rationale, and no risk analysis. It will be ignored and will fail.
- Strong Proposal: A user posts a multi-page proposal.
- **Title:** "ARC: Onboard XYZ Token as a New Collateral Asset"
- **Problem Statement:** It explains that Aave needs to diversify its collateral types.
- **Solution:** It proposes specific risk parameters for XYZ (LTV, Liquidation Threshold), backed by a quantitative risk analysis.
- **Rationale:** It outlines the benefits, such as attracting new users from the XYZ community.
- **Risks:** It honestly discusses the market risks of the new asset and suggests a conservative debt ceiling to mitigate them.
- **Temp Check:** It includes a poll to gauge initial community support.

This second proposal is a professional, comprehensive document that provides the DAO with everything it needs to make an informed decision.

Practical Application: Comparing Real Proposals

You can see the difference between successful and failed proposals on any major governance forum.

- **Try This How-To:**

1. Go back to a governance forum like gov.uniswap.org or governance.aave.com.
2. Find a proposal that has been successfully passed and has been implemented.
3. Now, find a proposal that was heavily debated but was ultimately rejected by the community.
4. Compare the structure and detail of the two original posts. You will almost certainly see that the successful proposal is a comprehensive, well-researched, and clearly written document that follows the structure we've outlined, while the failed one is often a poorly articulated or incomplete idea.

Key Takeaways

- A good proposal is a comprehensive document, not just an idea.
- It must clearly articulate the problem, solution, risks, and benefits.
- Socializing the proposal and gathering feedback before the vote is critical for success.

Bridge to the Next Lesson

Crafting proposals is about managing a DAO's internal politics. But as the Web3 ecosystem grows and becomes more interconnected, DAOs must also interact with each other. In our next lesson, we will explore the art of DAO diplomacy.

Lesson 03 - The Art of DAO Diplomacy

An Introduction to Digital Nation-States

No DAO is an island. In the maturing Web3 ecosystem, protocols are no longer isolated entities; they are interconnected "digital nation-states" that must compete, cooperate, and form alliances to survive and thrive. DAO diplomacy is the art and practice of negotiating and forming these strategic alliances with other protocols. It is a crucial meta-game of politics and economics that can create powerful network effects and strengthen a protocol's position in the market.

The Core Explanation: Building Alliances

DAO diplomacy involves negotiating and forming strategic alliances with other protocols. Just as nations form trade agreements, DAOs form on-chain partnerships to align their interests and work towards shared goals.

Common diplomatic actions include:

1. **Token Swaps:** This is a common practice where two DAOs agree to swap a small portion of their native governance tokens with each other. For example, the treasuries of DAO A and DAO B might exchange $1 million worth of their respective tokens. This gives both DAOs a direct financial stake in the other's success, aligning their incentives and encouraging future collaboration.
2. **Co-funding Public Goods:** DAOs often form coalitions to co-fund "public goods" that benefit the entire ecosystem, such as open-source software development or security research, often through grant programs like Gitcoin.

3. **Collaborating on Shared Technical Standards:** DAOs that are building in a similar sector might work together to create shared technical standards, improving interoperability and the user experience across their protocols.

Effective diplomacy can strengthen a protocol's economic moat, foster innovation, and create powerful, positive-sum network effects.

Case Study: The "Curve Wars"

The "Curve Wars" is the most famous and long-running example of protocol politics and DAO diplomacy in action.

- **The Battlefield:** Curve Finance is a DEX that is a critical piece of infrastructure for stablecoin liquidity in DeFi. It rewards its liquidity providers with its governance token, CRV.
- **The Goal:** The more CRV you hold and lock, the more you can "boost" the rewards paid out to a specific liquidity pool.
- **The Diplomacy:** This created a situation where other DeFi protocols (like Convex Finance and Frax Finance) began fiercely competing to acquire as much CRV as possible. They did this so they could direct Curve's rewards to their own stablecoin pools, making their products more attractive to users. This led to a complex ecosystem of alliances, bribes (on platforms like Votium), and strategic maneuvering that is a perfect, long-running example of protocol politics and inter-DAO diplomacy.

Practical Application: Observing a Token Swap

You can often see the results of these diplomatic actions

directly on-chain.

- **Try This How-To:**

1. Go to the treasury wallet for a major DeFi protocol on a portfolio viewer like Zapper.
2. Browse its token holdings.
3. Do you see it holding the governance tokens of other, seemingly unrelated protocols? This is often the result of a token swap or a strategic decision to acquire another protocol's tokens to participate in its governance.

This is a direct, on-chain footprint of a past act of DAO diplomacy.

Key Takeaways

- DAO diplomacy is the practice of forming strategic relationships between protocols.
- Common diplomatic actions include token swaps and collaborative funding initiatives.
- These alliances are crucial for navigating the competitive, multi-chain landscape.

Bridge to the Next Lesson

Diplomacy and governance rely on effective decision-making. But as we've discussed, one of the biggest challenges for large DAOs is getting their community to participate. In our next lesson, we will look at the primary solution to voter apathy: delegate systems.

Lesson 04 - Delegate Systems & Voter Apathy

An Introduction to Digital Democracy's Dilemma

Democracy doesn't work if nobody shows up to vote. This is a fundamental dilemma that large DAOs face. While token-based voting is a powerful tool, the reality is that most token holders do not have the time, expertise, or incentive to research and vote on every single proposal. This is known as voter apathy, and it can lead to governance stagnation. The primary solution to this problem is the delegate system, a model of liquid democracy that creates a new class of "protocol politicians."

The Core Explanation: Representative Digital Government

Large DAOs suffer from voter apathy. To solve this, many of the most successful protocols have implemented delegation systems.

The model works like this:

1. **Delegation:** Token holders who do not wish to vote directly can delegate their voting power to another wallet address they trust. This is a non-custodial process; they are only delegating the *vote*, not their actual tokens.
2. **Delegates:** The recipients of this delegated voting power are known as delegates. These are often individuals or organizations who have established themselves as informed and active community members. They effectively become 'protocol politicians'.
3. **Governance:** These delegates are then expected to stay up-to-date on all governance proposals, participate in debates, and vote on behalf of all the token holders who

have delegated to them.

This system has two major benefits:

- **It increases participation:** It dramatically boosts voter turnout, as the delegated votes are now active.
- **It improves the quality of decision-making:** It concentrates voting power in the hands of the most informed and engaged participants.

However, it also introduces a potential risk of centralization if a huge amount of voting power becomes concentrated among a few powerful, elite delegates.

Case Study: The Arbitrum DAO

The Arbitrum DAO, which governs the Arbitrum Layer 2 network, has one of the most active and professionalized delegate systems in all of crypto.

- When the DAO launched its ARB token via a massive airdrop, the claiming process actively prompted users to choose a delegate for their new voting power.
- Dozens of individuals and organizations had applied to be delegates, including university blockchain clubs (e.g., from MIT and Stanford), professional DAO governance teams, crypto research firms, and influential community members.
- These delegates actively campaign for votes, publish their voting philosophies, and publicly debate proposals on the governance forums. This has created a vibrant and functional system of representative governance for one of the largest DAOs in the world.

Practical Application: Finding a Delegate

You can see the landscape of these "protocol politicians" on governance dashboards.

- **Try This How-To:**

1. Go to the website Tally.xyz, a major governance dashboard for many DAOs.
2. Find a major DAO that uses delegation, such as Arbitrum, Uniswap, or Aave.
3. Navigate to the 'Delegates' tab.
4. You will see a leaderboard of the top delegates, ranked by how much voting power has been entrusted to them. You can click on their profiles to read their platforms and see their complete voting history.

This is a real-time list of the most powerful and influential "politicians" in that protocol's ecosystem.

Key Takeaways

- Delegation allows token holders to entrust their voting power to active experts.
- This system is a primary defence against voter apathy in large DAOs.
- The key risk of delegation is the potential for centralization of power if it becomes concentrated among too few delegates.

Bridge to the Next Lesson

Delegates and token holders make crucial decisions about how a DAO's treasury is used. But what if the treasury itself could be used not just as a budget, but as a powerful strategic weapon? In our final lesson of the entire curriculum, we will explore the advanced concept of treasury management as a strategy.

Lesson 05 - Treasury Management as Strategy

An Introduction to a DAO's Economic Weapon

A treasury is not just a bank account to pay bills; it is a powerful strategic tool. At the expert level, treasury management moves beyond simple diversification and budgeting into the realm of high-level economic strategy. This involves actively deploying a DAO's treasury to drive long-term growth, create a competitive moat, and enhance the value of its entire ecosystem. This final lesson will explore how the most sophisticated DAOs use their treasury as a strategic weapon.

The Core Explanation: From Defence to Offense

While prudent treasury management starts with defence (diversifying into stablecoins to ensure a long runway), expert-level treasury management is about playing offense. It views the DAO's treasury as a powerful instrument for directly influencing its own ecosystem and competitive landscape.

Advanced treasury strategies include:

1. **Strategic Acquisitions:** A DAO can use its treasury funds to acquire or merge with other protocols, absorbing their technology or community to accelerate its own growth.

2. **Protocol-Owned Liquidity (POL):** Instead of just relying on users to provide liquidity for its native token on DEXs, a DAO can deploy its own treasury assets (e.g., ETH and its own token) to create deep liquidity pools. This ensures its token always has a stable and liquid market.
3. **Ecosystem Grants:** A DAO can use its treasury to fund a grants program for third-party developers, paying them to build new applications and tools on top of its protocol. This is a powerful way to bootstrap a vibrant and innovative ecosystem.
4. **Buybacks and Burns:** As discussed previously, a DAO can allocate a portion of its protocol revenue to buy back its own tokens from the open market and burn them, creating deflationary pressure and returning value to token holders.

These actions directly use the treasury to enhance the protocol's long-term value and competitive position.

Case Study: Frax Finance's Strategic Treasury

Frax Finance, a decentralized stablecoin protocol, has one of the most aggressive and sophisticated treasury strategies in DeFi.

- Its protocol generates revenue, which flows into its treasury.
- It then uses this treasury offensively. For example, Frax has used its treasury to acquire a massive amount of other key governance tokens from the DeFi ecosystem, particularly CRV (from Curve) and CVX (from Convex).
- By holding these tokens, Frax is able to participate in the "Curve Wars" and direct the valuable CRV rewards to its

own stablecoin liquidity pools. This creates a powerful, self-reinforcing economic flywheel: protocol revenue is used to acquire influence in other protocols, which is then used to deepen the liquidity and utility of its own protocol. This is a prime example of a treasury being used for offense, not just defence.

Practical Application: Analysing a Grants Program

You can see this strategic use of treasury funds by observing a DAO's grant program.

- **Try This How-To:**

1. Find the governance forum or blog for a major protocol that has a grants program (e.g., Uniswap, Aave, Optimism).
2. Look for a post that announces the latest cohort of grant recipients.
3. You will see the DAO's treasury being used to fund a wide variety of projects: new developer tools, analytics dashboards, community initiatives, and educational content, all designed to make the main protocol more valuable.

This is a direct look into how a decentralized organization makes strategic capital allocation decisions to grow its ecosystem.

Key Takeaways

- A DAO's treasury can be used for strategic purposes

beyond just paying contributors.

- Actions like ecosystem grants, strategic acquisitions, and managing protocol-owned liquidity can drive long-term growth.
- Effective treasury management is a key differentiator for successful protocols, transforming the treasury from a simple budget into a powerful economic tool.

18

Module 3 Recap and Final Conclusion

You have now completed the final module of the Expert Level and the entire CryptoEaz Curriculum.

- You've explored the complex human layer of Web3, from the meta-game of Protocol Politics and the art of DAO Diplomacy to the practical skill of crafting effective governance proposals.
- You understand the solutions being developed to solve DAO challenges, such as delegate systems, and the most advanced treasury strategies that separate the leading protocols from the rest.

From the first lesson on "What is Money?" to these final thoughts on high-level strategy, you have completed a comprehensive journey. You started with the foundational principles of finance, mastered the core technology of the blockchain, learned to navigate the DeFi ecosystem, and have now explored the advanced strategic and technical concepts that define the cutting edge of Web3.

19

Next Steps

Take Your Web3 Journey Further

Congratulations on completing the CryptoEaz Curriculum! You're now equipped with a solid foundation in digital finance and Web3.

Here's how to continue exploring and contributing to this exciting ecosystem:

- Join Uniswap's DAO: Engage with the decentralized community at gov.uniswap.org. Participate in discussions, learn about governance proposals, and connect with like-minded enthusiasts shaping DeFi's future.
- Follow @VitalikButerin on X: Stay informed about Ethereum and Web3 developments by following this co-founder's insights. His posts offer a window into the technology's evolution and community trends.
- Contribute to Gitcoin: Explore open-source projects at gitcoin.co. Share your skills, collaborate with devel-

opers, and discover how the crypto community builds together—no financial commitment required.

- Explore Web3 Learning Communities: Dive into forums like the Bankless Discord or Reddit's r/Web3. Exchange ideas, ask questions, and learn from others' experiences in a supportive environment.
- Create Your Own Content: Share your newfound knowledge by starting a blog, X thread, or video series about Web3 topics. Inspire others and build your presence in the ecosystem.
- Attend Virtual Web3 Events: Look for online meetups or webinars on platforms like Eventbrite or Meetup. Network with enthusiasts and stay updated on industry discussions.

This is just the beginning! The Web3 space thrives on collaboration and curiosity—use these steps to deepen your understanding and connect with the global community. Visit www.cryptoeaz.com for more resources and to stay engaged.

About the Author

CryptoEaz is an education platform dedicated to demystifying the world of cryptocurrency and decentralized finance. We provide a clear, structured learning path designed to empower anyone, from absolute beginners to seasoned professionals, with the knowledge to navigate the future of digital finance confidently and safely. #NFA (Not Financial Advice).

You can connect with me on:

- https://cryptoeaz.com
- https://x.com/CryptoEaz

www.ingramcontent.com/pod-product-compliance
Lightning Source LLC
LaVergne TN
LVHW052218200926
848481LV00001B/144
* 9 7 9 8 2 3 2 7 5 9 0 0 1 *